John Josselyn,
Colonial Traveler

A Critical Edition of
Two Voyages to New-England

University Press of New England

Hanover and London, 1988

John Josselyn, Colonial Traveler

A Critical Edition of
Two Voyages to New-England

Edited and introduced by
Paul J. Lindholdt

University Press of New England

Brandeis University
Brown University
Clark University
University of Connecticut
Dartmouth College
University of New Hampshire
University of Rhode Island
Tufts University
University of Vermont

© 1988 by University Press of New England

Printed in the United States of America
∞

LIBRARY OF CONGRESS CATALOGING-IN-PUBLICATION DATA

Josselyn, John, fl. 1630–1675.
John Josselyn, colonial traveler.

Bibliography: p.
Includes index.
New England—Description and travel—To 1775.
2. Josselyn, John, fl. 1630–1675—Journeys—New England. I. Lindholdt, Paul J. II. Title.
F7.J85   1988   917.4'042   87–24271
ISBN 0–87451–428–2

5 4 3 2 1

Information for the map on p. xl was drawn from Cotton Mather, *Magnalia Christi Americana: or the Ecclesiastical History of New England from Its First Planting in the Year 1620 unto the Year of Our Lord, 1695*. Ed. Richard C. Robey. Research Library of Colonial Americana. New York: Arno Press, 1872, and Lois M. Rosenberry, *The Expansion of New England*. New York: Russell and Russell, Inc., 1962.

Contents

Acknowledgments

Editing the following text has produced many questions in the fields of history, science, literature, and bibliography. Accordingly I have appealed to experts without whose knowledge I should have had greater difficulty completing such a complex task. Whenever possible, I have availed myself of rare books and pamphlets in the libraries of the Pennsylvania State University and the University of Washington. Where I have been unable personally to investigate original texts, I have examined photofacsimiles or other photocopied materials kindly sent me by librarians.

For tutelage and advice in bibliographic matters, I am most grateful to Pennylvania State professors Harrison T. Meserole and Michael Kiernan, whose unselfish willingness to read and respond to the work in manuscript has aided me immensely. Both have also taught me much about the seventeenth century. For repeated correspondence on Josselyn as a historical figure, I thank Charles E. Clark of the University of New Hampshire and Alden T. Vaughan of Columbia University. Robert D. Arner at the University of Cincinnati has corresponded and spoken with me about Josselyn's literary accomplishments. Finally, my colleague Waller B. Wigginton at Idaho State University has translated the Latin passages and offered advice on etymological problems.

Among librarians to whom I owe gratitude, Charles Mann, curator of Pennsylvania State University's special collections, has my utmost respect for his cheerful and learned assistance. Grace Peréz of Pennsylvania State University's interlibrary loans has exceeded the bounds of duty to locate obscure Josselyn materials. Also very helpful were Gary Menges of the University of Washington Rare Books Division, Margot McCain of the Maine Historical Society, Shirley Thayer of the Maine State Library, James Lewis of the Houghton Reading Room at Harvard University, and Jennifer Lee of the John Hay Library at Brown University. Members of the New England Historic Genealogical Society have aided me as well, particularly George Sanborn, Jr. and Ralph Crandall. Malcolm Freiberg of the Massachusetts Historical Society has corresponded readily on the project.

This research was partially supported by Grant no. 611 from the Faculty Research Committee, Idaho State University, Pocatello, Idaho.

Pocatello, Idaho   P.J.L.
June 1987

Note on the Text

In editing John Josselyn's *Account of Two Voyages to New-England*,
I have chosen to present a scholarly edition in which the spelling
and punctuation of the copy text have not been modernized.
Rather, they have been preserved to retain the flavor of the book
originally offered to the public in 1674. The rationale for doing
so is my belief that much of the appeal in early American literature comes from the authors' pre-Websterian resourcefulness
in diction, syntax, and orthography. Also for this reason, despite
the availability of diplomatic modernizations, I cite original
seventeenth-century editions or unretouched facsimiles whenever
possible.

The publishing history of the book is straightforward. "LI-
CENSED BY Roger L'estrange Novem. the 28. 1673" (leaf
A1), the *Two Voyages* was offered for sale the following year. In
1675 it appeared in a "Second Addition," as the title page declares. Not until the nineteenth century was it published again.
Then, in 1833, the Massachusetts Historical Society offered a reprint in its *Collections*. The society included no introduction or
annotations, however, but only a brief statement of the copy text's
provenance (211n); this statement errs in declaring the book's
small octavo format to be 12mo, a mistake followed or committed
likewise by other, twentieth-century sources. Another reprint of
the book was offered for sale in 1865 by the Boston press of
William Veazie. This reprint appeared in numbered copies, both
small and medium quarto, to coincide that year with Veazie's re-
lease of *Rarities*, first edited by Edward Tuckerman in 1860 for
the *Transactions and Collections* of the American Antiquarian Society. Veazie's *Two Voyages* includes a three-page "Publisher's
Preface," which primarily treats the author's family. Both Veazie

and the Massachusetts Historical Society used the 1675 edition as copy texts.

My 1674 copy text, housed in the Special Collections Division of Pattee Library, Pennsylvania State University, is a small octavo, bound in brown morocco, with gilt leaf edges. This copy appears to have been "sophisticated," for it bears three loose leaves (U7, U8, X1) that are untrimmed and must have been inserted from another copy. The signature pattern otherwise corresponds exactly to bibliographic descriptions offered by standard early American reference sources, including the Church Catalogue of *Books Relating to the Discovery and Early History of North and South America*, the *Catalogue of the John Carter Brown Library*, and the *Thomas Winthrop Streeter Collection of Americana*. The one irregularity among these sources appears in the Church description, which records no signature on leaf B3, contrary to my copy text and other printed descriptions.

The "Second Addition" is not a separate edition at all. Some twenty copies of the first edition are extant in American university libraries, but only four copies of the second. Joseph Sabin's *Dictionary of Books Relating to America* accurately states the relationship of these books: "The second edition is the first, with a new title-page only" (9:340). This evidence, corroborated by my own research, has led me to collate my copy text against only the Massachusetts Historical Society reprint of the second. The few variants this collation revealed have been compared in turn against multiple copies of the 1675 text by means of correspondence with special collections librarians at Harvard University and at the John Carter Brown Library of Brown University. These variants are exclusively mispunctuations and misspellings, and they turn out to have been introduced by the 1833 editors. Since the book therefore exists in a single edition only, my apparatus includes no variants.

My editorial policy is as follows. The copy text anticipates modern practice in its use of "u" and "v," "f" and "s," "i" and "j." I have, of course, preserved that practice. All words, letters, and punctuation bracketed in the present edition—with the exception of numbered page breaks—represent exclusively my additions to, not emendations of, the copy text. These additions I have deemed necessary to prevent misreadings and to afford as few pauses as possible. My emendations, listed immediately after the text, supply intended readings as nearly as they can be ascertained. These include the correction of inaccurately cited biblical passages, unbalanced parentheses, and errors evidently committed by the typesetter in transcribing handwritten copy. "Thomas Goffe," for instance, appears as "Thomas Gosse" and "Cape Ann" as "Cape Aun"—the former error apparently due to the use of long "s" in the manuscript and the latter to an accidentally turned "n." Beyond the incorporation of the book's short list of errata, my only silent changes restore "*M*" to "M" in a number of cases where the printer appears to have suffered a shortage of the roman letter and had to substitute italics.

In presenting this text of early Americana, I intend as my audience primarily students and scholars. Thus I assume a degree of familiarity with those figures central to seventeenth-century New England—such figures as John Winthrop, William Bradford, and Thomas Morton. Throughout my notes and introduction I follow the 1984 edition of the *MLA Handbook for Writers of Research Papers*. Numbers in parentheses refer to page numbers of the copy text. For translations of the Vulgate passages I quote the King James Version. Finally, Bernhard Grizmek's *Encyclopedia* and Alfred J. Godin's *Wild Animals of New England*, both cited in the bibliography, serve as source for all natural history names.

Introduction

John Josselyn's reputation as a writer rests exclusively upon two books, *New-Englands Rarities Discovered* (1672) and *An Account of Two Voyages to New-England* (1674). Like Captain John Smith's earlier works, Josselyn's offer advice for the prospective colonist in America and have been variously classed as histories, promotion tracts, and travel accounts. The difference is that Josselyn wrote as an independent observer and thus was more receptive to the region's legends and marvels. At the same time, he was an accomplished scientist. In England his first book received a three-page notice in the Royal Society's *Philosophical Transactions*, and the present book is dedicated to the fellows of the society. His studies of the region's flora, including identification of several new genera, remained authoritative till 1785. Early in the present century a group of scientists honored him by founding the Josselyn Botanical Society of Maine.

Yet Josselyn's scientific accomplishments are overshadowed by his inclination to record the wonders of a paradise he envisioned in New England. From 1638 through 1639, and again from 1663 to 1671, he visited his elder brother Henry in the province of Maine. His royalist sympathies alienated him, like Thomas Morton, author of the *New English Canaan*, from the region's leaders. The ruin of his aristocratic family's fortunes, both in England and in Maine, thwarted achievement of his potential as a natural historian. Yet the *Two Voyages* remains fascinating reading because of Josselyn's awe before the mythical landscape of America. In the flux of this rough frontier, supernatural events may scarcely be distinguished from the natural. Fabulous creatures throng America's shores. Knowledge of these creatures sometimes comes from hearsay, whose credibility he graciously refuses either to endorse or deny. Such tantalizing details as lions, sea serpents, and mermen must have piqued the jaded curiosity of his English audience, especially since the author was a noble countryman so obviously well versed in natural philosophy.

Such details remain engaging today. Alongside the Puritan founders and their writing, Josselyn appears an eccentric swimmer against the tide of his time. Indeed, so-called promotion writers on the whole have been overlooked, although their contributions to American history, literature, and folklore are significant. Josselyn, however, defies categorization as a mere promoter by virtue of a colorful and often irascible personality. His study of the native Americans combines romantic admiration with antipathy to their savage ways. His pastoral preconceptions of the New World's natural history play against the adverse impacts of European immigration. His commitment to scientific objectivity wavers in the face of legendry and lore reported by the settlers he met. Addressing the critics who had scorned his first book, he chides their imagined tendency to cast a prejudiced eye upon his writing. Above all, he is just plain fun to read. Insofar as these features enrich the *Two Voyages*, Josselyn merits inclusion in the canon of American literature.

II

The extant biographical details help explain Josselyn's literary personality. An ancestor, Gilbertus Josselinus, had arrived in England with William the Conqueror and left descendants throughout the counties of Kent, Essex, and Hertfordshire. The site of Josselyn's birth, probably in 1608, appears to have been the imposing Torrell's Hall in the parish village of Willingale-Doe, Essex. His father, Thomas Josselyn, was successor to the manor; he received his knighthood from King James in 1603. Sir Thomas evidently was a poor manager of his affairs, however, for sometime between 1614 and 1618 he was forced to sell Torrell's Hall and relocate to the Isle of Ely, an administrative district bordered by the river Ouse and surrounded at that time by fens. Once again he became "so financially embarrassed" that he was forced to surrender up his estate. These are the circumstances under which John Josselyn grew up—a "scion of impoverished gentry" (Höltgen 44).

Despite such odds, his writing exhibits signs of a liberal education. He quotes the English poets, historians, and theologians; he borrows from American travel writers and promoters; he debates contemporary scientific issues. From all indications he had been trained as a physician, one with faith in the fruits of earth to salve man's wounds and even save his life. His studies of American natural history complement the seventeenth-century interest in *materia medica* (natural curatives), and the present book demonstrates his thorough familiarity with the English herbals of John Gerard, John Parkinson, and Thomas Johnson. We may picture Josselyn tramping the New England countryside, bending now and then to pluck a leaf, paging through his copy of Gerard's massive *Historie of Plantes* to study a woodcut. The coastal frontier offered him opportunities to practice medicine or, as he terms it, "physick" and "chyrurgery." But botany and medicine were only two of his many interests.

To understand his life and writing, we should recall the Restoration's widespread interest in the sciences. Francis Bacon, Thomas Browne, and Abraham Cowley in earlier decades had called for liberation from classical and medieval thought. Inherited beliefs were to be examined anew, and deductive approaches to "natural philosophy" were to be cast aside in favor of inductive observation and collection. Scientific writings at this time grew to emphasize the advancement of "Useful Knowledge"—learning with instrumental value—which accordingly gives many period pieces a utilitarian slant. English merchants quickly got involved, for the New Science facilitated trade in foreign commodities by clarifying the value and availability of herbs, furs, precious gems, and minerals. The Royal Society, founded in 1660, came to spearhead this scientific movement and to influence Josselyn's methodology.

Because they emphasized experimentation and specimen collection, the society's fellows had to rely upon contributors abroad. Settlement of the Americas, they recognized, could add greatly to their storehouse of raw materials. Thus from the outset, as R. W. Frantz has noted, "the voyager was drafted into the service of the

New Science" (17). The society enjoined all voyagers to record their observations carefully, and it offered amateurs the reward of favorable mention or even publication in the *Philosophical Transactions* beside such luminaries as Edmund Halley and Isaac Newton. Editors of the society's organ printed lengthy guidelines to be followed by the traveler and aspiring scientist, including a "Catalogue of Directions" for sea voyagers (January 1665/6) and "General Heads for a Natural History of a Countrey" (April 1666). In all cases they sought sobriety, skepticism, accuracy, and truth. How well Josselyn displayed these virtues may be estimated by the society's reception of his work.

Whether or not he designed *New-Englands Rarities* to appeal to the society, certainly Josselyn was gratified to find his book noticed in the pages of its official publication. In many ways his study was exactly what the fellows had called for. The author declares his ambition "to discover all along the Natural, Physical, and Chyrurgical Rarities of this New-found World" (12). He classifies these rarities as birds, mammals, fish, serpents, insects, plants and herbs, and minerals, between catalogs of which he scatters samples of his wit and frequent charm. The society's notice of the book was curt, objective, noncommittal—not actually a review at all. Without comment it presented his findings, including vehement assertions that native "Moose-deer" stand twelve feet high and sport horns equally far apart. As Raymond P. Stearns has argued in *Science in the British Colonies of America*, "some of the accounts of remarkable cures and wondrous beasts which he occasionally interpolated into his catalogue of rarities must have lifted the eyebrows of his most credulous follower" (140). Ingenuously encouraged by the society's attention, clearly seeking sanction and perhaps admission as a fellow, Josselyn quickly brought to press the longer and more political *Two Voyages*. This he dedicated "TO THE RIGHT HONOURABLE AND MOST ILLUSTRIOUS THE President & Fellows OF THE ROYAL SOCIETY." But the society granted him no further notice. Closely examining his work, we can see why.

Although he addressed an audience that demanded factuality and skepticism, John Josselyn nonetheless enthusiastically transmitted the myths and legends that continued to flourish alongside the New Science. Despite his pioneering botanical accomplishments, we should not be surprised that the virtuosos of the Royal Society received him so ambiguously. At worst, he is credulous. Viewed less harshly, he possesses a delightful gift for gathering the lore that sprang in such profusion from the strange new soil of America. His storytelling talent, combined with a predisposition toward ancient and medieval thought, a promoter's enthusiasm for the New England coast, and amorous verses praising Indian maids, undoubtedly were enough to have dissuaded the Royal Society and its patrons from according his work the genuine credit it deserved as natural history. In *Maine: A History*, Charles E. Clark has assessed Josselyn's image of America as "a version of the old European quest for an earthly paradise, Eden before the Fall" (37). To have seen the New World only through the spectacles of science would have been to describe a different land indeed.

Again, however, Josselyn's purposes for writing were complex. He was passionately concerned with the progress of Britain's dominions oversea. By 1638, when he began his journal of the first voyage, England's nonconforming Puritans were growing increasingly powerful; the American colonies at Plymouth and Massachusetts Bay already were challenging the crown. John's brother, Henry, felt these threats firsthand.

Henry Jocelyn (so he spelled his name) had graduated in 1623 from Corpus Christi College, Cambridge and probably served an apprenticeship in one of London's Inns of Court. Like his father, he allied himself with the colonizing enterprises of Sir Ferdinando Gorges, that indefatigable promoter of a feudal principality in Maine. Consequently, at about the same time that John Winthrop was setting out to found the city on a hill at Massachusetts Bay, Henry Jocelyn also took leave of his native England. He settled first near the Piscataqua River, which forms the boundary between present-day New Hampshire and Maine. There he served as an agent, and eventually a commissioner, under Sir Ferdinando's partner Captain John Mason. This collective enterprise they designated the Laconia Company.

In contemporary terms Mason and Gorges were "adventurers," speculators who financed settlements. They received their patent in 1622 from the Council for New England, a corporate and political body comprised of prominent leaders from the aristocracy.

They strove to follow Captain John Smith's advice by devoting their energies to the lumber and fish trade, and by dividing up their vast domain among fishermen and planters according to the principle of feudal benefice. Opposed thus to New England Congregationalism, Mason and Gorges found their Laconia Company forced into competition with the upstart colony at Massachusetts Bay. And competition proved difficult. As members of the British gentry, Mason and Gorges were poorly equipped to plant colonies. They lacked the practical experience necessary to outfit ships and gather immigrants; they were slow to recruit permanent settlers to northerly New England. When Mason died in 1635, he left his portion of the region (now New Hampshire) without direction or support. Henry Jocelyn consequently went to work for Gorges and by 1636 was living at Black Point (now Scarborough in Maine), where John visited him. There he served in various official capacities, attempted to resist inroads from the Puritans, and remained for most of his long life.

Meanwhile Gorges, who in his 85 years never traveled to America, was hard at work on plans to cripple the power of the Massachusetts Bay Colony and to strengthen his doomed province of New Somersetshire in Maine. In 1635 he persuaded Charles I to declare him "Lord Governor" of New England; at the same time the Council for New England disbanded, effectively nullifying the Massachusetts charter it had sold John Endecott in 1627. Yet the Puritans remained stubbornly in place, and Gorges' grand scheme came to naught. His error, which the Josselyns appear to have shared, lay in failing to acknowledge that British aristocrats were less fit than the middle classes to civilize a land so vast. Undaunted, in 1639 Gorges acquired a fresh grant to the province, whose seaboard capital (now York) he chose to christen Gorgeana. To govern this string of fishing villages and lumber camps by proxy, he appointed 43 municipal officers led by a commission of seventeen members, among them Henry Jocelyn.

Sir Thomas Josselyn, John's father, also served among Gorges' commissioners or agents when he accompanied John on the first voyage of 1638. This voyage, John tells us, was protracted by weather and illness, including a smallpox epidemic that evidently mandated a ship's quarantine in Boston Harbor from 3 until

10 July. A journal entry John Winthrop made for 1638 reports "Two ships," one probably the *New Supply* bearing the Josselyns, "which came over this year much pestered, and many fell sick after they landed, and many of them died" (1:27). John's father, that ragged nobleman, has left no record of his life beyond arrival. But arrive he certainly did. In a 1638 letter, reprinted in *The Trelawny Papers*, John Winter reported from the Richmond's Island plantation near Black Point that John and Sir Thomas had set up residence with Captain Thomas Cammock. The elder Josselyn, as a last ditch effort having surrendered his destiny to the Gorges enterprise, is characterized as "an ancyent old knight" of nearly eighty years (140). His name soon disappeared from Gorges' list of commissioners for New Somersetshire, probably because of his death or departure, and was replaced after 1640 by Sir Ferdinando's cousin Thomas Gorges.

John declares that the first voyage began on 26 April 1638, the height of the Great Migration of Puritans seeking asylum from the persecution of Anglican officials. In New England the battle at Mystic Fort had settled the fate of the Pequot Indians; the Antinomian rebel Anne Hutchinson was newly exiled to Rhode Island. Although John Josselyn must have wished for peace to study his natural history, and to avoid tangling himself in political affairs, from his comments in the *Two Voyages* it is obvious he harbored scant love for the Puritans. He distinguishes himself aboard ship from certain "Sectaries" whose pious enthusiasm prompts them, one Sunday morning, to throw back to the sea good cod their hungry servants had caught in violation of the Sabbath (9). He praises the Episcopalian promoter Samuel Maverick of Noddle's Island in Boston Harbor, "the only hospitable man in all the Countrey," who opposed the Massachusetts Bay Colony in person and indicted it in print (12). Ruefully he notes the precision of Vincent Potter, later condemned as a regicide, who quibbles over a biblical passage explicated in a shipboard sermon (30). His second account offers a firsthand glimpse of New England through eyes not glazed with admiration for its strain of Congregationalism.

Perhaps most worthy of note among his interactions with the New England leaders were the "respects" he presented to Governor Winthrop and the translations of certain Hebrew "Psalms into *English* Meeter" he delivered to the Reverend John Cotton. The respects were probably perfunctory, but he tells us that the Psalms were definitely the work of English poet Francis Quarles. Remembered best for his 1635 collection *Emblemes*, Quarles was an acquaintance and neighbor of the Josselyn family in Essex. He apparently had heard that the Massachusetts Bay Colony's ecclesiastical leaders were compiling an edition of the Psalms, and thus he recruited Josselyn as his emissary. Visiting among the "grose *Goddons*," as he terms them elsewhere (180), Josselyn found himself "civilly treated" (20) in 1638 Boston. However, Quarles's translations apparently were deemed unfit for inclusion in the metrically primitive but doctrinally pure *Bay Psalm Book*; its wooden verses proved to be the work of a "committee" including Richard Mather, John Eliot, Thomas Welde, and perhaps some others. Josselyn's efforts as a go-between were unsuccessful.

His epistemological beliefs differ notably from those of his Puritan peers. Unlike them, he does not read supernatural events as evidence of a battle between evil forces and the Bible commonwealth. A case in point is the birth of a "monster" child to Mary Dyer. Both John Winthrop (1: 266–69) and Edward Johnson (187) profess that this rebellious Quakeress and follower of Anne Hutchinson was merely suffering the just effects of God's displeasure. Hutchinson, they report, was punished likewise. Josselyn, on the other hand, registers the event with all the objectivity of a scientist and folklorist. The birth of Mary Dyer's "thornback" offspring is a biological marvel and little more, recounted briefly by a sailor before the Boston landfall, and again in considerably more detail by "a grave and sober person" after arriving (11, 27). Josselyn was not less gullible than other period writers. He merely saw no need to accommodate his materials to a didactic design.

Whereas his literary contemporaries are best remembered for their contributions to theology, Josselyn adds principally to the region's lore. Increase and Cotton Mather, interpreting American history as a series of remarkable providences, sought to chasten and instruct their congregations to good works. They set themselves above their audience and were proud they had been trained to piece together the puzzle of an invisible world. For Josselyn, however, the perplexities of New England serve to keep in view

the boundless potency of nature, as distinct from the bounded
scope of human endeavor. Again in 1638 some neighboring fishermen notified him they had spied a sea serpent "that lay quoiled
up like a Cable upon a Rock at *Cape-Ann*." The superstitious Indians in the boat construed the creature as a powerful omen and
cautioned vehemently against its harm. Such details Josselyn declines either "to impeach or enforce," instead allowing his readers
to arrive at their own conclusions (23–24). Many of his details
stuck in the New England mind. By committing the sea serpent
story to print, he became the original reporter of a now standard
regional legend repeated even in the present century.

Perhaps Josselyn's most memorable firsthand experience was to
mistake a wasp nest for a pineapple, an error that resulted in an
upper lip "swell'd so extreamly" that his friends could recognize
him only by his clothes (29). Thus he remained for Henry
Wadsworth Longfellow. In his verse play "John Endicott," from
The New England Tragedies, Longfellow has the beleaguered inn-
keeper Samuel Cole exclaim,

> I feel like Master Josselyn when he found
> The hornets' nest, and thought it some strange fruit,
> Until the seeds came out, and then he dropped it.
>
> (576)

This humorous image gains archetypal dimensions when viewed
against its proper backdrop of European preconceptions of the
New World. Like many hopeful colonists, Josselyn expected to
find rich fruits. Instead he suffered stings.

His first voyage to New England lasted fifteen months, and he
was then some thirty years of age. Perhaps he hoped soon to return to the New World and try his luck anew. But within three
years the Civil War began in his homeland, immigration to New
England all but ceased, and his life appears an utter void until his
eight-year removal to Maine after the Restoration. His brother
Henry continued to serve the Gorges interests and soon advanced
to the post of deputy governor. In 1643 he fell heir to the fifteen-
hundred-acre Black Point grant awarded to his comrade Thomas
Cammock, another agent for Gorges, who had been taken ill and
died en route to the West Indies. He also married Cammock's
widow, Margaret. Evidently Henry was no better as a manager

of his financial affairs than Sir Thomas had been, for by 1663 he found it necessary to mortgage his lands to the Puritan business-man Joshua Scottow, and later he surrendered them to Scottow outright. The Old World curse of impoverishment afflicted the Josselyns even in America.

Prior to this period, Henry had found himself increasingly enmeshed in a series of legal and political battles over jurisdiction in Maine. In 1646, George Cleeve successfully defended the so-called Plough Patent, which rendered powerless the Gorges claims. The Massachusetts Bay Colony—emboldened perhaps by the death of Gorges in 1647 and the execution two years later of Charles I—began to annex the region in 1652. Yet by all accounts Henry was a fair administrator, and the civil deci-sions over which he presided "disclose a noteworthy effort to cre-ate a law abiding community out of an honest but often unruly body of people" (Andrews 1:427). Unlike the typecast Yankee, Henry found prosperity elusive and therefore did not economi-cally threaten the powerful Massachusetts Bay Colony's merchant saints. Massachusetts retained his services as a commissioner, and, after the intercession of Charles II, he became Maine's first and only chief magistrate ever appointed by royal authority. At this period John Josselyn's eight-year visit began.

Although the account of the second voyage contains few first-person statements, its author clearly clashed with the Puritan au-thorities. In 1665, 1667, and 1668 he was fined for neglecting to attend church services in Maine. Henry was chief justice of the province at this time, and the condemnatory records of the court and province use his spelling of the surname: "Wee present Mr. John Jocelyn for absenting himself from publique Meeteing on the Lords days" (Libby 1:334). John declines to discuss his per-sonal confrontations with the authorities, but he gnashes teeth in noting that the lawmakers "judge every man and woman to pay Five shillings *per* day, who comes not to their Assemblies" (179). A possible motive for his recurrent attacks on the New England theocracy was to ingratiate himself with New England's enemy, the court of Charles II. Above all, however, he was nettled by the recurrent Puritan intrusions into his brother's government in Maine. He details one incident from among the Massachusetts trespasses and usurpations, alludes briefly to other "foul proceedings," and concludes by pleading for "some consideration of the great losses, charge and labour" exacted from Henry and the other faithful representatives of "his Sacred Majesties Dominion" in America (198).

The king may have heard his pleas. In the several years just prior to Josselyn's appearance in print, the descendants of Mason and Gorges had approached the king and Privy Council many times about the legal muddle in New England. Between 1676 and 1680, possibly in response to growing unrest, the Council for Trade and Plantations in England compiled a list of pertinent publications that included both of Josselyn's books. Also in 1676, two years after the appearance of *Two Voyages*, the crown sent out Edward Randolph to attempt to wrestle the Massachusetts Bay into submission. Josselyn's writings may have contributed to this decision, which the British patriots in New England certainly applauded. Perhaps he was rewarded for his support of royal affairs. In a rare biographical interlude, he hints that he enjoyed court patronage after completing his last voyage: "I am now return'd into my Native Countrey, and by the providence of the Almighty, and the bounty of my Royal Soveraigness am disposed to a holy quiet of study and meditation" (151). This reprieve from workaday affairs probably allowed him to produce his books.

The impression is strong in the conclusion of his second voyage that the weary traveler sensed the inevitability of Puritan rule in New England. Overwhelmed by politics, feeling the weight of his six decades, he returned home in 1671 to fulfil "the *French* proverb, Travail where thou canst, but dye where thou oughtest, that is, in thine own Countrey" (215). Exactly where and when he died remain untraced. The best biographical information would make him sixty-six or sixty-seven in 1674, after which all is conjectural, although Horace P. Beck (26) has connected him with a tombstone in Willingale Doe that bears his name and a death date of 1700. If this is indeed the author's grave, then he lived to an age of ninety-two or more, perhaps authenticating the efficacy of his herbal restoratives and cures.

III

Josselyn's contributions to early American culture have been undervalued. Admittedly, his intentions in writing were utilitarian. He hoped to offer practical advice for the settler, natural history for the amateur scientist, political commentary for the British court. In the process of accomplishing these goals, however, he indulges an aesthetic impulse in more ways than he probably supposed. Interpolated among the catalogs and ostensibly factual narratives of his experience are passages lyrical, satirical, and humorous. In addition to his verses praising Indian women and a storm at sea, he furnishes prose odes upon the virtues of tobacco, the magnitude of moose, and the skills of savage natives untainted by white ways. As a Cavalier gentleman, he pronounces roundly and with irony against planters' sloth and Puritan hypocrisy and greed. Playing to a homebound British audience, he depicts New England's natural features with an exaggeration often extravagant, thus spoofing the innocence of those for whom America, willy nilly, defied imagination's boundaries. Not all readers could have possessed the skills to appreciate his fantastic incongruities; for those who sought mere facts, he protests his veracity and thereby shrewdly implicates their doubt. The complex and engaging personality behind the *Two Voyages* allows it to transcend the common shuffle of seventeenth-century travel accounts.

The stylistic vagaries of his prose may prove perplexing to the uninitiated. He reveals only sporadic concern for splicing clauses, and his paragraphs sometimes bulk interminably, but by and large his style contrasts refreshingly with the sober architectonics of contemporaries like William Bradford and Increase Mather. His language rhythms simulate native speech, and his homespun diction is a joy. Deliberate unsophistication is evident especially in the *Two Voyages*, which opens with a recital of names, dates, figures, and places germane to the departure of his ship for New England. "At *Gravesend* I began my Journal," he writes (2), and the eleven pages that follow are evidently unhewn journal entries. Pages 12–19, comprised of supply lists for the prospective planter, are scarcely more sophisticated; many critical judgments of Josselyn probably have been founded on the basis of these first few pages only. Thereafter the author exercises greater care and entertains his audience with more colorful details, including many marvels. Form follows function in sentences relating continuous action. A confrontation with marauding wolves is described in a virtually nonstop flow of words (20–22) equalled only by his account of Indians pursuing a bull moose (136–38). The latter narrative features a 430-word sentence that engagingly approximates the action of the chase.

His book is a rich resource for the etymologist. Many words antedate their earliest citations in the *Oxford English Dictionary* (*OED*), others correspond only inexactly to the definitions listed there, and still others constitute unrecorded variant forms. His use of "*Cawdimawdie*" (8), probably to denote the common curlew, is recorded elsewhere only by the Romantic laborer-poet of Northamptonshire, John Clare. The author fortunately glosses "transcendentia," of which no other record exists, to mean creatures of extraordinary size "which are the indelible Characters of God, and which discover God" (89). Henry David Thoreau read Josselyn and noted this word in his journal. Another interesting form, "*Famacides*" (149), receives no citation in the *OED*, although its context and familiar roots clearly indicate Josselyn intended to denote persons who kill by slander or defamation, persons who, as it were, murder fame. "Gally-patch" (38), a section of a turtle's shell, represents an obscure variant of *calipash*, whose tangled origins may be unwoven by comparison with Josselyn's use, which precedes the earliest record by fifteen years. These samples represent only a few of the book's linguistic treasures.

Josselyn was also a poet. *New-Englands Rarities* ends with complimentary verses included "by way of Divertisement, or Recreation" upon an "*Indian* SQUA, or Female *Indian*, trick'd up in all her bravery" (99). Erotic in theme, metaphysical in tone and diction, these twenty lines contrast dark and sensuous Indian women with their fair Caucasian counterparts. Josselyn reasons that his English readers, having endured the book's anatomy of plant and animal species, had earned the lyric diversion that the poem provides. Teasingly he notes that the native maidens are "seldome without a *Come to me*, or *Cos Amoris*, in their Countenance," despite which most are "of a modest deportment" (100). The rough lines on a sea storm from the *Two Voyages* are much different. They borrow the strength of Anglo-Saxon rhythms and alliteration to simulate the terror evoked by thunder and lightning on the high seas. Again drawing from his travel experiences, Josselyn vividly illustrates how the natural event acquired supernatural dimensions, the passengers grew desperate and confused, and the pilot's "Art stood amaz'd in Ambiguity" (31). Scholars of American literature have praised both poems, and a recent dictionary terms the sea storm verse "one of the finest short poems in early American literature" (*American Writers before 1800* 2: 847).

Equally valuable to the student of American culture are Josselyn's fascinating records of Indian life. Unaccountably, this aspect of his writings has been largely overlooked. The narratives of Mary Rowlandson and other captives of the Indians form the basis for so many generalizations about racial interactions during the seventeenth century that the more sympathetic accounts of Josselyn, William Wood, Thomas Morton, and Roger Williams are unfairly overshadowed. Like these literary predecessors, Josselyn admires the native Americans for their craft and self-reliance. This admiration he qualifies, however, with reservations about their want of husbandry and Christian faith. Unlike the Puritans, he is openly responsive to Indian women, whom he assesses in the *Two Voyages* as "very comely, having good features, their faces plump and round, and generally plump of their Bodies, . . . as soft and smooth as a mole-skin" (124). Here again he insists the Indians "are of a modest demeanor . . . and indeed do shame our *English* rusticks whose rudeness in many things exceedeth theirs" (124–25). As both books illustrate, he came to know the natives well and occasionally served as their physician.

The European settlers—greedy merchants and "droanish" planters alike—suffer by comparison with the New England tribes. Trading among the Indians for furs, the mercenary French and English wrongly charm them with rum, he laments. "Thus instead of bringing of them to the knowledge of Christianitie, we have taught them to commit the beastly and crying sins of our Nation, for a little profit" (139). This passage significantly overturns the standard Puritan rhetoric, which figures American natives as base and beastly when placed beside the Europeans.

English society is tainted, Josselyn implies, while the native American is pure. As J. A. Leo Lemay has shown, many early accounts of the culture reflect belief in a "stage theory" of human civilization, according to which "the Indians are living in the 'heroic' stage of civilization" (206). This fact serves to explain the voyager's quaint observation that Indian braves are natural poets whose formal speeches run "sometimes an hour long, the last word of a line riming with the last word of the following line" (135), a claim that links them with the bardic tradition of ancient Greece. As elsewhere in his books, New England represents a virgin land besmirched by contact with the Old World. Writing well before Jean Jacques Rousseau, Josselyn illustrates that the concept of the noble savage had ample literary precedent.

If not for the ravages of European immigration, the American Indian still would be residing in a golden age. To enforce this point, Josselyn borrows from the ancients. His account of the Indians' lengthy pursuit of a bull moose inspires a sentence of epic proportions and a learned quotation in Latin from Virgil's *Aeneid* (137). Having slain the beast at last, "they make their *Vulcan* or fire near to a great Tree" and settle in to feast (138). Elsewhere, "you would think it strange to see, yea admire if you saw the bold *Barbarians* in their light *Canows* rush down the swift and head-long stream with desperate speed, but with excellent dexterity" in the face of imminent danger (142). The Indians dwell in a primitive but inherently virtuous state of cultural evolution once matched by the pagan peoples of Europe. Lucan's historical poem *Pharsalia* comes to point up similarities between the ancient Britons, as the conquering Romans found them, and the aboriginal Americans as discovered by the English (145). Writing from a neoclassical perspective, Josselyn draws upon Greek and Roman literature to depict the American Indian. His respectful portrait differs immensely from those of his Puritan peers.

For Josselyn, the native Americans are privy to an intimate correspondence with worlds invisible to the settler from oversea. The wonders that this correspondence reveals are valuable not only in themselves, Josselyn reasons, but also insofar as they contribute knowledge useful to the prospective colonist. The Protestant Reformation had emphasized the ubiquity of Satan within the pale of Christian faith; all the more plausible, therefore, was the presence of evil among unsuspecting heathens. Worshiping a wrathful and capricious creator, New England Puritans constantly sought proof of election; the Indians, in paradoxically similar fashion, "live in a wretched consternation worshipping the Devil for fear" (133). On the other hand, "they dye patiently both men and women, not knowing of a Hell to scare them, nor a Conscience to terrifie them" (132). The European missionary performed a dubious service when he began acquainting American natives with religious principles, especially sin and damnation. Knowledge of these fruits is harmful, while ignorance of Old World beliefs is bliss. After their evil god Cheepie appears to several Indians, they report that he resembled an Englishman, "clothed with hat and coat, shooes and stockins," an association whose irony is not lost on Josselyn (133).

More useful to prospective colonists are bits of lore conferred upon them by the natives. As Squanto had shown the hungry Plymouth pilgrims how best to grow maize, so Josselyn's kindly tribesmen share more arcane knowledge. To rid gardens of harmful worms, Maine Indians gather them in bowls, which then they float to sea upon the ebbing tide. The remaining worms respond sympathetically to this magic, and "within a day or two if you go into your field you may look your eyes out sooner than find any of them" (116). Likewise the natives capture precious sturgeon by luring them at night to birch-bark fires suspended from the sides of their canoes (141). They convey knowledge of "an admirable rare Creature" called a tree buck, which, if spied "walking upon the branches of an *Oake* when they go out in a morning to hunt, they shall have good luck that day" (61–62). Josselyn's response to Indian lore divides between the objectivity of the folklorist and the dutiful utilitarianism of the Restoration travel writer. His point of view makes him a more valuable source to later folklorists than more rational or more religious observers. In fuller fashion than anyone of the period, he catalogs the wisdom and folkways of the native tribes.

"Chronological Observations of America, From the year of the World to the year of Christ" is an exhaustive chronicle of the New World that concludes both books and rests squarely in the tradition of the earliest English literature. The first four pages prove most interesting for what they reveal about their compiler, whose ambitious design belies his vows of modesty. The remaining pages are a valuable synthesis of historical sources relating to the exploration, settlement, and political proceedings of the New World. Greatly expanded and revised for inclusion in the *Two Voyages*, this document may have been intended originally for individual publication; it disrupts the pagination and bears a separate title page. As though in conscious imitation of King Alfred's *Anglo-Saxon Chronicle*, Josselyn opens with Caesar's invasion of Britain, an event that bears tangentially at best upon America itself. His assumption may be that the British, in emulation of the ancient Romans, were striving to wield a civilizing influence over the savages of North America. Like the British antiquarian John Stow, compiler of *A Generall Chronicle of England, from Brute unto this present Yeare of Christe* (1580), Josselyn is predisposed to lend credence to fabulous and providential events. Thomas Prince's numerous elections as governor of the New Plymouth Colony, for example, appear alongside such surprising accounts as this one, for 1671: an unnamed Dutch shipmaster who had just returned from his travels reported "two Islands never before discovered, where were men all hairy, Eleven foot in height" (279).

No educated Englishman of the seventeenth century could have been ignorant of the body of fables pertaining to the New World. By the time Josselyn wrote, literary treatments had traveled full circuit from frothing hyperbole to satire and back again. Such familiarity both complicated and facilitated the writer's task. On the one hand, it invited disbelief among the reading public. On the other, it made available thematic and rhetorical conventions that built upon America's magnitude, abundance, natural exotica, and economic opportunity.

Nonetheless, contemporary book buyers relished fantastic stories, and the strange New World experience afforded Josselyn the opportunity to capitalize upon a popular readership as yet unaffected by the New Science. Travel accounts commonly were printed in London for the delectation of the small but literate middle class. The expense of securing approval for publication forced travel writers to treat safe political, commercial, and theological causes. As a consequence, the modern critic often judges their books to be subliterary. But the provincial British reader was not aesthetically fastidious; he cared more for prodigies, marvels, and sensation than for plays or epic poems. This enthusiasm liberated travelers and promoters from strict adherence to the truth, allowing them to experiment with the tall tales, legends, hearsay, and myths that contributed to the rise of the novel.

Certainly Josselyn embarked upon his voyages bearing a fair share of preconceptions, some of which he saw fulfilled. Grasses rose "man-high unmowed, uneaten and uselessly withering" (43); valleys were "infinitely thick set with Trees . . . under the shades whereof you may freely walk two or three mile together" (44); radishes sown there grow "as big as a mans Arm" (188). Such images, reported as fact, matched or exceeded the bounds of English pastoral myth and romance. But Josselyn also confesses to having seen a number of his wishful preconceptions foiled by the adverse impacts of immigration. Turkeys, formerly flourishing in flocks of "threescore," had been all but destroyed within twenty-five years (*Rarities* 9); passenger pigeons, once innumerable, were "much diminished, the *English* taking them with Nets" (99). A belated traveler, following the tracks of John Smith and others, Josselyn laments the changes wrought by rapid colonization. Nonetheless, he eagerly exploits the fables that still enchanted British audiences.

With the authority of a physician and scientist, both of which he actually was by Restoration standards, Josselyn extravagantly plays up the natural productions of the New World. He argues that the whale "feeds upon *Ambergreece*," actually a vomited excrescence, but defined with mock objectivity as "a kind of Mushroom growing at the bottom of some Seas" (*Rarities* 36). Arrived in Maine, he reports lakes so large and deep that "in one of them huge fishes like Whales are to be seen" (203). This tantalizing detail helps explain Ben Franklin's practical hoax about the Great Lakes whaling industry, made possible when the hungry beasts chase codfish up Niagara Falls. Whereas William Wood had promoted the manly New England sport of bearbaiting, Josselyn cautions that bear brains are "venomous," and the beasts quite fierce in mating season when "they walk the Country twenty, thirty, forty in a company, making a hideous noise with roaring, which," happily for visiting Europeans, "you may hear a mile or two before they come so near to endanger the Traveller" (*Rarities*

13). Frequently he claims to distinguish between what he's heard and what he has observed firsthand. Pond frogs, he flatly states, "when they set upon their breech are a Foot high," although "the *Indians* will tell you, that up in the Country there are Pond *Frogs* as big as a Child of a year old" (*Rarities* 38). Without a wobble he tosses off many similar comparisons, which later would become the stock-in-trade of American humorists.

Josselyn's ability to imbue the land with wonder gives his work its most attractive dimension. Cataloging fauna, he raises the curtain upon his diverse species as though they were players in a pageant drama, thereby modifying and enriching the familiar promoters' theme of overabundance: "The fish are swum by, and the serpents are creeping on, terrible creatures, carrying stings in their Tails" (114). Striving to engage his audience, he builds in details that contradict the facts of natural history as he had presented them in *Rarities*, where the rattlesnake more accurately "poysons with a Vapour that comes thorough two crooked Fangs" (38). The supernatural attributes of this land also include witches, fairies, and other "strange apparitions if you will believe report" (182). Did his seventeenth-century readers "believe report"? The New England that Josselyn depicts is more a region to be wondered at from a distance than easily harnessed and bent to human will. If he hoped to attract settlers to the New World, he chose peculiar means to do so. One of the book's foremost effects must have been to amaze and, in some cases, to dissuade its audience from considering immigration.

Nor do his passing barbs at the Puritans appear designed to attract prospective planters. Disaffected by the civil and ecclesiastical strictures of the New England theocracy, Josselyn depicts its leaders as exceedingly complacent and illiberal. He is not specifically anticlerical, however, nor does he employ derisive allegory of the sort that shapes so much of the *New English Canaan*, published thirty-seven years before by Thomas Morton, who had greater cause to dislike the "cruel schismatics" who had fined, jailed, and banished him. In Josselyn's view the Puritans ruled with too heavy a hand and hypocritically exhibited excessive pride: "The grose *Goddons*, or great masters, as also some of their Merchants are . . . inexplicably covetous and proud, they receive your gifts but as an homage or tribute due to their transcendency, which is a fault their Clergie are also guilty of, whose living is upon the bounty of their hearers" (180). They are collectively the most powerful figures in New England, and the most self-satisfied. In *The Puritans*, Thomas H. Johnson and Perry Miller have corroborated Josselyn: "though sketched in pique his outline does not seriously misrepresent the composite Yankee" (2:379). Nonetheless, his candid character profiles would not have served to spur colonization.

Robert D. Arner has accurately noted that Josselyn's verbal abuse is "especially focused on the Puritans' pretense of otherworldliness while they keep their eyes squarely on the main chance" (186). Josselyn describes how the Massachusetts merchant piously decries drunkenness among planters and fishermen, endorses fining or committing violators to stocks, and yet, "to increase his gains," will tempt them with liquors from his "walking Tavern" (211). Also, he lacks Christian charity. Husbandmen unable to pay debts often find themselves bereft of plantation and cattle, thrust "out of house and home, poor Creatures, to look out for a new habitation in some remote place where they begin the world again" (212). Self-righteous and exclusive, the churchmen forbid nonmembers to partake in holy sacraments. As a result, "Many hundred Souls there be amongst them grown up to men & womens estate that were never Christened" (179), a fact of ecclesiastical history modified by the Half-Way Covenant of 1662. The Puritans are "great Syndics, or censors, or controllers of other mens manners, and savagely factious amongst themselves." Merchants and churchmen alike are "full of ludification and injurious dealing, and cruelty the extreamest of all vices" (181). Josselyn's withering denunciations anticipate the anti-Yankee sketches by such later American writers as Washington Irving and James Russell Lowell.

Just as the author's fine treatment of the Indians has been overlooked, so too has a unique aspect of his literary personality. Recurrently in the *Two Voyages* he berates those readers who, he knows, will cast a skeptical eye upon his writing. This feature of the book is confined to the second voyage, which took place some twenty-five years after the first and therefore reflects his advanced age and disillusionment. By 1671, when he returned for good to England, "heartily weary and expecting the approach of winter," he had witnessed "the Government of the province turned topsi-turvy" (213); the peace and prosperity envisioned for the Gorges enterprise in Maine were not forthcoming. Probably also, by the time he wrote, he was bitter over negative criticism directed toward *Rarities*.

Reports of American exotica had become suspect, even when couched in scientific terms. In reaction against such suspicion, the author mounts a complex strategy of challenging the doubts he senses his readers uttering. His tone grows irascible and adds a measurable tension to his work. The first and most abusive attack opens the second voyage. There he charges that "a sort of stagnant stinking spirits, who, like flyes, lye sucking at the botches of carnal pleasures, and never travelled so much Sea, as is between *Heth-ferry*, and *Lyon-Key*; yet notwithstanding, (sitting in the Chair of the scornful over their whifts and draughts of intoxication) will desperately censure the relations of the greatest Travellers" (34). These harsh words appear designed to offend and alienate, and certainly in some instances they had such an effect. Yet they also constitute a sly rhetorical appeal implicating all skeptics as drunkards, hypocrites, and debauchees. This specious indictment must have served to polarize his audience into believers and nonbelievers, perhaps converting some gullible few who secretly had harbored doubts. By associating incredulity with want of temperance, Josselyn shrewdly vanquishes the doubts of his less sophisticated followers.

As his books' numerous tall tales illustrate, readers had just cause for incredulity. Troculuses, Josselyn assures us, are small fowl possessed of sharp feathers "which they stick into the sides of the Chymney" where they nest; upon departure for the season, "they never fail to throw down one of their young Birds into the room by way of Gratitude" (*Rarities* 7). Spawned by the medieval bestiary, Josselyn's portrait of this bird (presumably the chimney swift) relies for its impact upon anthropomorphic exaggeration. As elsewhere, he intimates that New Englanders enjoy cozy familiarity with their larger-than-life fellow creatures. The moose indigenous to Maine, he claims in the *Two Voyages*, is "a Monster of superfluity" whose vast dimensions "hath been taken by some of my *sceptique* Readers to be monstrous lyes" (89). His first book had reported similarly on this beast, and Josselyn's self-defense here proves he still felt wounded by his critics. Accordingly, he challenges their skepticism and reviles their unwillingness to take his report on faith.

Trust is the commodity the traveler seeks to gain. Appealing to the authority of the Roman historian Pliny, Josselyn protests that owl eggs placed in a drunkard's cup "will make him loath drunkenness ever after" (96–97). (This cure presumably effects teetotalism because the owl is such a sober bird.) Anticipating disbelief, he mounts a complex argument in which Athens figures as an academy for the advancement of God's wondrous ways. The curse of aspersion has sprung from among "a Generation of men and women in this prophane age that despise God's learning and his Ushers to the *Athenians*, choosing to wallow in the pleasures of sin for a season" (98). Identifying himself here as a sacred official in the academy of natural philosophy, he charges that those who doubt his word are sinfully denying the miracles of creation. Playing thus upon his readers' lack of faith, he borrows techniques from the sermon to affirm his most preposterous claims. Nearly two centuries later, Herman Melville's confidence man would exploit similar appeals to defraud his listeners of their reluctant faith in humankind.

His numerous lapses into censure call upon Josselyn's greatest resources as a writer. Indeed, so recurrent are these features of the book that they constitute variations on a prevalent theme. Repeatedly he indicts his disbelievers for moral turpitude and atheism; despite his political and religious connections to the Cavaliers, his rhetoric appears to league him rather with the Puritans. Perhaps the many years he spent in New England, forced to attend the lengthy sermons all along, had had more impact than he could acknowledge. Upon reporting ten thousand alewives caught in two hours by a pair of fishermen, he adverts to miracles and the problem of belief, observing that reactions to his claim likely will take the form of "an Adulterate construction from those that are somewhat akin to St. *Peters* mockers, such as deny the last judgement" (108). The terms of this analogy identify the author with the beleaguered Saint Peter; he yearns to banish his detractors along with those of Christ's foremost disciple. Again the implications are weighty: failure to accredit his travel account signifies a more thoroughgoing skepticism of the Christian faith.

Josselyn's apostrophes to the malcontents among his audience create an ongoing war with the reader—a war of wit, challenge, charge, and countercharge. These fictive exchanges betoken a rhetorical strategy arising from his desire to offset the reputation of travel writers as liars, a reputation under which he appears particularly to have smarted. His sensitivity thus manifests itself in irascibility. However, that he was sensitive to critical response even in so abrasive a manner should serve as index of the forethought that went into shaping his account. Earlier writers on America likewise had exhibited traces of combat against skepticism, most notably William Wood and John Smith, with both of whose works Josselyn was demonstrably familiar. In the *Two Voyages*, however, this feature of early American literature gains its fullest expression, a sort of secular version of the jeremiad. At the conclusion of his report on Indian culture, the most extended instance of vituperation occurs.

As if to justify having examined the Indians in such detail, he points out that New England previously had been "solely possesst" by them. Again he creates a hypothetical dialogue with his detractors: "methinks I hear my skeptick Readers muttering out of their scuttle mouths, what will accrew to us by this rambling *Logodiarce*? You do but bring straw into *Egypt*, a Countrey abounding with Corn" (149). Once again adversity, imagined or otherwise, prompts his richest diction and most striking metaphors. A scuttle operates as a hatch in the side of a ship, and thus the word figuratively images a mouth forever open and exclaiming. But it also suggests the verb, which denotes sinking a craft by piercing its hull, as though his book were a boat the critics hoped to swamp. "*Logodiarce*" is an unrecorded variant of the Greek *logodiarrhe*, a flux or flow of words, and its use by his imagined detractors heightens the tension of his apologia. Conscious that they wished to "accrew" useful or profitable knowledge from his account, Josselyn thus intricately defends his tendency to convey knowledge from which no material benefit may be gained. Obliquely he confesses his aesthetic motives: "I have done what I can to please you, I have piped and you will not dance. I have told you as strange things as ever you or your Fathers have heard" (149–50). Limited by the strictures of factuality and instrumentalism, Josselyn appears to be a frustrated artist trapped in the mode of travel literature.

At this point in the book he becomes so engaged in countering his presumed accusers that he forgets to accommodate the larger audience and resorts to the second-person point of view. Closing a carefully contrived sequence of metaphors, he exclaims with exasperation, "'tis the poyson of *Asps* under your tongue that swells you: truly, I do take you rather to be Spider catchers than Spiders, such as will not laudably employ themselves, nor suffer others" (150). The first image graphically conveys his aggravation before those critics whom he figures as snakes so swollen with venom that they involuntarily strike the faultless traveler. The second draws upon familiar English proverbs extolling the industry of spiders, creatures that the slothful critic cannot countenance and therefore must restrain from their endeavors. Again Josselyn waxes most allusive and metaphorical—most literary—when berating his audience for its alleged skepticism. His war with the reader serves to structure the book and to contribute further dimension to an account already more complex and appealing than its peers.

A close reading of the *Two Voyages* also reveals the author's familiarity with earlier writers in New England, especially John Smith, William Wood, Thomas Morton, and Edward Johnson. Neither Wood nor his *New Englands Prospect* (1634) is ever mentioned by name, but borrowings are evident throughout. Wood's promotional tract, composed in lively Elizabethan verse and prose, appears to have served as Josselyn's foremost American model. Morton's *New English Canaan* (1637) was also influential, especially in the area of Indian culture; but in most other respects it is a less thorough, albeit more unified, account than the *Two Voyages*. Josselyn certainly was familiar with Smith's *Description of New England* (1616), and probably with his *Generall Historie* (1621) as well. Several echoes from Roger Williams argue his familiarity with *A Key into the Langage of America* (1643). But the most surprising source is Edward Johnson's *Wonder-Working Providence* (1654), an influence previously unnoted by scholars but one that served for many geographical descriptions and historical statistics. Josselyn eschews Johnson's militant Puritan pieties when borrowing from the book. He was well aware of his predecessors and conscious of the tradition in which he wrote.

If Josselyn's work is promotional in purpose, it may understandably have failed to draw settlers because it so candidly describes the political and domestic hardships of seventeenth-century New England. That he follows promotional conventions—lists of supplies to be brought from England, catalogs of flora and fauna, portraits of the native Americans—may be evidence only that he hoped thereby to gain an audience. Although many commentators have condemned his alleged credulity, more recent writers believe that Josselyn operates instead by slyly ridiculing the gullibility of his unversed British readers. Perhaps the truth lies somewhere between these extreme points of view. Perhaps Josselyn refuses either to "impeach or enforce" the validity of his reported legendry and lore because he sensed that from this tension of equivocation his book could derive its modest art.

Two Voyages to New-England

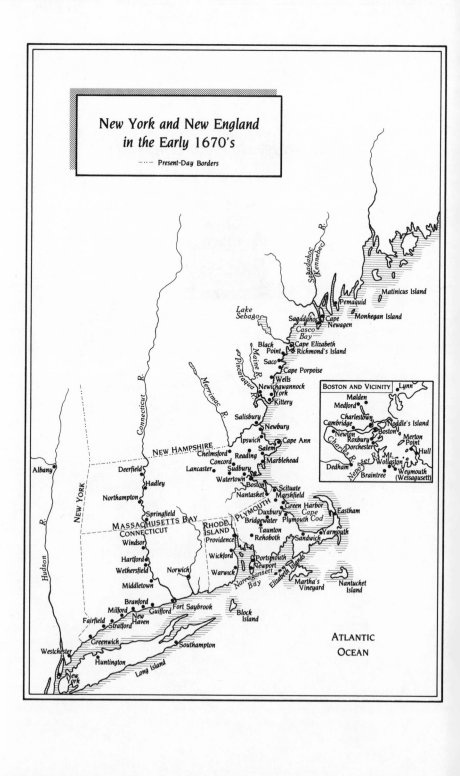

New York and New England
in the Early 1670's
---- Present-Day Borders

BOSTON AND VICINITY

AN ACCOUNT OF
TWO VOYAGES TO
NEW-ENGLAND.

Wherein you have the setting out of a Ship, with the charges; The prices of all necessaries for furnishing a Planter and his Family at his first coming; A Description of the Countrey, Natives and Creatures, with their Merchantil and Physical use; The Government of the Countrey as it is now possessed by the *English, &c.* A large Chronological Table of the most remarkable passages, from the first discovering of the Continent of *America*, to the year 1673.[1]

BY
John Josselyn Gent.

Memner. distich rendred English by Dr. *Heylin.*

> *Heart, take thine ease,*
> *Men hard to please*
> *Thou haply might'st offend,*
> *Though one speak ill*
> *Of thee, some will*
> *Say better; there's an end.*[2]

London, Printed for *Giles Widdows,* at the *Green-Dragon* in St. *Paul's* Church-yard, 1674.

I

Notes to title page

1. Among the minor revisions of the title page for the "Second Addition," the most significant is the exclusion of "with their Merchantil and Physical use." Josselyn may have had some second thoughts about his book's otherwise pervasive utilitarianism.

2. Seventh-century Greek poet Mimnermus (Memner) authored the couplet (distich) of which these lines are a translation. Evidently they are not, however, the translation of the Royalist theologian Peter Heylyn (1600–1662), in whose *History of . . . St. George of Cappadocia* the couplet is rendered thus: "Soule, be at rest: though some offended be, / And speake thee foule; others will cherish thee" (9). It is unlikely Heylyn gave the lines a second translation. Thus either Josselyn's memory or his journal failed him, and the lines evidently originate elsewhere.

To the

Right Honourable,

and

Most Illustrious

the

President & Fellows

of the

ROYAL SOCIETY:

The following Account of Two

Voyages

to

New-England,

Is Most Humbly presented

By the Authour

John Josselyn

A RELATION
OF TWO VOYAGES TO
New-England.

The first Voyage.

ANNO Dom. 1638. *April* the 26th being *Thursday*, I came to *Gravesend* and went aboard the *New Supply, alias,* the *Nicholas* of *London,* a Ship of good force, of 300 Tuns burden, carrying 20 Sacre and Minion,[3] man'd with 48 Sailers, the Master *Robert Taylor,* the Merchant or undertaker Mr. *Edward Tinge,* with 164 Passengers men, women and children.

[p. 2] At *Gravesend* I began my Journal,[4] from whence we departed on the 26. of *April,* about Six of the clock at night, and went down into the *Hope.*

The 27. being *Fryday,* we set sail out of the *Hope,* and about Nine of the clock at night we came to an anchor in *Margaret*-Road in three fathom and a half water: by the way we past a States man of war, of 500 Tun, cast away a month before upon the *Good-win,*[5] nothing remaining visible above water but her main mast top, 16 of her men were drowned, the rest saved by Fishermen.

---

3. Saker (Sacree) and minion were small kinds of cannon. The bore of a saker was three and one-half inches; that of the minion, generally three.

4. Josselyn's journal is not extant.

5. States man of war: Dutch military ship. Goodwin Sands, dangerous shoals along the north Straits of Dover.

The 28. we twined into the Downs, where Captain *Clark* one of his Majesties Captains in the Navy, came aboard of us in the afternoon, and prest two of our Trumpeters.[6] Here we had good store of Flounders from the Fishermen, new taken out of the Sea and living, which being readily gutted, were fry'd while they were warm; me thoughts I never tasted of a delicater Fish in all my life before.

The Third of *May* being *Ascension* day, in the afternoon we weighed out of the *Downs*, the wind at *E.* and ran down into *Dover* Road, and lay by the lee, whilst they sent the Skiffe ashore for one of the Masters mates: by the way we past *Sandwich* in the [p. 3] *Hope, Sandown-Castle, Deal*; so we steered away for *Doniesse*, from thence we steered *S.W.* ½ *S.* for the *Beachie*, about one of the clock at night the wind took us a stayes[7] with a gust, rain, thunder and lightning, and now a Servant of one of the passengers sickned of the small pox.

The Fifth day in the afternoon we Anchored, the *Isle* of *Wight W.N.W.* 10 leagues off, *Beachie E.N.E.* 8 leagues off, rode in 32 fathom water at low water, at 8 of the clock at night the land over the Needles bore *N.W.* 4 leagues off, we steered *W.* afore the Start, at noon the Boult was *N.W.* by *W.* about 3½ leagues off, we were becalmed from 7 of the clock in the morning, till 12 of the clock at noon, where we took good store of *Whitings*, and half a score *Gurnets*,[8] this afternoon an infinite number of *Porpisces* shewed themselves above water round about the ship, as far as we could kenn, the night proved tempestuous with much lightning and thunder.

The Sixth day being *Sunday* at five of the clock at night the *Lizard* was *N.W.* by *W.* 6 leagues off, and the *Blackhead* which is to the westward of *Falmouth* was *N.W.* about 5 leagues off.

The Seventh day the uttermost part of *Silly* was *N.E.* 12 leagues off, and now we began to sail by the logg.[9]

---

6. Twined: turned. The heralds were forced or impressed into service, since military matters took priority over private enterprises.

7. That is, put the ship on another tack.

8. Whitings: a name for various species of croaker, hake, and cod. "*Gurnets*" now are gurnards, genus *Prionotus*.

9. Scilly Isles: group of 140 islands off Land's End, Cornwall. The "logg" was a floating apparatus used to determine the rate of a ship's motion.

[p. 4] The Eighth day, one *Boremans* man a passenger was duck'd at the main yards arm (for being drunk with his Masters strong waters which he stole) thrice, and fire given to two whole *Sacree*, at that instant. Two mighty Whales we now saw, the one spouted water through two great holes in her head into the Air a great height, and making a great noise with puffing and blowing, the Seamen called her a Soufler;[10] the other was further off, about a league from the Ship, fighting with the Sword-fish, and the Flail-fish, whose stroakes with a fin that growes upon her back like a flail, upon the back of the Whale, we heard with amazement:[11] when presently some more than half as far again we spied a spout from above, it came pouring down like a River of water; So that if they should light in any Ship, she were in danger to be presently sunk down into the Sea, and falleth with such an extream violence all whole together as one drop, or as water out of a Vessel, and dured[12] a quarter of an hour, making the Sea to boyle like a pot, and if any Vessel be near, it sucks it in. I saw many of these spouts afterwards at nearer distance. In the afternoon the Mariners struck a Porpice, called also a *Marsovious* or Sea-hogg, with an harping iron, and hoisted her aboard, [p. 5] they cut some of it into thin pieces, and fryed, it tasts like rusty Bacon, or hung Beef, if not worse; but the Liver boiled and soused sometime in Vinegar is more grateful to the pallat.[13] About 8 of the clock at night, a flame settled upon the main mast, it was about the bigness of a great Candle, and is called by our Seamen St. *Elmes* fire, and is commonly thought to be a Spirit; if two appear they prognosticate safety: These are known to the learned by the names of *Castor* and *Pollux*, to the *Italians* by St. *Nicholas* and St. *Hermes*, by the *Spaniards* called *Corpos Santos*.[14]

10. This is the only *OED* incidence of the word, used to designate a whale, from French *souffler*, "to blow."

11. The "Flail-fish" is perhaps a species of ray, whose tail resembles a whip or flail. Certainly not a sailfish, however, which Josselyn catalogs separately (113).

12. Continued, endured.

13. Harping iron: harpoon. Rusty: reisty or rancid.

14. Corposant (from *Corpos Santos*) is now most commonly known as Saint Elmo's fire, an electrical phenomenon that occurs during thunderstorms. According to myth, the twins Castor and Pollux saved the Argonauts from a tempest when two flames appeared above the twins' heads and caused the wind to

The Ninth day, about two of the clock in the afternoon, we found the head of our main mast close to the cap twisted and shivered, and we presently after found the fore-top-mast crackt a little above the cap; So they wolled them both, and about two of the clock in the morning 7 new long Boat oars brake away from our Star-board quarter with a horrid crack.[15]

The Eleventh day, they observed and made the Ship to be in latitude 48 degrees 46 minuts, having a great Sea all night; about 6 of the clock in the morning we spake with Mr. *Rupe* in a Ship of *Dartmouth*, which came from *Marcelloes*; and now is *Silly N.E.* by *E.* 34 leagues off; [p. 6] about 9 of the clock at night we sounded, and had 85 fathom water, small brownish pepperie sand, with a small piece of *Hakes* Tooth, and now we are 45 leagues off the *Lizard*, great Seas all night, and now we see to the *S.W.* six tall Ships, the wind being *S.W.*

The Twelfth day being *Whitsunday*, at prayer-time we found the Ships trine a foot by the stern,[16] and also the partie that was sick of the small pox now dyed, whom we buried in the Sea, tying a bullet (as the manner is) to his neck, and another to his leggs, turned him out at a Port-hole, giving fire to a great Gun. In the afternoon one *Martin Ivy* a stripling, servant to Captain *Thomas Cammock* was whipt naked at the Cap-stern, with a Cat with Nine tails, for filching 9 great Lemmons out of the *Chirurgeons* Cabbin, which he eat rinds and all in less than an hours time.[17]

---

abate; thus they became the patron deities of mariners. Saints Nicholas and Hermes also appear mythically as guardians of travelers.

15. The cap is a block of wood used to hold two masts together. Wolled: strengthened by winding with rope or chain.

16. Josselyn's precise meaning is unclear. *Trine* denotes a group of three, a triad, often with religious associations; since the company discovered the trine misplaced at prayer time, it may have been an object symbolizing the Christian Trinity. The 1833 editors suggest a misprint for *trim*, however, whereas Beck (28) conjectures that the ship had sprung a leak in the foregoing storm and that the term denotes "freeboard."

17. An agent for the Council for New England under John Mason and Sir Ferdinando Gorges, Thomas Cammock received a grant in 1631 of fifteen hundred acres of land at Black Point (now Prout's Neck, part of Scarborough) in Maine. He was nephew, by marriage, to the influential Robert Rich, Earl of Warwick (1587–1658). He died on a voyage to the West Indies in 1643, and

The Thirteenth day we took a Sharke, a great one, and hoisted him aboard with his two Companions (for there is never a Sharke, but hath a mate or two)[,] that is the Pilot-fish or Pilgrim, which lay upon his back close to a long finn; the other fish (somewhat bigger than the Pilot) about two foot long called a *Remora*, it hath no scales and sticks close to the Sharkes belly. [p. 7] So the Whale hath the Sea-Gudgeon, a small fish for his mate, marching before him, and guiding him; which I have seen likewise. The Seamen divided the Sharke into quarters, and made more quarter about it than the Purser, when he makes five quarters of a Oxe, and after they had cooked him, he proved very rough Grain'd, not worthy of wholesome preferment; but in the afternoon we took store of *Bonitoes*, or Spanish *Dolphins*, a fish about the size of a large Mackarel, beautified with admirable varietie of glittering colours in the water, and was excellent food.

The Fourteenth day we spake with a *Plimouth* man (about dinner time) bound for *New-found-land*, who having gone up westward sprang a leak, and now bore back for *Plimouth*. Now was *Silly* 50 leagues off, and now many of the passengers fall sick of the small Pox and Calenture.[18]

The Sixteenth Mr. *Clarke*, who came out of the *Downs* with us, and was bound for the Isle of *Providence*, one of the summer Islands; the *Spaniards* having taken it a little before, though unknown to *Clarke*, and to Captain *Nathaniel Butler* going Governour, they now departed from us the wind *N.W.* great Seas and stormie winds all night.[19]

[p. 8] The Seventeenth day, the wind at *N.W.* about 8 of the clock we saw 5 great Ships bound for the *Channel*, which was to the Westward of us, about two leagues off, we thought them to be

---

Henry Jocelyn married his widow, Margaret, thus becoming owner of his property. Cap-stern: capstan, a device for hauling in rope aboard the ship.

18. Severe fever, influenza.

19. Nathaniel Butler was governor of the Somers Isles (now Bermuda) from 1619 to 1622. In October 1638, under the auspices of the Providence Company, he arrived at Providence Island off the coast of Nicaragua to serve as governor, and he therefore must have been en route when Josselyn met him. Butler governed Providence until the Spanish takeover of May 1641.

Flemmings; here we expected to have met with Pirates, but were happily deceived.[20]

The One and twentieth day, the wind *S.* by *W.* great Seas and Wind in'd our courses,[21] and tryed from 5 of the clock afternoon, till 4 in the morning, the night being very stormie and dark; we lost Mr. *Goodlad* and his Ship, who came out with us, and bound for *Boston* in *New-England.*

The Eight and twentieth day, all this while a very great grown Sea and mighty winds.

June the first day in the afternoon, very thick foggie weather, we sailed by an inchanted Island, saw a great deal of filth and rubbish floating by the Ship, heard *Cawdimawdies,*[22] *Sea-gulls* and *Crowes,* (Birds that always frequent the shoar) but could see nothing by reason of the mist: towards Sunset, when we were past the Island, it cleared up.

The Fourteenth day of *June,* very foggie weather, we sailed by an Island of Ice (which lay on the Star-board side) three leagues in length mountain high, in form of [p. 9] land, with Bayes and Capes like high clift land, and a river pouring off it into the Sea. We saw likewise two or three Foxes, or Devils skipping upon it. These Islands of Ice are congealed in the North, and brought down in the spring-time with the Current to the banks on this side *New-found-land,* and there stopt, where they dissolve at last to water; by that time we had sailed half way by it, we met with a *French* Pickeroon.[23] Here it was as cold as in the middle of *January* in *England,* and so continued till we were some leagues beyond it.

The Sixteenth day we sounded, and found 35 fathom water, upon the bank of *New-found-land,* we cast out our hooks for Cod-

20. Compare the work of the English poet and traveler George Sandys, who wrote of his adventures near the Greek island of Rhodes, where "we expected to have met with Pirats, but were happily deceived," in *Travels* (72), originally titled *A Relation of a Journey Begun Anno. Dom. 1610,* the seventh edition of which appeared in 1673.

21. That is, caused the sailors to gather or take in the sails attached to the ship's lower yards.

22. Cawdy-mawdy: British dialect for the common curlew (*Numenius arquata*).

23. Picaroon: pirate ship or corsair.

fish, thick foggie weather, the Codd being taken on a Sunday morning, the Sectaries aboard threw those their servants took into the Sea again, although they wanted fresh victuals,[24] but the Sailers were not so nice, amongst many that were taken, we had some that were wasted fish, & it is observable and very strange, that fishes bodies do grow slender with age, their Tails and Heads retaining their former bigness; Fish of all Creatures have generally the biggest heads, and the first part that begins to taint in a fish is the head.

The nineteenth day, Captain *Thomas* [p. 10] *Cammock* (a near kinsman of the Earl of *Warwicks*)[25] now had another lad *Thomas Jones*, that dyed of the small pox at eight of the clock at night.

The Twentieth day, we saw a great number of Sea-bats, or Owles, called also flying fish, they are about the bigness of a Whiting, with four tinsel wings, with which they fly as long as they are wet, when pursued by other fishes. Here likewise we saw many Grandpisces[26] or Herring-hogs, hunting the scholes of Herrings, in the afternoon we saw a great fish called the *vehuella* or Sword fish, having a long, strong and sharp finn like a Swordblade on the top of his head, with which he pierced our Ship, and broke it off with striving to get loose, one of our Sailers dived and brought it aboard.

The One and twentieth day, we met with two *Bristow* men bound for *New-England*, and now we are 100 and 75 leagues off *Cape-Sable*, the sandy *Cape*, for so *Sable* in French signifieth, off of which lyeth the Isle of *Sable*, which is beyond *New-found-land*, where they take the *Amphibious* Creature, the *Walrus*, *Mors*, or *Sea-Horse*.

The Two and twentieth, another passenger dyed of a Consumption. Now we passed by the Southern part of *New-found-land*, [p. 11] within sight of it; the Southern part of *New-found-land* is said to be not above 600 leagues from *England*.

24. By "Sectaries," Josselyn intends members of a dissenting religious group, such as the Puritans or Quakers.

25. Robert Rich, second Earl of Warwick and governor in chief of the colonies.

26. The mammalian grampus (*Grampus griseus*). The term also was used during the period for both the pilot whale (*Globicephala melaena*) and the killer whale (*Orcinus orca*).

The Six and twentieth day, Capt. *Thomas Cammock* went aboard of a barke of 300 Tuns, laden with Island Wine, and but 7 men in her, and never a Gun, bound for *Richmonds* Island, set out by Mr. *Trelaney* of *Plimouth*, exceeding hot weather now.[27]

The Eight and twentieth, one of Mr. *Edward Ting's* the Undertakers men now dyed of the Phthisick.[28]

The Nine and twentieth day, sounded at night, and found 120 fathome water, the head of the Ship struck against a rock; At 4 of the clock we descryed two sail bound for *New-found-land*, and so for the *Streights*, they told us of general Earth-quake in *New-England*, of the birth of a Monster at *Boston*, in the *Massachusetts-Bay* a mortality, and now we are two leagues off *Cape Ann*.

The Thirtieth day proved stormie, and having lost the sight of Land, we saw none untill the morning; doubtfully discovering the Coast, fearing the Lee-shore all night we bore out to Sea.

July the first day, we sounded at 8 of the clock at night, and found 93 fathome water, descried land.

The Third day, we anchored in the *Bay* [p. 12] of *Massachusets* before *Boston*. Mr. *Tinges* other man now dyed of the small pox.

The Tenth day, I went a shore upon *Noddles* Island to Mr. *Samuel Maverick* (for my passage)[,] the only hospitable man in all the Countrey, giving entertainment to all Comers *gratis*.[29]

27. Richmond's Island figures prominently in early New England history. Lying just off Cape Elizabeth, Maine, it was part of the 1631 grant made to Robert Trelawny and Moses Goodyear of Plymouth, England, who sent agents there in 1632 to establish the long-lived trading plantation. There they employed some sixty men in fishing and furring.

One of Thomas Morton's followers, Walter Bagnall of Richmond's Island, engaged in trade among the Indians before being murdered by them in 1631. Governor Winthrop refused to dispatch troops to avenge the crime, and soon thereafter an innocent Indian, Black Will, was discovered on the island and hanged. More than two centuries later, a plowman overturned a stone vessel containing period coins believed to have been Bagnall's.

28. Tuberculosis.

29. Noddle's Island is now part of East Boston. Samuel Maverick (1602–c. 1676) was associated with the colonizing ventures of Mason and Gorges and is the author of *A Briefe Discription of New England* (written 1660; pub. 1885). He came to Massachusetts Bay in 1623. Edward Johnson in *Wonder-Working Providence* profiles him as "a man of a very loving and curteous behaviour, very ready to entertaine strangers, yet an enemy to the Reformation in hand" (64).

Now before I proceed any further, it will not be Impertinent to give the intending planter some Instructions for the furnishing of himself with things necessary for undertaking the Transport of his Family, or any others.

To which end observe, that a Ship of 150 Tuns, with 2 Decks and a half, and 26 men, with 12 pieces of Ordnance, the charge will amount *per* moneth, with the Mariners, to 120 pound *per* moneth. It is better to let the owners undertake for the Victualling of the Mariners, and their pay for Wages, and the Transporter only to take care of the passengers.

> *The common proportions of Victuals for the Sea to a Mess,*
> *being 4 men, is as followeth;*

Two pieces of Beef, of 3 pound and ¼ *per* piece.

Four pound of *Bread.*

One pint of *Pease.*

[p. 13] Four Gallons of *Bear*, with *Mustard* and *Vinegar* for three flesh dayes in the week. For four fish dayes, to each mess *per* day.

Two pieces of *Codd* or *Habberdine*,[30] making three pieces of a fish.

One quarter of a pound of *Butter.*

Four pound of *Bread.*

Three quarter of a pound of *Cheese.*

> *Bear* as before.

Oatmeal per day, for 50 men, Gallon 1. and so proportionable for more or fewer.

Thus you see the Ships provision, is *Beef* or *Porke*, *Fish*, *Butter*, *Cheese*, *Pease*, *Pottage*, *Water-gruel*, *Bisket*, and six shilling *Bear*.

For private fresh provision, you may carry with you (in case you, or any of yours should be sick at Sea) Conserves of *Roses*, *Clove-gilliflowers*, *Wormwood*, *Green-Ginger*, *Burnt-Wine*, English *Spirits*, *Prunes* to stew, *Raisons* of the *Sun*, *Currence*, *Sugar*, *Nutmeg*, *Mace*, *Cinnamon*, *Pepper* and *Ginger*, White *Bisket*, or *Spanish rusk*, *Eggs*, *Rice*, *juice of Lemmons* well put up to cure, or

30. Haddock?

prevent the Scurvy. Small *Skillets*, *Pipkins*, *Porrengers*, and small *Frying pans*.[31]

To prevent or take away Sea sickness, Conserve of *Wormwood* is very proper, but these following Troches I prefer before it.[32]

First make paste of *Sugar* and *Gum-Dragagant* mixed together, then mix therewith [p. 14] a reasonable quantitie of the powder of *Cinnamon* and *Ginger*, and if you please a little *Musk* also, and make it up into Roules of several fashions, which you may gild, of this when you are troubled in your Stomach, take and eat a quantity according to discretion.[33]

Apparel for one man, and after the rate for more.

	l.	*s.*	*d.*[34]
One Hatt	0	3	0
One *Monmouth* Cap	0	1	10
Three falling bands[35]	0	1	3
Three Shirts	0	7	6
One Wastcoat	0	2	6
One suit of Frize[36]	0	19	0
One suit of Cloth	0	15	0
One suit of Canvas	0	7	6
Three pair of *Irish* Stockins	0	5	0
Four pair of Shoos	0	8	0
One pair of Canvas Sheets	0	8	0
Seven ells of course Canvas to make a bed at Sea for two men, to be filled with straw	0	5	0
One course Rug at Sea for two men	0	6	0
Sum Total.	4	0	0

31. Gilliflowers are most often a clove-scented species of the pink (genus *Dianthus*); but see Felter's exhaustive note (38n) on other denotations of the word. Wormwood: the plant *Artemisia absinthium*, which yields a dark green oil formerly used in medicine as a tonic. Green ginger is the undried root, usually in preserve, of the tropical plant *Zingiber officinale*. "*Currence*" are currants; and "*rusk*" is small bread, often refired to be hard and crisp. *Pipkins*: small earthenware pots.

32. Troches: medicinal tablets, lozenges, or pastes.

33. "*Gum-Dragagant*" is resin of the tragacanth plant (genus *Astragalus*),

[p. 15]

Victuals for a whole year to be carried out of England *for one man, and so for more after the rate.*

	l.	*s.*	*d.*
Eight bushels of Meal	2	0	0
Two bushels of *Pease* at three shillings a bushel	0	6	0
Two bushels of *Oatmeal*, at four and six pence the bushel	0	9	0
One Gallon of *Aqua Vitae*	0	2	6
One Gallon of *Oyl*	0	3	6
Two Gallons of *Vinegar*	0	2	0

NOTE.

Of *Sugar* and *Spice*, 8 pound make the stone, 13 stone and an half, *i.e.* 100 pound maketh the hundred, but your best way is to buy your *Sugar* there, for it is cheapest, but for Spice you must carry it over with you.

	l.	*s.*	*d.*
A Hogshead[37] of *English* Beef will cost	5	0	0
A Hogshead of *Irish* Beef will cost	2	10	0
A Barrell of *Oatmeal*	0	13	0
A Hogshead of *Aqua vitae* will cost	4	0	0
A Hogshead of *Vinegar*	1	0	0
A Bushel of *Mustard-seed*	0	6	0

[p. 16] A *Kental* of fish, Cod or Habberdine is 112 pound, will cost if it be merchantable fish, Two or three and thirty Rials a *Kental*, if it be refuse you may have it for 10 or 11 shillings a *Kental*.[38]

---

used in early medicine. By *musk* Josselyn perhaps intends leaves of the musk flower (*Mimulus moschatus*). To gild is to soften or tone down something unpleasant.

34. British abbreviations for pounds, shillings, and pence.

35. Bands or collars worn around the neck during the seventeenth century.

36. Frieze, heavy wool cloth with a shaggy nap on one side, formerly woven in the Dutch province of Friesland.

37. A large gallon or cask, especially one equal to 63 gallons liquid measure.

38. Quintal: 112-pound weight. The rial was a gold coin current in England, its value about ten shillings at the time.

Wooden Ware.

	l.	*s.*	*d.*
A pair of Bellowes	0	2	0
A Skoope	0	0	9
A pair of Wheels for a Cart, if you buy them in the Countrey, they will cost 3 or 4 pound	0	14	0
Wheelbarrow you may have there, in *England* they cost	0	6	0
A great pail in *England* will cost	0	0	10
A Boat called a Canow, will cost in the Countrey (with a pair of Paddles) if it be a good one	3	0	0
A shorte Oake ladder in *England* will cost but	0	0	10
A Plough	0	3	9
An Axletree	0	0	8
A Cart	0	10	0
For a casting shovel	0	0	10
For a shovel	0	0	6
For a Sack	0	2	4
For a Lanthorn	0	1	3

For Tobacco pipes short steels, and great bouls 14 *pence and* 16 *pence the grose.*

[p. 17]

	l.	*s.*	*d.*
For clipping an hundred sheep in *England*	0	4	6
For winding the Wool	0	0	8
For washing them	0	2	0
For one garnish of Peuter [39]	2	0	0

Prizes [40] of Iron Ware.

Arms for one man, but if half of your men have Armour it is sufficient, so that all have pieces and swords.

One Armour compleat, light	0	17	0

39. Garnish of pewter: a set of vessels for table use.
40. Prices.

One long piece five foot, or five and a half near Musket bore	1	2	0
One Sword	0	5	0
One Bandaleer[41]	0	1	6
One Belt	0	1	0
Twenty pound of powder	0	18	0
Sixty pound of shot or lead, pistol and Goose shot	0	5	0

Tools for a Family of Six persons, and so after the rate for more.

Five broad howes at two shillings a piece	0	10	0
Five narrow howes at 16 pence the piece	0	6	8

[p. 18]

Five felling Axes at 18 pence a piece	0	7	6
Two steel hand-sawes at 16 pence the piece	0	2	8
Two hand-sawes at 5 shillings a piece	0	10	0
One whip saw, set and filed with box	0	10	0
A file and wrest[42]	0	0	10
Two Hammers 12 pence a piece	0	2	0
Three shovels 18 pence a piece shod	0	4	6
Two spades 18 pence a piece	0	3	0
Two Augars	0	1	0
Two broad axes at 3 shillings 8 pence a piece	0	7	4
Six Chissels	0	3	0
Three Gimblets[43]	0	0	6
Two Hatchets One and twenty pence a piece	0	3	6
Two froues to cleave pail at 18 pence a piece[44]	0	3	0
Two hand-bills at 20 pence a piece[45]	0	3	4
Nails of all sorts to be valued	2	0	0
Two pick-Axes	0	3	0

41. Bandoleer: a belt worn over the shoulder and across the breast, frequently used to suspend a wallet.

42. "The *wrest* was an instrument for bending the teeth of the saw outward. It is now called a *saw-set*" (*Trelawny Papers* 305n).

43. Gimlet: a small drill resembling a corkscrew.

44. Froe or frow: a wedge-shaped tool used to split posts or stakes (pales).

45. Hand bills were tools for pruning bushes and trees.

Three Locks, and 3 pair of Fetters	0	5	10
Two Currie Combs	0	0	10
For a Brand to brand Beasts with	0	0	6
For a Chain and lock for a Boat	0	2	2
For a Coulter weighing 10 pound	0	3	4
For a Hand-vise	0	2	6
[p. 19] For a Pitch-fork	0	1	4
For one hundred weight of Spikes			
Nails and pins 120, to the hundred	2	5	0
For a share	0	2	11

*Houshould Implements for a Family of six persons,
and so for more or less after the rate.*

One Iron Pot	0	7	0
For one great Copper Kettle	2	0	0
For a small Kettle	0	10	0
For a lesser Kettle	0	6	0
For one large Frying-pan	0	2	6
For a small Frying-pan	0	1	8
For a brass Morter	0	3	0
For a Spit	0	2	0
For one Grid-Iron	0	1	0
For two Skillets	0	5	0
Platters, dishes, & spoons of wood	0	4	0
For Sugar, Spice and fruits at Sea for six			
men	0	12	10

The fraught will be for one man half a Tun.

Having refreshed myself for a day or two upon *Noddles-Island*, I crossed the Bay in a small Boat to *Boston*, which then was rather a Village, than a Town, there being [p. 20] not above Twenty or thirty houses; and presenting my respects to Mr. *Winthorpe* the Governour, and to Mr. *Cotton* the Teacher of *Boston* Church, to whom I delivered from Mr. *Francis Quarles* the poet, the Translation of the 16, 25, 51, 88, 113, and 137. Psalms into *English* Meeter, for his approbation, being civilly treated by all I had occasion to converse with, I returned in the Evening to my lodging.[46]

46. John Winthrop (1588–1649) was the first elected governor of the Massachusetts Bay Colony; John Cotton (1584–1644), minister of the First Church

The Twelfth day of *July*, after I had taken my leave of Mr. *Maverick*, and some other Gentlemen, I took Boat for the Eastern parts of the Countrie, and arrived at *Black point* in the Province of *Main*, which is 150 miles from *Boston*, the Fourteenth day, which makes my voyage 11 weeks and odd dayes.

The Countrey all along as I sailed, being no other than a meer Wilderness, here and there by the Sea-side a few scattered plantations, with as few houses.

About the Tenth of *August*, I hapned to walk into the Woods, not far from the Sea-side, and falling upon a piece of ground over-grown with bushes, called there black Currence, but differing from our Garden Currence, they being ripe and hanging in lovely bunches; I set up my piece against a stately Oake, with a resolution to fill my [p. 21] belly, being near half a mile from the house; of a sudden I heard a hollow thumping noise upon the Rocks approaching towards me, which made me presently to recover my piece, which I had no sooner cock'd, than a great and grim over-grown she-Wolf appears, at whom I shot, and finding her Gor-belly[47] stuft with flesh newly taken in, I began presently to suspect that she had fallen foul upon our Goats, which were then valued (our she Goats) at Five pound a Goat; Therefore to make further discovery, I descended (it being low water) upon the Sea sands, with an intent to walk round about a neck of land where the Goats usually kept. I had not gone far before I found the footing of two Wolves, and one Goat betwixt them, whom they had driven into a hollow, betwixt two Rocks, hither I followed their footing, and perceiving by the Crowes, that there was the place of slaughter, I hung my piece upon my back, and upon all four clambered up to the top of the Rock, where I made ready my piece and shot at the dog Wolf, who was feeding upon the remainder of the Goat, which was only the fore shoulders, head and horns, the rest being devoured by the she-Wolf, even to the very hair of the Goat: and it is very observable, that when [p. 22] the Wolves have kill'd a Beast, or a Hog, not a Dog-

---

in Boston; Francis Quarles (1592–1644), Anglican poet. Quarles's translations apparently were deemed unfit for inclusion in the *Bay Psalm Book*, which was then being put together (Höltgen).

47. Protuberant belly.

Wolf amongst them offers to eat any of it, till the she-Wolves have filled their paunches.

The Twenty fourth of *September*, being Munday about 4 of the clock in the afternoon, a fearful storm of wind began to rage, called a *Hurricane*. *It is an impetuous wind that goes commonly about the Compass in the space of* 24 *hours*, it began from the W.N.W. and continued till next morning, the greatest mischief it did us, was the wracking of our Shallop,[48] and the blowing down of many tall Trees, in some places a mile together.

December the Tenth, happened an Eclipse of the Moon at 8 of the clock at night, it continued till after 11 as near as we could guess; in old *England* it began after midnight, and continued till 4 of *the clock in the morning; if Seamen would make observation of the time, either of the beginning or ending of the Eclipse, or total darkness of Sun and Moon in all places where they happen to be, and confer their observations to some Artist, hereby the longitude of all places might be certainly known, which are now very uncertainly reported to us.*

1639. *May*, which fell out to be extream hot and foggie, about the middle of *May* I [p. 23] kill'd within a stones throw of our house, above four score Snakes, some of them as big as the small of my leg, black of colour, and three yards long, with sharp horn on the tip of their tail two inches in length.

June the Six and twentieth day, very stormie, Lightning and Thunder. I heard now two of the greatest and fearfullest thunder-claps that ever were heard, I am confident. At this time we had some neighboring Gentlemen in our house who came to welcome me into the Countrey; where amongst variety of discourse they told me of a young *Lyon* (not long before) kill'd at *Piscataway*[49] by an *Indian*, of a *Sea-Serpent* or *Snake*, that lay quoiled up like a Cable upon a Rock at *Cape-Ann*: a Boat passing by with *English* aboard, and two *Indians*, they would have shot the *Serpent*, but the *Indians* disswaded them, saying, that if he were not kill'd outright, they would be all in danger of their lives.

One Mr. *Mittin* related of a *Triton* or *Mereman* which he saw

48. That is, the wrecking of their boat. Throughout the text, when Josselyn italicizes at length, he is usually quoting, often without citing his source.

49. The general area of the Piscataqua River mouth in New Hampshire.

in *Cascobay*, the Gentleman was a great Fouler,[50] and used to goe out with a small Boat or Canow, and fetching a compass about a small Island, (there being many small Islands in the Bay) for the advantage of a shot, was encountred [p. 24] with a *Triton*, who laying his hands upon the side of the Canow, had one of them chopt off with a Hatchet by Mr. *Mittin*, which was in all respects like the hand of a man, the *Triton* presently sunk, dying the water with his purple blood, and was no more seen. The next story was told by Mr. *Foxwell*, now living in the province of *Main*, who having been to the Eastward in a Shallop, as far as *Cape-Ann* a Waggon[51] in his return was overtaken by the night, and fearing to land upon the barbarous shore, he put off a little further to Sea; about midnight they were wakened with a loud voice from the shore, calling upon *Foxwell*, *Foxwell* come a shore, two or three times: upon the Sands they saw a great fire, and Men and Women hand in hand dancing round about it in a ring, after an hour or two they vanished, and as soon as the day appeared, *Foxwell* puts into a small *Cove*, it being about three quarters floud, and traces along the shore, where he found the footing of Men, Women and Children shod with shoos; and an infinite number of brands-ends thrown up by the water, but neither *Indian* nor *English* could he meet with on the shore, nor in the woods; these with many other stories they told me, the credit whereof I will neither impeach nor inforce, but shall [p. 25] satisfie my self, and I hope the Reader hereof, with the saying of a wise, learned and honourable Knight, *that there are many stranger things in the world, than are to be seen between* London *and* Stanes.

September the Sixth day, one Mr. *John Hickford* the Son of Mr. *Hickford* a Linnen-Draper in *Cheapside*, having been sometime in the province of *Main*, and now determined to return for *England*, sold and kill'd his stock of Cattle and Hoggs, one great

50. Michael Mitton (c. 1607–60) came over from England with George Cleeve in 1637 and resided at Cape Elizabeth. As Josselyn attests, he was a great fowler, for business accounts of the Richmond's Island trading station show repeated payments to him for delivery of ducks and geese.

51. Richard Foxwell (c. 1605–77) was at this time engaged in the fur and fish trade at Black Point; a landowner, he served variously as deputy, clerk, and commissioner until 1668. Below, "*Cape-Ann* a Waggon" should read Cape Anawagen, which is now Cape Newagen.

Sow he had which he made great account of, but being very fat, and not suspecting that she was with pig, he caused her to be kill'd, and they found 25 pigs within her belly; verifying the old proverb, As fruitful as a white sow. And now we were told of a sow in *Virginia* that brought forth six pigs; their fore-parts Lyons, their hinder-parts hogs. *I have read that at* Bruxels, Anno 1564. *a sow brought forth six pigs, the first whereof (for the last in generating is alwayes in bruit beasts the first brought forth) had the head, face, arms and legs of a man, but the whole trunck of the body from the neck, was of a swine, a sodomitical monster is more like the mother than the father in the organs of the vegetative soul.*[52]

The Three and twentieth, I left *Black-point*, and came to *Richmonds* Island about [p. 26] three leagues to the Eastward, where Mr. *Tralanie* kept a fishing, Mr. *John Winter* a grave and discreet man was his Agent, and imployer of 60 men upon that design.[53]

The Four and twentieth day being *Munday*, I went aboard the *Fellowship* of 100 and 70 Tuns a Flemish bottom, the Master *George Luxon* of *Bittiford* in *Devonshire*, several of my friends came to bid me farewell, among the rest Captain *Thomas Wannerton* who drank to me a pint of kill-devil *alias* Rhum at a draught, at 6 of the clock in the morning we weighed Anchor and set sail for the *Massachusetts-bay.*[54]

The Seven and twentieth day being *Fryday*, we Anchored in the afternoon in the *Massachusetts-bay* before *Boston*. Next day I went aboard of Mr. *Hinderson*, Master of a ship of 500 Tuns, and Captain *Jackson* in the *Queen of Bohemia* a privateer, and from thence I went ashore to *Boston*, where I refreshed myself at

52. Standard dictionaries of proverbs by Morris Tilley and Bartlett Whiting show no instances of the white sow proverb. Vegetative soul: the faculty of growth or reproduction.

53. In 1640 a Maine court found against Winter, Trelawny's agent, for fixing fur prices and for wrongly evicting settlers from the Cape Elizabeth grant.

54. Bittiford: Bideford. Thomas Wannerton was originally a notary public in London, and after 1629 a leader of the Laconia Company. He resided near what is now Portsmouth, New Hampshire, and was killed in 1644 at Penobscot during a skirmish between the rival French traders Charles La Tour and D'Aulney de Charnisy. On Wannerton's antipathy to the Massachusetts Bay Company, see Reid (92).

an Ordinary.[55] Next morning I was invited to a fishermans house somewhat lower within the *Bay*, and was there by his wife presented with a handful of small Pearl, but none of them bored nor orient. From thence I crost the Bay to *Charles-town*, where at one *Longs* Ordinary I met with Captain *Jackson* and others, walking on the back side we spied a rattle [p. 27] Snake a yard and half long, and as thick in the middle as the small of a mans leg, on the belly yellow, her back spotted with black, russet, yellow and green, placed like scales, at her tail she had a rattle which is nothing but a hollow shelly bussiness joynted, look how many years old she is, so many rattles she hath in her tail, her neck seemed to be no bigger than ones Thumb; yet she swallowed a live Chicken, as big as one they give 4 pence for in *England*, presently as we were looking on. In the afternoon I returned to our Ship, being no sooner aboard but we had the sight of an *Indian*-Pinnace sailing by us made of *Birch-bark*, sewed together with the roots of *spruse* and white *Cedar* (drawn out into threads) with a deck, and trimmed with sails top and top gallant very sumptuously.

The Thirtieth day of *September*, I went ashore upon *Noddles*-Island, where when I was come to Mr. *Mavericks* he would let me go aboard no more, until the Ship was ready to set sail; the next day a grave and sober person described the Monster to me, that was born at *Boston* of one Mrs. *Dyer* a great Sectarie, *the Nine and twentieth of* June, *it was (it should seem) without a head, but having horns like a Beast, and ears, scales on a rough skin like a fish* [p. 28] *called a* Thornback, *legs and claws like a* Hawke, *and in other respects as a Woman-Child.*[56]

55. William Jackson of London was a privateer and a commissioner for the Providence Company. He was charged in 1645 with having pillaged Jamaica and various towns in the West Indies. Ordinary: inn or tavern. Josselyn's use of this word precedes the earliest printed American instance (1774) cited by the *OED*.

56. Mary Dyer was a follower of the Antinomian leader Anne Hutchinson, who was also reputed to have borne a badly deformed stillborn child; both women were banished from Boston on 22 March 1638. Dyer became a Quaker, repeatedly returned to Boston, finally was condemned for sedition and hanged in 1660. John Winthrop (1:266–69) and Edward Johnson also report the births. As Johnson explains it, "the Lord had poynted directly to their sinne by a very

The Second of *October*, about 9 of the clock in the morning, Mr. *Mavericks* Negro woman came to my chamber window, and in her own Countrey language and tune sang very loud and shril, going out to her, she used a great deal of respect toward me, and willingly would have expressed her grief in *English*; but I apprehended it by her countenance and deportment, whereupon I repaired to my host, to learn of him the cause, and resolved to intreat him in her behalf, for that I understood before, that she had been a Queen in her own Countrey, and observed a very humble and dutiful garb used towards her by another Negro who was her maid. Mr. *Maverick* was desirous to have a breed of Negroes, and therefore seeing she would not yield by perswasions to company with a Negro young man he had in his house; he commanded him will'd she nill'd she to go to bed to her, which was no sooner done but she kickt him out again, this she took in high disdain beyond her slavery, and this was the cause of her grief.[57] In the afternoon I walked into the Woods on the back side of the house, and happening into a [p. 29] fine broad walk (which was a sledg-way) I wandered till I chanc't to spye a fruit as I thought like a pine Apple plated with scales, it was as big as the crown of a Womans hat; I made bold to step unto it, with an intent to have gathered it, no sooner had I toucht it, but hundreds of Wasps were about me; at last I cleared my self from them, being stung only by one upon the upper lip, glad I was that I scaped so well; But by that time I was come into the house my lip was swell'd so extreamly, that they hardly knew me but by my Garments.

The Tenth of *October*, I went aboard and we fell down to *Nantascot*,[58] here Mr. *Davies* (Mr. *Hicks* the Apothecarie in *Fleet-streets* Son-in law) dyed of the Phthisick aboard on a Sunday in the afternoon. The next day Mr. *Luxon* our Master having been

---

fearful monster, that another of these women brought forth" (187). See Anne Jacobson Schutte, who studies historical precedents and scientific bases for "monster" births.

57. William Prescott Greenlaw has written that Samuel Maverick "was one of the earliest slaveholders in Massachusetts" (237), which makes Josselyn's sympathetic anecdote particularly significant. Will'd she, nill'd she: willy-nilly, whether she desired or not.

58. Nantasket.

ashore upon the Governours Island gave me half a score very fair
Pippins which he brought from thence, there being not one
Apple-tree, nor Pear planted yet in no part of the Countrey, but
upon that Island.⁵⁹

The Fifteenth day, we set sail from *Nantascot.*

The Sixteenth day Mr. *Robert Foster*, one of our passengers
Preached aboard upon [p. 30] the 113 Psalm; *The Lord shall preserve thy going out, & thy coming in*; The Sectaries began to quarrel with him, especially Mr. *Vincent Potter*, who was afterwards
questioned for a Regicide.⁶⁰

The Seventeenth day, toward Sun-set a Lanner⁶¹ settled upon
our main Mast-top, when it was dark I hired one of the Sailers to
fetch her down, and I brought her into *England* with much ado,
being fain to feed her with hard Eggs. After this day we had very
cold weather at Sea, our deck in a morning ore-spread with hoarie
frost, and dangling Isickles hung upon the Ropes. *Some say the
Sea is hotter in winter, than in summer; but I did not find it so.*

November the Fifth day, about three of the clock in the afternoon, the Mariners observed the rising of a little black cloud in
the *N.W.* which increasing apace, made them prepare against a
coming storm, the wind in short time grew to boisterous, bringing after us a huge grown Sea, at 5 of the clock it was pitchie
dark.

> *And the bitter storm augments; the wild winds wage*
> *War from all parts; and joyn with the Seas rage.*

[p. 31]
> *The sad clouds sink in showers; you would have thought,*
> *That high-swoln-seas even unto Heaven had wrought;*
> *And Heaven to Seas descended: no star shown;*
> *Blind night in darkness, tempests, and her own*

59. Governor's Island was the site of Fort Winthrop, located within Boston
Harbor. Pippins: any of a variety of apples.

60. Potter was one of the original members of the Massachusetts Bay Company, and apparently a very rigid Puritan. Thomas Hutchinson reports that he
"came to Boston but returned to England and was one of the Kings Judges"
(1:17n). The biblical passage comes in fact from Psalms 121.8 which promises
eternal bounty and beneficence from the Lord, a point of view perhaps incom-
patible with strict interpretations.

61. Female falcon.

> *Dread terrours lost; yet this dire lightning turns*
> *To more fear'd light; the Sea with lightning Burns.*
> *The Pilot knew not what to chuse or fly,*
> *Art stood amaz'd in Ambiguity.*[62]

The storm augmenting still, the next day about 4 of the clock afternoon we lost our Rudder, and with that our hopes, so necessary a part it is, that a ship without it, is like a wild horse without a bridle; yet *Aristotle* that *Eagle*-ey'd *Philosopher could not give a reason, why so small a thing as a Helm should rule the ship.*[63]

[p. 32] The Seventh day at night, the wind began to dye away, the next day we had leasure to repair our breaches; it continued calm till the 13 day, and all the while we saw many dead bodies of men and women floating by us.

The Four and twentieth, we arrived before *Bittiford*, having past before under *Lundee*-Island.[64]

62. The poem evidently is Josselyn's creation (Meserole 403–4).
63. This allusion is untraced, though possibly an extrapolation from Aristotle's *De Anima*, which contains numerous seafaring analogies.
64. Lundy Isle.

The Second Voyage

[p. 33] I have heard of a certain Merchant in the west of *England*, who after many great losses, walking upon the Sea-bank in a calm Sun-shining day; observing the smoothness of the Sea, coming in with a chequered or dimpled wave: Ah (quoth he) thou flattering Element, many a time hast thou inticed me to throw my self and my fortunes into thy Arms; but thou hast hitherto proved treacherous; thinking to find thee a Mother of encrease, I have found thee to be the Mother of mischief and wickedness; yea the Father of prodigies; therefore, being now secure, I will trust thee no more: But mark this mans resolution a while after, *periculum maris spes lucri superat.*[1] So fared it with me, that having escaped the dangers of one Voyage, must needs put on a resolution for a second, wherein I plowed many a churlish billow [p. 34] with little or no advantage, but rather to my loss and detriment. In the setting down, whereof I purpose not to insist in a methodical way, but according to my quality, in a plain and brief relation as I have done already; for I perceive, if I used all the Art that possibly I could, it would be difficult to please all, for all mens eyes, ears, faith, judgement, are not of a size. There be a sort of stagnant stinking spirits, who, like flyes, lye sucking at the botches of carnal pleasures, and never travelled so much Sea, as is between *Heth-ferry*, and *Lyon-Key*; yet notwithstanding, (sitting in the

1. Hope for money overcomes the danger of the sea.

Chair of the scornful over their whifts and draughts of intoxication) will desperately censure the relations of the greatest Travellers. It was a good *proviso* of a learned man, never to report
wonders, for in so doing, of the greatest he will be sure not to be
believed, but laughed at, which certainly bewraies[2] their ignorance and want of discretion. Of Fools and Mad-men then I shall
take no care, I will not invite these in the least to honour me with
a glance from their supercilious eyes; but rather advise them to
keep their inspection for their fine-tongu'd Romances, and playes.
This homely piece, I protest ingenuously, is prepared for such
only who well know how to make use of their [p. 35] charitable
constructions towards works of this nature, to whom I submit my
self in all my faculties, and proceed in my second voyage.

Anno 1663. *May* the Three and twentieth, I went down to
Gravesend, it being *Saturday* I lay ashore till *Monday* the fifth,
about 11 a clock at night, I went aboard the *Society* belonging to
Boston in the *Massachusetts* a Colony of *English* in *New-England*,
of 200 and 20 Tun, carrying 16 Iron Guns most unserviceable,
man'd with 33 sailers, and 77 passengers, men, women and
children.

The Six and twentieth day, about 6 of the clock in the morning
we weighed Anchor, and fell down with the tide three or four
miles below *Gravesend*.

The Seven and twentieth in the afternoon, we weighed Anchor
and came into the *Hope* before *Deal-Castle*, there we were wind
bound till

The 30 day, we set sail out of the *Downs*, being *Saturday* about
9 of the clock in the morning, about 4 of the clock in the afternoon we came up with *Beachy* by *W.* at *Nore*.

The One and thirtieth at 4 of the clock in the morning we
came up with the Isle of *Wight*, at 4 of the clock in the afternoon
[p. 36] we had *Portland* N.N.W. of us, 6 leagues off, the wind
being then at *N.W.* by *N.* at 5 of the clock we came to *Dartmouth*, the wind *W.S.W.*

June the first day, being *Monday* about 4 of the clock *Plimouth*
was about 9 leagues off, our course *W.S.W.* the Start bore North

2. Exposes.

distant about 6 leagues from whence our reckonings began; the wind now *E.N.E.* a fair gale.

The second day the *Lizard* bore *N.N.W.* in the latitude 51. 300 leagues from *Cape-Cod* in *New-England*, our course *W.* and by *S.* One of our passengers now dyed of a Consumption.

The Fifth day we steered *S.W.* observed and found the ship in latitude 47 degrees, and 44 minutes.

The Tenth day observed and found the ship in latitude 49 degrees, and 24 minutes.

The Five and twentieth day, about 3 of the clock in the morning we discovered land, about 6 of the clock *Flowers*,[3] so called from abundance of flowers, and *Corvo* from a multitude of *Crowes*; two of the *Azores* or western Islands, in the *Atlantique Ocean* not above 250 leagues from *Lisbon* bore *N.W.* of us some 3 leagues off, we steered away *W.* by *W.* observed and found *Flowers* to be in the Southern part in latitude 39 de- [p. 37] grees 13 minuts, we descryed a Village and a small Church or Chappel seated in a pleasant valley to the Easter-side of the Island, the whole Island is rockie and mountainious about 8 miles in compass, stored with Corn, Wine and Goats, and inhabited by outlaw'd *Portingals*, the town they call *Santa Cruz*. *Corvo* is not far from this, I supposed two or three leagues, a meer mountain, and very high and steep on all sides, cloathed with tall wood on the very top, uninhabited, but the *Flowreans* here keep some number of Goats.

The Seven and twentieth day, 30 leagues to the westward of these Islands we met with a small Vessel stoln from *Jamaico*, but 10 men in her, and those of several nations, *English, French, Scotch, Dutch* almost famish'd, having been out as they told us, by reason of calms, three moneths, bound for *Holland*.

July the sixth, calm now for two or three dayes, our men went out to swim, some hoisted the *Shallop* out and took divers Turtles, there being an infinite number of them all over the Sea as far as we could ken, and a man may ken at Sea in a clear Air 20 miles, they floated upon the top of the water being a sleep, and driving gently upon them with a *Shallop*, of a sudden [p. 38] they took

3. Flores, the westernmost island in the Azores.

hold of their hinder legs, and lifted them into the boat, if they be
not very nimble they awake and presently dive under water; when
they were brought aboard they sob'd and wept exceedingly, continuing to do so till the next day that we killed them, by chopping
off their heads, and having taken off their shells (that on their
back being fairest, is called a Gally patch)[4] we opened the body
and took out three hearts in one case, and (which was more
strange) we perceived motion in the hearts ten hours after they
were taken out. I have observed in *England* in my youthful dayes
the like in the heart of a *Pike*, and the heart of a *Frog*, which will
leap and skip as nimbly as the *Frog* used to do when it was alive
from whom it was taken. Likewise the heart of a *Pig* will stir
after it is exenterated. Being at a friends house in *Cambridg-shire*,
the Cook maid making ready to slaughter a *Pig*, she put the
hinder parts between her legs as the usual manner is, and taking
the snout in her left hand with a long knife stuck the *Pig* and cut
the small end of the heart almost in two, letting it bleed as long as
any bloud came forth, then throwing of it into a Kettle of boyling
water, the *Pig* swom twice round about the kettle, when taking of
it out to [p. 39] the dresser she rubd it with powdered *Rozen* and
stript off the hair, and as she was cutting off the hinder pettito,
the *Pig* lifts up his head with open mouth, as if it would have
bitten: well, the belly was cut up, and the entrails drawn out, and
the heart laid upon the board, which notwithstanding the wound
it received had motion in it, above four hours after; there were
several of the Family by, with my self, and we could not otherwayes conclude but that the *Pig* was bewitched; but this by the
way. Of the Sea Turtles there be five sorts, first the Trunck-turtle
which is biggest, Secondly, the Logggerhead-turtle. Thirdly, the
Hawk-bill-turtle, which with its bill will bite horribly. Fourthly,
the Green-turtle which is best for food, it is affirmed that the
feeding upon this Turtle for twelve moneth, forbearing all other
kind of food will cure absolutely Consumptions, and the great
pox;[5] They are a very delicate food and their Eggs are very
wholesome and restorative, it is an *Amphibious* Creature[;] going

4. Calipash: upper shell or carapace of a turtle.
5. Josselyn names only four marine turtles. These are the trunkback (*Der-
mochelys coriacea*), now endangered, called also the leatherback because it has no
proper shell; the loggerhead (*Caretta caretta*); the hawksbill (*Eretmochelys im-*

ashore, the male throws the female on her back when he couples
with her, which is termed cooting,[6] their Eggs grown to perfection the female goes ashore again and making a hole in the sand,
there layes her Eggs which are numerous, I have seen a peck
[p. 40] of Eggs taken out of one Turtle; when they have laid they
cover the hole again with sand, and return to the Sea never looking after her Eggs, which hatching in the sand and coming to
some strength break out and repair to the Sea. Having fill'd our
bellies with Turtles and Bonito's, called *Spanish* Dolphins excel-
lently well cooked both of them, the wind blowing fair,

The Eighth day we spread our sails and went on our voyage,
after a while we met with abundance of Sea-weeds called Gulf-
weed coming out of the Bay of *Mexico*, and firr-trees floating on
the Sea, observed and found the Ship to be in 39 degrees and 49
minuts.

The Fifteenth day we took a young Sharke about three foot
long, which being drest and dished by a young Merchant a passenger happened to be very good fish, having very white flesh in
flakes like Codd but delicately curl'd, the back-bone which is perfectly round, joynted with short joynts, the space between not
above a quarter of an inch thick, separated they make fine Table-
men,[7] being wrought on both sides with curious works.

The One and twentieth thick hasie weather.

The Five and twentieth we met with a [p. 41] *Plimouth* man
come from St. *Malloes* in *France*, 10 weeks out, laden with
cloath, fruit, and honey, bound for *Boston* in *New-England*.

The Six and twentieth we had sight of land.

The Seven and twentieth we Anchored at *Nantascot*, in the afternoon I went aboard of a *Ketch*, with some other of our passengers, in hope to get to *Boston* that night; but the Master of the
Ketch would not consent.

The Eight and twentieth being *Tuesday*, in the morning about
5 of the clock he lent us his *Shallop* and three of his men, who

---

bricata); and the green turtle (*Chelonia mydas*), still processed to make soups.
The great pox: syphilis.

6. A verb coined in the seventeenth century and applied exclusively to copu-
lation of tortoises. The first incidence of its use listed in the *OED* is from a
1667 issue of the Royal Society's *Philosophical Transactions*.

7. Pieces used in board games.

brought us to the western end of the town where we landed, and having gratified the men, we repaired to an Ordinary (for so they call their Taverns there) where we were provided with a liberal cup of burnt Madera-wine, and store of plum-cake, about ten of the clock I went about my Affairs.

Before I pursue my Voyage to an end, I shall give you to understand what Countrie *New-England* is. *New-England* is that part of *America*, which together with *Virginia*, *Mary land*, and *Nova-scotia* were by the Indians called by one name *Wingadacoa*, after the discovery by Sir *Walter* [p. 42] *Rawleigh* they were named *Virginia*,[8] and remained until King *James* divided the Countrey into Provinces. *New-England* then is all that tract of land that lyes between the Northerly latitudes of 40 and 46, that is from *De-la-ware-Bay* to *New-found-land*, some will have it to be in latitude from 41 to 45[;] in King *Jame's* Letters Patents to the Council of *Plimouth* in *Devonshire* from 40 to 48 of the same latitude, it is judged to be an Island, surrounded on the North with the spacious River of *Canada*,[9] on the South with *Mahegan* or *Hudsons* River, having their rise, as it is thought, from two great lakes not far off one another, the Sea lyes East and South from the land, and is very deep, some say that the depth of the Sea being measured with line and plummer, seldom exceeds two or three miles, except in some places near the *Swevian*-shores, and about *Pontus*, observed by *Pliny*.[10] Sir *Francis Drake* threw out 7 Hogsheads of line near *Porto-bello* and found no bottom,[11] but whether this be true or no, or that they were deceived by the Currants carrying away their lead and line, this is certainly true,

8. *Wingadacoa:* otherwise Wingandacoa. Sir Walter Raleigh (c. 1552–1618) received a grant from Queen Elizabeth and in 1584 sent the first of his abortive colonizing expeditions to Virginia.

9. Josselyn's claim is perhaps the latest instance of the persistent tradition that northeastern North America was an island (Smith 1:325n). The River of *Canada*: Saint Lawrence River.

10. The plummet is a weighted line used to measure depths. Swevian: Swedish. Pontus, now part of Armenia, was an ancient country in Asia Minor. Pliny: Gaius Plinius Secundus, the Elder (A.D. 23–79), Roman scholar and natural historian from whose *Historia Naturalis* Josselyn garnered a great deal of lore.

11. Francis Drake (c. 1545–96) died aboard ship and was buried at sea near Puerto Bello on the Caribbean coast of Panama.

that there is more Sea in the Western than the Eastern *Hemi-sphere*, on the shore in more places than one at spring-tides, that is at the full or new of the moon, [p. 43] the Sea riseth 18 foot perpendicular, the reason of this great flow of waters I refer to the learned, onely by the way I shall acquaint you with two reasons for the ebbing and flowing of the Sea; the one delivered in Common conference, the other in a Sermon at *Boston* in the *Massachusets-Bay* by an eminent man; The first was, *that God and his spirit moving upon the waters caused the motion*; the other, *that the spirit of the waters gathered the waters together; as the spirit of Christ gathered Souls.* [12]

The shore is Rockie, with high cliffs, having a multitude of considerable Harbours; many of which are capacious enough for a Navy of 500 sail, one of a thousand, the Countrie within Rockie and mountanious, full of tall wood, one stately mountain there is surmounting the rest, about four score mile from the Sea: The description of it you have in my rarities of *New-England*, between the mountains are many ample rich and pregnant valleys as ever eye beheld, beset on each side with variety of goodly Trees, the grass man-high unmowed, uneaten and uselesly withering; within these valleys are spacious lakes or ponds well stored with Fish and Beavers, the original of all the great Rivers in the Countrie, of which there are many with lesser [p. 44] streams (wherein are an infinite of fish) manifesting the goodness of the soil which is black, red-clay, gravel, sand, loom, and very deep in some places, as in the valleys and swamps, which are low grounds and bottoms infinitely thick set with Trees and Bushes of all sorts for the most part, others having no other shrub or Tree growing, but spruse, under the shades whereof you may freely walk two or three mile together; being goodly large Trees, and convenient for masts and sail-yards. The whole Countrie produceth springs in abundance replenished with excellent waters, having all the properties ascribed to the best in the world.

> *Swift is't in pace, light poiz'd, to look in clear,*
> *And quick in boiling (which esteemed were)*

12. This passage, of course, derives from Genesis 1.2, which reads, in part, "the Spirit of God moved upon the face of the waters."

Such qualities, as rightly understood
Withouten these no water could be good.[13]

One Spring there is at Black-point in the *Province of* Main, *coming out of muddy-clay that will colour a spade, as if hatcht*[14] *with silver, it is purgative and cures scabs and Itch,* &c.

The mountains and Rocky Hills are richly furnished with mines of Lead, Silver, [p. 45] Copper, Tin, and divers sorts of minerals, branching out even to their summits, where in small Crannies you may meet with threds of perfect silver; yet have the *English* no maw to open any of them, whether out of ignorance or fear of bringing a forraign Enemy upon them, or (like the dog in the manger)[15] to keep their Soveraign from partaking of the benefits, who certainly may claim an interest in them as his due, being eminently a gift proceeding from divine bounty to him; [right-hand marginalia inset: "*Isa.* 45.3."][16] no person can pretend interest in Gold, Silver, or Copper by the law of Nations, but the Soveraign Prince; but the subjects of our king have a right to mines discovered in their own Lands and inheritances; So as that every tenth Tun of such Oar is to be paid to the proprieters of such lands, and not to the state, if it be not a mine-Royal: if it prove to be a mine-Royal, every fifth Tun of all such Oar as shall hold Gold or Silver worth refining, is to be rendered to the King. *The learned Judges of our Kingdom have long since concluded, that although the Gold or Silver conteined in the base mettals of a mine in the land of a Subject, be of less value than the baser mettal; yet if the Gold or Silver do countervail the charge of refining it, or be more worth than the base mettal spent* [p. 46] *in refining it, that then it is a mine-Royal, and as well the base mettal as the Gold and Silver in it belongs by prerogative to the Crown.*

The stones in the Countrey are for the most *mettle*-stone, freestone, pebble, slate, none that will run to lime, of which they

13. Another verse that has been received as Josselyn's creation (Meserole 404).

14. Inlaid.

15. Josselyn's is the earliest American reference to this proverb (Whiting D233), which may be read as an indictment of those who covet valuable materials only so that others may gain no good from them. Officially the crown claimed rights to one-fifth of all ore discovered in the colonies.

16. Isaiah 45.3: "And I will give thee the treasures of darkness, and hidden

have great want, of the slate you may make Tables easie to be split to the thickness of an inch, or thicker if you please, and long enough for a dozen men to sit at. Pretious stones there are too, but if you desire to know further of them, see the Rarities of *New-England*; onely let me add this observation by the way, that Crystal set in the Sun taketh fire, and setteth dry Tow or brown Paper on fire held to it. There is likewise a sort of glittering sand, which is altogether as good as the glassie powder brought from the *Indies* to dry up ink on paper newly written. The climate is reasonably temperate, hotter in Summer, and colder in Winter than with us, agrees with our Constitutions better than *hotter Climates, these are limbecks* [17] *to our bodies, forraign heat will extract the inward and adventitious heat consume the natural, so much more heat any man receives outwardly from the heat of the Sun, so much more wants he the same inwardly,* which is one reason why [p. 47] they are able to receive more and larger draughts of Brandy, & the like strong spirits than in *England* without offence. *Cold is less tolerable than heat, this is a friend to nature, that an enemy. Many are of opinion that the greatest enemies of life, consisting of heat and moisture, is cold and dryness, the extremity of cold is more easie to be endured than extremity of heat, the violent sharpness of winter, than the fiery raging of Summer. To conclude, they are both bad, too much heat brings a hot Feaver, too much cold diminisheth the flesh, withers the face, hollowes the eyes, quencheth natural heat, peeleth the hair, and procureth baldness.*

Astronomers have taken special knowledge of the number of 1024 of the principal apparent noted Stars of all the rest, besides the 7 Planets, and the 12 Signs, and it is agreed upon that there are more Stars under the Northern-pole, than under the Southern, the numbers of Stars under both poles are innumerable to us; but not to the Almighty Creator of Heaven and Earth, who calleth them all by their names. *Isai[ah]. 40. Levate in excelsum oculos vestros & videte* [;] *quis creavit hæc? quis educit in numero militiam eorum & omnia fuis numinibus vocat?* [18] In *January* 1668.

---

riches of secret places, that thou mayest know that I, the Lord, which call thee by thy name, am the God of Israel."

17. Alembic: anything that transforms, purifies, or refines.

18. A corruption of the Vulgate for Isaiah 40.26. Among other errors, the

two Suns appeared and two Moons. The year before was published the Suns Prerogative, vindicated by [p. 48] *Alexander No-
wel* a young student at *Harvard-Colledge* in the *Massachusets*
Colony, which was as followeth.[19]

*Mathematicians have that priviledge above other Philosophers,
that their foundations are so founded upon, and proved by demonstra-
tion, that reason* volens nolens[20] *must approve of them, when they
are once viewed by the eye of the intellect,* ipso facto *it grants a pro-
batum est;* [21] *if upon these foundations he raises famous Architectures,
which are inseparably joynted in, and joyned to their ground-works,
yet are not their Elements of such vast extensions, as to have their
dimensions adequated with the machine of the* primum mobile,[22] *and
so include the Fabrick of created beings; but there are sphears above
the sphear of their Activity, and Orbs placed above the reach of their
Instruments, which will* non-plus *the most acute inquisitors, at least
in reference to an accurate scrutiny: hence dissentions about Celestial
bodies, whether the planets have any natural light, has been a question, proving that they borrow their light from the Sun: he being
the primitive, they derivatives; he the* Augmentum primum, *they*
Orta, *who though they have light* in se, *yet not* ex se.[23] *This assertion
is not expugned by* Geocentricks *who produce sense and Antiquity to
support their suppositions; nor oppugned by* Heliocentricks, [p. 49]
who deduce their Hypothesis *from reason, and new observations:
for,* quicquid in ambitu alicujus circuli actu diffusum, compre-
henditur, id in centro ejusdem continetur potentia collectum.[24]

---

verse should read *nominibus* in place of *numinibus*, although the latter word
makes a certain medieval sense ("properties" or "powers" instead of "names").
According to the King James Version: "Lift up your eyes on high, and behold
who hath created these things, that bringeth out their host by number: he calleth
them all by names by the greatness of his might, for that he is strong in power;
not one faileth."

19. Alexander Nowell (c. 1645–72), son of Increase and brother of Samuel, graduated from Harvard in 1664 and published in the next year's Cambridge almanac "The Suns Prerogative Vindicated," which Josselyn reprints.

20. Willy-nilly.   21. Proven truth.

22. First moving thing.

23. *Augmentum primum*: prime mover. *Orta*: offshoots. *In se:* in themselves.
Ex se: of themselves.

24. Whatever is understood to spread out through the circumference of any
circle in act, is held concentrated together at its center in potency.

Should I put the question to the vote, questionless the major part of modern Astronomers would carry it affirmatively; but a testimony being Inartificialis Argumentum,[25] *I shall found my position upon a more Artificial Basis. As for the multiplication of Eclipses which some fear, it's needless, for the extent of the* Cone *of the earths shaddow* (à Centro terræ)[26] *being* 250 Semidiameters, *it cannot reach* Mars; Venus *and* Mercury *never oppose the Sun. It has been observed by the help of* Optick Tubes,[27] *that* Venus *has divers faces, according to her diverse position to the Sun. Some affirm the same of* Mercury, *but he's not so liable to observation, being seldom clear of the radiancy of the Sun. The superior Planets being above the Sun, turn the same side to the Sun, as they do to us.* Venus *and* Mars *are more lucid in their* Parhelion, *than in their* Aphelion.[28] *The* Telescope *may convince us of this truth;* Evincit enim crassa, opaca & dissimilium plane partium corpora, planetas esse.[29] *Lastly God made the Sun and Moon, the two greater lights (though not the greater lucid bodies)[;] that the Moons light is adventitious, followes from her invisibilitie* [p. 50] *in a central Eclipse: hence the other planets are destitute of native light;* nam à majore ad minus valet consequentia negativè.[30]

In the year 1664. a Star or Comet appeared in *New-England* in *December* in the *South-East*, rising constantly about one of the clock in the morning, carrying the tail lower and lower till it came into the *West*, and then bare it directly before it; the Star it self was of a duskish red, the tail the colour of *via lactea*, or the milkie way. A fortnight after it appeared again rising higher near the *Nadir* or point over our heads, of the same form and colour, of which hear the former Scholar.

Comets (say Naturalists) proceed from natural causes, but they oft preceed preternatural effects. That they have been Antecedents to strange consequents is an universal truth, and proved by particulars, viz. *That which hung over* Hierusalem *before its extirpation by*

---

25. Inartistic proof.   26. From the center of the earth.
27. Telescopes.
28. *Parhelion*: the point of orbit nearest to the sun. *Aphelion*: point of orbit farthest from the sun.
29. It demonstrates the planets to be dense, opaque bodies of clearly dissimilar parts.
30. For the influence of a negative consequence goes from the greater to the less.

Vespatian,[31] *that vertical to* Germany, *before those bloudy Wars &c.
So that experience Attests, and reason Assents, that they have served
for sad Prologues to Tragical Epilogues. For the future, preludiums to
what events they'l prove, may be proved by consequence, if they han't
suffered a privation of their powerful Energie. Dr.* Ward[32] *to salve
Contests, distinguishes between Cometœidae, which are* [p. 51] *Sub-
lunary exhalations, and Cometœ, which are heavenly bodies, coevous
with the Stars; the cause of the inequality of whose motion, is their
Apoge and Periges. Concerning the height of the late Comets Orb,
because of the deficiency of Instruments, here's* pars deficiens.[33] *As for
its motion* December 10. *'twas about the middle of* Virgo. Jan. 24.
26 deg. Aries. *Some observe that comets commonly follow a Con-
junction of the superiour planets. Astronomers attribute much to the
predominancy of that planet which rules it, which they judge by the
Colour; a dull leaden colour, claims* Saturn *for his Lord; bright,*
Jupiter; *Red,* Mars; *Golden,* Sol; *Yellow,* Venus; *variable,* Mercury; *pale,* Luna. *Also to the Aspects it receives from other planets,
the sign it is in, and the house of the Heavens in which it first was.
Hence some may judge a scheam of the Heavens necessary, but unless
Calculated for its certain rise (which is uncertain) it's adjudged by the
judicious, superfluous. Some put much trust or virtue in the tail, ter-
ming it the Ignomon,* &c. *But that is probable of all, which has been
observed of some, that it's always opposite to the Sun; hence when the
Sun is at the Meridian of the Antipodes it turns,* &c. *Which* Regio-
mont *observed of that in* 1475. *and* Keckerman *of that in* 1607.
Longomontanus *observes of that in* 1618. *that its first* [p. 52] *appearance was vertical to* Germany *and went* Northward, *so its effect
began there, and made the like progress:*[34] *it's rational, that as a*

31. Titus Flavius Sabinus Vespasianus (A.D. 9–79), Roman commander
(later emperor) sent by Nero to conduct war against the Jews.

32. Seth Ward (1617–89), English bishop and professor of astronomy at
Oxford who propounded a theory of planetary motion.

33. *Coevous: coaevous* or contemporary. Pars deficiens: the failing part.

34. Regiomontanus, or Johann Müller (1436–76), was a German astrono-
mer and mathematician. Bartholomäus Keckerman (1571–1609), was a German scholar and rhetorician whose works were used extensively in the early days
of Harvard. Longomontanus was Christian Severin (1562–1647), Danish as-
tronomer and assistant to the more famous Tycho Brahe (1546–1601), termed
"noble Ticho" below. Brahe was the founder of an observatory at Copenhagen
and discoverer of a "new star" in the constellation Cassiopeia.

cause, it should operate most powerfully on those in whose Zenith it is, as the meridional Altitude; nor is it irrational, that as a sign, it should presage somewhat to all those, in whose Horizon it appears; for in reason, Relata se mutuo inferunt,[35] *hence* signum *infers* signatum, *and the signifier implies a signified. Diverse desire to be certified of the event; but he is wise that knowes it. Some presume prophetically to specificate from generals truths; others desperately deny generals and all; of all whom it's a truth,* Incidunt in Scyllam, &c.[36] *Noble* Ticho *concludes, (with whom I conclude) that it's not rational particularly to determine the sequel; for should any, it would be only in a contingent Axiom, and proceed from fancie; therefore of no necessary consequence, and would produce only opinion.*

A friend of mine shewed me a small Treatise written and printed in the *Massachusetts*-Bay by *B.D.*[37] intituled *An Astronomical description of the late Comet, or Blazing-Star, as it appeared in* New-England *in the Ninth, Tenth, Eleventh, and the beginning of the Twelfth moneth, 1664. printed at* Cambridge *by* Samuel Green 1665. An ingenious piece, but because I could not perswade my [p. 53] friend to part with it, I took out some short notes being straitned in time, which are as followes.

Comets are distinguished in respect of their figure, according to the divers aspects of the Sun, into *Barbate, Caudate,* and *Crinite.*[38] 1. When the stream like a beard goes before the body. 2. When the stream followes the body. 3. When the stream goes right up into the Heavens.

A Comet is said to be vertical to any people, when the body of the Comet passeth over their heads.

The light of the Comet alters and varies according to the diverse Aspects of the Sun enlightning it.

Some took notice of it in the beginning of *November.*

In *Anno Dom.* 1668. *July* the Fifteenth happened an Eclipse of the moon from 9 of the clock at night, till after 11, digits 9, and 35 minutes.

35. Related things reciprocally infer each other.
36. They fall upon Scylla.
37. Actually "*S. D.*" for Samuel Danforth I. In the popular 122-page tract from which Josselyn borrows, the American colonist Danforth argues that comets portend various events and move according to mathematical laws.
38. That is, beardlike, taillike, and hairlike.

In *November* following appeared a Star between the horns of the Moon in the midst.[39]

In *Anno Dom.* 1669. about the middle of *June* at 4 of the clock in the afternoon, appeared a Rain-bow reverst, and at night about 10 of the clock we had a *Lunar* Rain-bow.

[p.54] The *Indians* so far as I could perceive have but little knowledge of the Stars and Planets, observing the Sun and Moon only, the dividers of time into dayes and years: they being nearer to the Equintoctial-line by 10 degrees, have their dayes and nights more equally divided, being in Summer two hours shorter, in Winter two hours longer than they are in *England*. The 11 of *June* the Sun riseth at 4 and 26 minutes, and setteth at 7 & 34 minutes; in *December*, the 13 the shortest day, the Sun riseth at 7 and 35 minutes, and setteth at 4 and 27 minutes.

Mid-*March* their Spring begins, in *April* they have Rain and Thunder; So again at *Michaelmas*, about which season they have either before *Michaelmas* or after outrageous storms of Wind and Rain. It's observable that there is no part of the World, which hath not some certain times of outrageous storms. We have upon our Coast in *England* a *Michaelmas* flaw,[40] that seldom fails: in the *West-Indies* in *August* and *September* the forcible *North*-wind, which though some call *Tuffins* or *Hurricanes* we must distinguish, for a right *Hurricane* is (as I have said before) an impetuous wind that goes about the Compass in the space of 24 hours, in such a storm the Lord *Willoughby* [p. 55] of *Parham* Governour of the *Barbadoes* was castaway, going with a Fleet to recover St. *Christophers* from the *French, Anno Dom* 1666 *July*.[41] Cold weather begins with the middle of *November*, the winter's perpetually freezing, insomuch that their Rivers and salt-Bayes are frozen over and passable for Men, Horse, Oxen and Carts: *Aequore cum gelido zephyrus fert xenia Cymbo.*[42] The *North-west* wind is the

---

39. See Lowes (389, 432–33), who traces this image from Josselyn, to Cotton Mather's communications to the Royal Society, and ultimately to Samuel Taylor Coleridge's poem "The Rime of the Ancient Mariner."

40. That is, a sudden squall of wind on 29 September.

41. Francis Willoughby (c. 1613–66), fifth Baron Willoughby of Parham, assumed governorship of Barbados on 7 May 1650 and was lost later at sea as Josselyn relates.

42. When the west wind carries gifts from the cold sea to Cymbo.

sharpest wind in the Countrie. In *England* most of the cold winds and weathers come from the Sea, and those that are nearest the Sea-coasts in *England* are accounted unwholsome, but not so in *New-England*, for in the extremity of winter the *North-East* and *South*-wind coming from the Sea produceth warm weather, only the *North-West*-wind coming over land from the white mountains[43] (which are alwayes (except in August) covered with snow) is the cause of extream cold weather, alwayes accompanied with deep snowes and bitter frosts, the snow for the most part four and six foot deep, which melting on the superficies with the heat of the Sun, (for the most part shining out clearly every day) and freezing again in the night makes a crust upon the snow sufficient to bear a man walking with snow shoos[44] upon it. And at this [p. 56] season the *Indians* go forth on hunting of Dear and Moose twenty, thirty, forty miles up into the Countrie. Their Summer is hot and dry proper for their *Indian* Wheat; which thrives best in a hot and dry season, the skie for the most part Summer and Winter very clear and serene; if they see a little black cloud in the *North-West*, no bigger than a man may cover with his Hat, they expect a following storm, the cloud in short time spreading round about the Horizon accompanied with violent gusts of wind, rain, and many times lightning and terrible thunder. In all Countries they have observations how the weather will fall out, and these rules following are observable in *New-England*. If the moon look bright and fair, look for fair weather, also the appearing of one Rainbow after a storm, is a known sign of fair weather; if mists come down from the Hills, or descend from the Heavens, and settle in the valleys, they promise fair hot weather; mists in the Evening show a fair hot day on the morrow: the like when mists rise from waters in the Evening. The obscuring of the smaller Stars is a certain sign of Tempests approaching; the oft changing of the wind is also a fore-runner of a storm; the resounding of the Sea from the shore, and murmuring of [p. 57] the winds in the woods without apparent wind, sheweth wind to follow: shooting of the Stars (as they call it) is an usual sign of

43. Part of the Appalachian range, northern New Hampshire.
44. This is the earliest example of *snow-shoe* in the language (*OED*). See also 128−29.

wind from that quarter the Star came from. So look whether the resounding of the Sea upon the shore be on the *East* or *West* side of the dwelling, out of that quarter will the wind proceed the next day. The redness of the sky in the morning, is a token of winds, or rain or both: if the Circles that appear about the Sun be red and broken they portend wind; if thick and dark, wind, snow and rain; the like may be said of the Circles about the moon. If two rainbowes appear, they are a sign of rain; If the Sun or Moon look pale, look for rain; if a dark cloud be at Sun rising, in which the Sun soon after is hid, it will dissolve it, and rain will follow; *nebula ascendens indicat imbres, nebula descendens serenitatem.*[45] If the Sun seem greater in the *East*, than in the *West* about Sun-setting, and that there appears a black cloud, you may expect rain that night, or the day following.

> *Serò rubens Cælum cras indicat esse serenum,*
> *Sed si manè rubet venturos indicat Imbres.*[46]

[p. 58] To conclude; if the white hills look clear and conspicu-ous, it is a sign of fair weather; if black and cloudy, of rain; if yellow, it is a certain sign of snow shortly to ensue.

In *Anno Dom.* 1667. *March*, appeared a sign in the *Heavens* in the form of a Sphear, pointing directly to the *West*: and in the year following on the third day of *April* being *Friday*, there was a terrible Earthquake, before that a very great one in 1638. and another in 58 and in 166⅔. *January* 26, 27, & 28. (which was the year before I came thither) there were Earthquakes 6 or 7 times in the space of three dayes. Earthquakes are frequent in the Countrie; some suppose that the white mountains were first raised by Earthquakes, they are hollow as may be guessed by the re-sounding of the rain upon the level on the top. The *Indians* told us of a River whose course was not only stopt by an Earthquake in 1668. (as near as I can remember) but the whole River swallowed up. And I have heard it reported from credible persons, that (whilst I was there in the Countrie) there happened a terrible

45. A rising cloud indicates rain, a falling cloud calm.
46. A rendering of the common proverb, one variation of which reads: "Red sky in the night is sailors' delight; red sky in the morning gives sailors warning."

Earthquake amongst the *French*, rending a huge Rock asunder even to the center wherein was a vast hollow of an immeasurable depth, out of which came many infernal Spirits. I shall [p. 59] conclude this discourse of Earthquakes, with that which came from the Pen of our Royal Martyr King *Charles* the First; *A storm at Sea wants not its terrour, but an Earthquake, shaking the very foundation of all, the World hath nothing more of horrour.*[47] And now I come to the plants of the Countrie.

The plants in *New England* for the variety, number, beauty, and vertues, may stand in Competition with the plants of any Countrey in Europe. *Johnson* hath added to *Gerard's* Herbal 300. and *Parkinson* mentioneth many more; had they been in *New England* they might have found 1000 at least never heard of nor seen by any *Englishman* before:[48] 'Tis true, the Countrie hath no *Bonerets*, or *Tartarlambs*, no glittering coloured *Tuleps*; but here you have the *American Mary-Gold*, the *Earth-nut* bearing a princely Flower, the beautiful leaved *Pirola*, the honied *Colibry*, &c.[49] They are generally of (somewhat) a more masculine vertue,[50] than any of the same species in *England*, but not in so terrible a degree, as to be mischievous or ineffectual to our *English* bodies. *It is affirmed by some that no forraign Drugg or Simple*

47. Paraphrased from *Eikon Basilike*, allegedly written by Charles I in prison. The specific passage details the "tumults" of opposition to Charles's rule, "which were not like a storm at sea, which yet wants not its terror, but like an earthquake, shaking the very foundations of all, than which nothing in the world hath more of horrour."

48. The English botanist and surgeon John Gerard (1545–1612) published his well-known *Herball or Generall Historie of Plantes* in 1597. Thomas Johnson (d. 1644), "citizen and apothecarye of London," enlarged and amended Gerard's book in 1633. John Parkinson (1567–1650) published *Paradisi in sole paradisus terrestris* in 1629, and *Theatrum Botanicum* in 1640.

49. *Bonerets*: no *OED* entry, although perhaps derived from *bonair*, well-bred, gentle, courteous. *Tartarlambs*: no *OED* entry. Josselyn's "*Mary-Gold*" in fact is a sunflower (genus *Helianthus*), of which he provides a sketch in *Rarities* (82). The "*earth-nut*" or groundnut is *Apios americana*, although in other early writings it is perhaps the Jerusalem artichoke, which was cultivated by the Indians. Pirola: *Pyrola* or shinleaf. The word *colibry* is recorded elsewhere in the language only to denote the hummingbird, and thus probably here means jewelweed or impatiens, to which hummingbirds are particularly attracted.

50. By "masculine vertue," strength or potency is intended (Latin *virtus*).

can be so proper to Englishmen as their own, for the quantity of
Opium *which Turks do safely take will kill four Englishmen, and
that which will* [p. 60] *salve their wounds within a day, will not
recure an Englishman in three.* To which I answer that it is custom
that brings the *Turks* to the familiar use of *Opium.* You may have
heard of a *Taylor* in *Kent,* who being afflicted with want of sleep
ventured upon *Opium,* taking at first a grain, and increasing of it
till it came to an ounce, which quantitie he took as familiarly as a
Turk, without any harm, more than that he could not sleep without it. The *English* in *New-England* take white *Hellebore,*[51] which
operates as fairly with them, as with the *Indians,* who steeping of
it in water sometime, give it to young lads gathered together a
purpose to drink, if it come up they force them to drink again
their vomit, (which they save in a Birchen-dish) till it stayes with
them, & he that gets the victory of it is made Captain of the other
lads for that year. There is a plant likewise, called for want of a
name *Clownes wound wort* by the *English,* though it be not the
same, that will heal a green wound in 24 hours, if a wise man
have the ordering of it.[52] Thus much for the general, I shall now
begin to discover unto you the plants more particularly, and I
shall first begin with Trees, and of them, first with such as are
called in Scripture Trees of God, that is great Trees, [p. 61] that
grow of themselves without planting. Psal[ms]. 104.16, 17. *Sa-
tiantur arbores Jehovæ, cedri libani quas plantavit; (ubi aviculæ
nidificent) abietes domicilia ciconiæ.*[53] The Herons take great delight to sit basking upon the tops of these Trees. And I shall not
be over large in any, having written of them in my Treatise of the
rarities of *New England,* to which I refer you.

The *Oake* I have given you an account of, and the kinds; I
shall add the ordering of Red *Oake* for Wainscot. When they
have cut it down and clear'd it from the branches, they pitch the
body of the Tree in a muddy place in a River, with the head

51. American hellebore (*Veratrum viride*), a highly poisonous plant still
used medicinally today.
52. Called "clownes all-heal" in *Rarities* (69), this is probably a species of
verbena.
53. Psalms 104.16, 17: "The trees of the Lord are full of sap; the cedars of
Lebanon, which he hath planted; / Where the birds make their nests: as for the
stork, the fir trees are her house."

downward for some time, afterwards they draw it out, and when
it is seasoned sufficiently, they saw it into boards for Wainscot,
and it will branch out into curious works.

There is an admirable rare Creature in shape like a *Buck*, with
Horns, of a gummy substance, which I have often found in the
fall of the leaf upon the ground amongst the withered leaves; a
living Creature I cannot call it; having only the sign of a mouth
and eyes: seldom or never shall you meet with any of them whole,
but the head and horns, or the hinder parts, broken off from the
rest; the *Indians* call them Tree *Bucks*, and have a superstitious
saying (for I believe [p. 62] they never see any of them living)
that if they can see a Tree-*Buck* walking upon the branches of an
Oake when they go out in a morning to hunt, they shall have
good luck that day. What they are good for I know not, but certainly there is some more than ordinary vertue in them. It is true
that nothing in nature is superfluous, and we have the Scripture
to back it, that God created nothing in vain. The like Creatures
they *have at the* Barbadoes *which they call* Negroes *heads, found in
the Sands, about two inches long, with forehead, eyes, nose, mouth,
chin, and part of the neck, they are alwayes found loose in the Sands
without any root, it is as black as Jet, but whence it comes they know
not.* I have read likewise, *that in the* Canaries *or* Fortunate-
Islands, *there is found a certain Creature, which Boys bring home
from the mountains as oft as they would, and named them* Tudes-
quels, *or little* Germans: *for they were dry'd dead Carcases, almost
three footed, which any boy did easily carry in one of the palms of his
hand, and they were of a humane shape; but the whole dead Carcase
was clearly like unto Parchment, and their bones were flexible, as it
were gristles: against the Sun, also, their bowels and intestines were
seen. Surely (saith my Authour) the destroyed race of the* Pigmies
was there.[54] There is [p. 63] also many times found upon the
leaves of the *Oake* a Creature like a *Frog*, being as thin as a leaf,
and transparent, as yellow as Gold, with little fiery red eyes, the
English call them Tree-frogs or Tree-toads (but of Tree-toads I
shall have occasion to speak in another place)[;] they are said to
be venomous, but may be safely used, being admirable to stop

---

54. Josselyn's "Author," from whom he gleans the foregoing lore, remains
untraced.

womens over-flowing courses[55] hung about their necks in a Taffetie bag.

Captain Smith *writes that in* New-England *there growes a certain berry called* Kermes, *worth 10 shillings a pound, and had been formerly sold for 30 or 40 shillings a pound, which may yearly be gathered in good quantity.* I have sought for this berry, he speaks of, as a man should seek for a needle in a bottle of Hay,[56] but could never light upon it; unless that kind of *Solomon-seal* called by the *English* Treacle-berry be it.[57] *Gerard* our famous Herbalist *writes that they grow upon a little Tree called* Scarlet-Oake, *the leaves have one sharp prickle at the end of it; it beareth small* Acorns: *But the grain or berry growes out of the woody branches, like an excrescence of the substance of the* Oake-Apple, *and of the bigness of Pease, at first white, when ripe of an* Ash-colour, *which ingenders little Maggots, which when it begins* [p. 64] *to have wings are put into a bag and boulted up and down till dead, and then made up into lumps, the Maggot as most do deem is* Cutchenele; *So that* Chermes *is* Cutchenele: *the berries dye scarlet.* Mr. George Sands *in his Travels saith (much to the same purpose) that scarlet dye growes*[58] *like a blister on the leaf of the Holy* Oake, *a little shrub, yet producing* Acorns, *being gathered they rub out of it a certain red dust, that converteth after a while into worms, which they kill with Wine, when they begin to quicken.* See farther concerning Treacle-berries and *Cutchinele* in the rarities of *New-England.*

The Pine-tree challengeth the next place, and that sort which is called Board-pine is the principal, it is a stately large Tree, very tall, and sometimes two or three fadom about: of the body the *English* make large *Canows* of 20 foot long, and two and a half

55. Excessive menstrual flow.

56. John Smith's discussion of the so-called Alkermes berry (1:336) reveals his misconstruction of the pregnant female insect *Kermes quercus*, which resembles a fruit. Bottle of hay: bundle of hay. This is the earliest recorded American instance of the figure of speech concerning the needle in a haystack.

57. Josselyn's earlier editor, Edward Tuckerman, is certainly correct (176n) in identifying this as false Solomon's seal, *Smilacina racemosa*, which bears striking red berries (*Rarities* 45).

58. To the end of this sentence Josselyn quotes accurately from George Sandys' *Travels* (4). Cochineal is a dye product found in the insect *Dactylopius coccus*, which feeds on prickly pear cactus and is distinct from the oak-feeding species (genus *Kermes*) described by Sandys and Gerard.

over, hollowing of them with an Adds, and shaping of the outside like a Boat.[59] Some conceive that the wood called *Gopher* in Scripture, of which *Noah* made the Ark, was no other than Pine, *Gen. 6.14.*[60] The bark thereof is good for Ulcers in tender persons that refuse sharp medicines. The inner bark of young board-pine cut small and stampt and boiled in a Gallon of water is a very soveraign medicine for burn [p. 65] or scald, washing the sore with some of the decoction, and then laying on the bark stampt very soft: or for frozen limbs, to take out the fire and to heal them, take the bark of the Board-pine-Tree, cut it small and stamp it and boil it in a gallon of water to Gelly, wash the sore with the liquor, stamp the bark again till it be very soft and bind it on. The Turpentine is excellent to heal wounds and cuts, and hath all the properties of *Venice* Turpentine, the Rosen is as good as Frankincense, and the powder of the dryed leaves generateth flesh; the distilled water of the green Cones taketh away wrinkles in the face being laid on with Cloths.

The Firr-tree is a large Tree too,[61] but seldom so big as the Pine, the bark is smooth, with knobs or blisters, in which lyeth clear liquid turpentine very good to be put into salves and oyntments, the leaves or Cones boiled in Beer are good for the Scurvie, the young buds are excellent to put into Epithemes for Warts and Corns, the Rosen is altogether as good as Frankincense; out of this Tree the Poleakers[62] draw Pitch and Tarr; the manner I shall give you, for that it may (with many other things contained in this Treatise) be beneficial to my Countrymen, either there already seated, or that [p. 66] may happen to go thither hereafter. Out of the fattest wood changed into Torch-wood, which is a disease in that Tree they draw Tarr, first a place must be paved with stone or the like, a little higher in the middle, about which there

59. The board pine is the eastern white pine (*Pinus strobus*), widely used also in colonial times for mast timbers. Fadom: fathom. Adds: adz, an axlike tool with a blade at right angles to the handle, used for shaping wood.

60. Genesis 6.14: "Make thee an ark of gopher wood; rooms shalt thou make in the ark, and shalt pitch it within and without with pitch."

61. No firs are native to the far northeast. The pitch pine (*Pinus rigida*) is probably the one being referred to; it was the principal tree used for making tar and pitch.

62. Epithemes: poultices. Poleakers: Polish.

must be made gutters, into which the liquor falls, then out from them other gutters are to be drawn, by which it may be received, then is it put into barrels. The place thus prepared, the cloven wood must be set upright, then must it be covered with a great number of firr and pitch bowes; and on every part all about with much lome and sods of earth, and great heed must be taken, lest there be any cleft or chink remaining, only a hole left in the top of the furnace, through which the fire may be put in, and the flame and smoak to pass out: when the fire burneth, the Pitch or Tarr runneth forth first thin, and then thicker; of which when it is boiled is made pitch: the powder of dried pitch is used to generate flesh in wounds and sores. The knots of this Tree and fat-pine are used by the *English* instead of candles, and it will burn a long time, but it makes the people pale.

The Spruce-tree I have given you an account of in my *New-England* rarities.[63] In the North-east of *Scotland* upon the banks [p. 67] of *Lough-argick*, there hath been formerly of these Trees 28 handful about at the Root, and their bodies mounted to 90 foot of height, bearing at the length 20 inches diameter. At *Pascata-way* there is now a Spruce-tree brought down to water-side by our Mass-men of an incredible bigness, and so long that no skipper durst ever yet adventure to ship it, but there it lyes and Rots.[64]

The Hemlock-tree[65] is a kind of spruce or pine; the bark boiled and stampt till it be very soft is excellent for to heal wounds, and so is the Turpentine thereof, and the Turpentine that issueth from the Cones of the Larch-tree, (which comes nearest of any to the right Turpentine) is singularly good to heal wounds, and to draw out the malice (or Thorn, as *Helmont*

---

63. The tree here is presumably the Norway spruce, *Picea excelsa*. See *Rarities* (63–64).

64. "Mass-men" may be a misprint for *mast-men*, that is, men who cut trees suitable for use as ship masts. The crown reserved all pines over 24 inches in diameter for use as mast timber (Cronon 110–11) and shipped them in great quantities from northern New England in special ships loaded through bow ports. Consequently, logs of larger than two feet cannot be found in New England buildings from the period. See page 44 above where Josselyn discusses the use of spruces for masts.

65. The eastern hemlock, *Tsuga canadensis*.

phrases it) of any Ach, rubbing the place therewith, and strowing upon it the powder of *Sage*-leaves.[66]

The white Cedar is a stately Tree, and is taken by some to be *Tamarisk*,[67] this Tree the *English* saw into boards to floor their Rooms, for which purpose it is excellent, long lasting, and wears very smooth and white; likewise they make shingles to cover their houses with instead of tyle, it will never warp. This Tree, the Oak and the [p. 68] Larch-tree are best for building. Groundsels made of Larch-tree will never rot, and the longer it lyes the harder it growes, that you may almost drive a nail into a bar of Iron as easily as into that.[68] Oh, that my Countreymen might obtain that blessing with their buildings, which *Esay* [Isaiah] prophesied to the *Jewes* in the 65 Chapter and 22 verse. *Non ædificabunt & alius inhabitabit, non plantubunt & alius comedet: sed ut sunt dies Arboria, dies erunt populi mei, & opus manuum suarum deterent electi mei.*[69]

The Sassafras-tree is no great Tree, I have met with some as big as my middle, the rind is tawny and upon that a thin colour of Ashes, the inner part is white, of an excellent smell like Fennel, of a sweet tast with some bitterness; the leaves are like Fig-leaves of a dark green. A decoction of the Roots and bark thereof sweetned with Sugar, and drunk in the morning fasting will open the body and procure a stool or two, it is good for the Scurvie taken some time together, and laying upon the legs the green leaves of white *Hellebore*. They give it to Cows that have newly calved to make them cast their Cleanings.[70] This Tree growes not beyond

66. "Malice" here means poison or infection. *Helmont*: Jean Baptista van Helmont (c. 1577–1644), Flemish physician and chemist whose works were published by his son in 1648 as *Ortus Medicinæ*.

67. A member of the cypress family, the white cedar (*Chamaecyparis thyoides*) is not related to the genus *Tamarix*.

68. The tamarack or eastern larch is *Latrix laricina*. Groundsels: ground sills or foundation timbers.

69. Isaiah 65.22: "They shall not build, and another inhabit; they shall not plant, and another eat: for as the days of a tree are the days of my people, and mine elect shall long enjoy the work of their hands."

70. *Sassafras albidum* contains the toxin safrole, a carcinogen. During the colonial period, however, sassafras was a very important New World export, widely used by Europeans in attempts to cure syphilis (Crosby 154–55). On

Black-point Eastward: it is observed, that there is no province but produces Trees and plants not growing in other Regions.

[p. 69]   *Non omnis fert omnia tellus.*[71]

The Walnut which is divers, some bearing square nuts, others like ours, but smaller: there is likewise black Walnut of precious use for Tables, Cabinets and the like. The Walnut-tree is the toughest wood in the Countrie, and therefore made use of for Hoops and Bowes, there being no Yew there growing; In *England* they made their Bowes usually of Witch Hasel, Ash, Yew, the best of outlandish Elm, but the Indians make theirs of Walnut.[72]

The Line-tree with long nuts, the other kind I could never find: the wood of this Tree, Laurel, Rhamnus, Holly and Ivy are accounted for woods that cause fire by attrition;[73] Laurel and Ivy are not growing in *New-England*: the *Indians* will rub two sear'd sticks of any sort of wood, and kindle a fire with them presently.

The Maple-tree, on the boughs of this Tree I have often found a jellied substance like *Jewes-Ears*,[74] which I found upon tryal to be good for sore throats &*c.*

The Birch-tree is of two kinds, ordinary Birch, and black Birch, many of these Trees are stript of their bark by the *Indians*, who make of it their Canows, Kettles, [p. 70] and Birchen-dishes: there is an excrescence growing out of the body of the Tree called spunck, or dead mens Caps,[75] it growes at the Roots of Ash, or Beech, or Elm; but the best is that which growes upon the black Birch, this boiled and beaten, and then dried in an Oven maketh excellent Touch-wood, and Balls to play with.

---

the great sassafras hunts of early New England, see Carroll (42–44). Glean or gleanings: placenta or afterbirth.

71. Not every ground bears all things.

72. These walnuts are probably the butternut and the black walnut (*Juglans cinera* and *J. nigra*).

73. The line tree is either the linden or the American basswood (*Tilia americana*). Rhamnus is the buckthorn (*Rhamnus cathartica*). By attrition: when rubbed together.

74. Jew's ears: folk term for various edible fungi known today as wood ear (genus *Auricula*).

75. Shelf fungus.

Alder, of which wood there is abundance in the wet swamps: the bark thereof with the yolke of an Egg is good for a strain; an *Indian* bruising of his knee, chew'd the bark of Alder fasting and laid it to, which quickly helped him. The wives of our West-Countrey English make a drink with the seeds of alder, giving it to their Children troubled with the *Alloes*. I have talk'd with many of them, but could never apprehend what disease it should be they so name, these Trees are called by some Sullinges.

The *Indians* tell of a Tree that growes far up in the land, that is as big as an Oake, that will cure the falling-sickness infallibly, what part thereof they use, Bark, Wood, leaves or fruit, I could never learn; they promised often to bring of it to me, but did not.[76] I have seen a stately Tree growing here and there in valleys, not like to any Trees in Europe, having a smooth bark of [p. 71] a dark brown colour, the leaves like great Maple, in *England* called Sycamor, but larger, it may be this Tree they brag of.

Thus much concerning Trees, now I shall present to your view the Shrubs; and first of the Sumach Shrub, which as I have told you in *New-Englands* rarities, differeth from all the kinds set down in our *English* herbals; the root dyeth wool or cloth reddish, the decoction of the leaves in wine drunk, is good for all Fluxes of the belly in man or woman, the whites, &c.[77] For galled places stamp the leaves with honey, and apply it, nothing so soon healeth a wound in the head as Sumach stampt and ap-plyed once in three dayes, the powder strewed in stayeth the bleeding of wounds: The seed of Sumach pounded and mixt with honey, healeth the Hemorrhoids, the gum put into a hollow tooth asswageth the pain, the bark or berries in the fall of the leaf, is as good as galls to make Ink of.[78]

Elder in *New-England* is shrubbie, & dies once in two years: there is a sort of dwarf-Elder that growes by the Sea-side that

76. Falling-sickness: epilepsy. (Is "infallibly" a pun?) The tree referred to is apparently the American sycamore (*Platanus occidentalis*), formerly called buttonwood and plane tree.

77. Smooth sumac (*Rhus glabra*) is the most widespread of the New England genuses. The whites: a common name for leucorrhea, a condition charac-terized by a whitish vaginal discharge.

78. Galls: tumors on plant tissue, often having a high tannic acid content.

hath a red pith, the berries of both are smaller than *English*-Elder, not round but corner'd, neither of them smell so strong as ours.

Juniper growes for the most part by the Sea-side, it bears abundance of skie-co- [p. 72] loured berries fed upon by Partridges, and hath a woodie root, which induceth me to believe that the plant mentioned in Job 30.4. *Qui decerpebant herbas e salsilagine cum stirpibus: etiam radices Juniperorum cibo erant illis*, was our *Indian* plant *Cassava*.[79] They write that *Juniper*-coals preserve fire longest of any, keeping fire a whole year without supply, yet the *Indian* never burns of it.

Sweet fern, see the rarities of *New England*, the tops and nucaments[80] of sweet fern boiled in water or milk and drunk helpeth all manner of Fluxes, being boiled in water it makes an excellent liquor for Inck.

Current-bushes are of two kinds red and black, the black currents which are larger than the red smell like cats piss, yet are reasonable pleasant in eating.

The Gooseberry-bush, the berry of which is called Grosers or thorn Grapes, grow all over the Countrie, the berry is but small, of a red or purple colour when ripe.

There is a small shrub which is very common, growing sometimes to the height of Elder, bearing a berry like in shape to the fruit of the white thorn, of a pale yellow colour at first, then red, when it is ripe of a deep purple, of a delicate Aromatical tast, somewhat stiptick: to conclude, al- [p. 73] wayes observe this rule in taking or refusing unknown fruit: if you find them eaten of the fowl or beast, you may boldly venture to eat of them, otherwise do not touch them.

Maze, otherwise called *Turkie*-wheat, or rather *Indian*-wheat, because it came first from thence; the leaves boiled and drunk helpeth the pain in the back; of the stalkes when they are green you may make *Beverage*, as they do with *Calamels*, or Sugar-

79. The verse from Job 30.4 reads: "Who cut up mallows by the bushes, and juniper roots for their meat." Cassava or manioc (*Manihot esculenta*) is the South American shrub from whose roots tapioca is made. Since the discovery of this New World food, it has become a staple around the globe (Crosby 173–74).

80. Catkins or amenta.

canes. The raw Corn chewed ripens felons or Cats hairs, or you may lay Samp to it: The *Indians* before it be thorow ripe eat of it parched.[81] Certainly the parched Corn that *Abigail* brought to *David* was of this kind of grain, I Sam[uel]. 25.18.[82] *The Jewes manner was (as it is delivered to us by a learned Divine) first to parch their corn, then they fryed it, and lastly they boiled it to a paste, and then tempered it with water, Cheese-Curds, Honey and Eggs, this they carried drye with them to the Camp, and so wet the Cakes in Wine or milk; such was the pulse too of* Africa.

French-beans, or rather *American*-beans, the Herbalists call them kidney beans from their shape and effects, for they strengthen the kidneys; they are variegated much, some being bigger a great deal than others; some [p. 74] white, black, red, yellow, blew, spotted; besides your *Bonivis* and *Calavances* and the kidney-bean, that is proper to *Ronoake*, but these are brought into the Countrie, the other are natural to the climate.[83] So the *Mexico* pompion which is flat and deeply camphered, the flesh laid to, asswageth pain of the eyes. The water-mellon is proper to the Countrie, the flesh of it is of a flesh colour, a rare cooler of Feavers, and excellent against the stone. *Pomum spinosum* and *palma Christi* too growes not here, unless planted, brought from *Peru*;[84] the later is thought to be the plant, that shaded Jonah *the Prophet*, Jonas 4.6. *Paraverat enim* Jehova *Deus ricinum qui ascenderet supra* Jonam, *ut esset umbra super caput ejus ereptura eum a malo ipsius; lætabaturque* Jonas *de ricino illo lætitia magna.*[85] *Ricinum*, that is *palma Christi*, called also *cucurbita*, and therefore translated a Gourd.

Tobacco, or *Tabacca* so called from *Tabaco* or *Tobago*, one of

81. *Calamels*: perhaps derived from the Latin *calamellus*, "little tube," after the plant's tubular stalk. Felons: small abscesses or sores. Samp: a coarse porridge of Indian corn.

82. I Samuel 25.18 reads in part: "Then Abigail made haste, and took . . . five measures of parched corn."

83. Bonavist is a species of tropical legume; Josselyn's use precedes the earliest *OED* entry of 1700. Calavance: another variety of tropical legume or bean.

84. Pompion: pumpkin. Camphered: chamfered, grooved or furrowed. *Palma Christi* is medieval Latin for the castor oil plant (*Ricinus communis*).

85. Jonah 4.6: "And the Lord God prepared a gourd, and made it to come up over Jonah, that it might be a shadow over his head, to deliver him from his grief. So Jonah was exceeding glad of the gourd."

the *Caribbe*-Islands about 50 *English* miles from *Trinidad*. The right name, according to *Monardus*,[86] is *picielte*, as others will *petum*, *nicotian* from *Nicot*, a Portingal, to whom it was presented for a raritie in *Anno Dom.* 1559. by one that brought it from *Florida*. Great contest there is about the time when it was first [p. 75] brought into *England*, some will have Sir *John Hawkins* the first, others Sir *Francis Drake's* Mariners; others again say that one Mr. *Lane* imployed by Sir *Walter Rawleigh* brought it first into *England*; all conclude that Sir *Walter Rawleigh* brought it first in use. *It is observed that no one kind of forraign Commodity yieldeth greater advantage to the publick than Tobacco, it is generally made the complement of our entertainment, and hath made more slaves than* Mahomet. There is three sorts of it Marchantable, the first horse Tobacco, having a broad long leaf piked at the end; the second round pointed Tobacco; third sweet scented Tobacco. These are made up into Cane, leaf or ball; there is little of it planted in *New-England*, neither have they learned the right way of curing of it. It is sowen in *April* upon a bed of rich mould sifted, they make a bed about three yards long, or more according to the ground they intend to plant, and a yard and a half over; this they tread down hard, then they sow their seed upon it as thick as may be, and sift fine earth upon it, then tread it down again as hard as possible they can, when it hath gotten four or six leaves, they remove it into the planting ground; when it begins to bud towards flowring, they crop off the [p. 76] top, for the Flower drawes away the strength of the leaf. For the rest I refer you to the Planter, being not willing to discover their mysteries. The *Indians* in *New England* use a small round leafed Tobacco, called by them, or the Fishermen Poke. *It is odious to the* English. *The vertues of Tobacco are these, it helps digestion, the Gout, the Toothach, prevents infection by scents, it heats the cold, and cools them that sweat, feedeth the hungry, spent spirits restoreth, purgeth the stomach, killeth nits and lice, the juice of the green leaf healeth green wounds although poysoned, the Syrup for many diseases, the smoak for the Phthisick, cough of the lungs, distillations of Rheume, and all diseases*

86. Nicolas Monardes (1493–1578), Spanish botanist and physician, whose account of American commodities was translated by John Frampton in 1577, with subsequent editions, as *Joyfull News out of the Newfounde World*.

of a cold and moist cause, good for all bodies cold and moist taken upon an emptie stomach, taken upon a full stomach it precipitates digestion, immoderately taken it dryeth the body, enflameth the bloud, hurteth the brain, weakens the eyes and the sinews.[87]

White *Hellebore* is used for the scurvie by the *English*. A friend of mine gave them first a purge, then conserve of Bearberries, then fumed their leggs with vinegar, sprinkled upon a piece of mill-stone made hot, and applied to the sores white *Hellebore* leaves; drink made of *Orpine* and *sorrel* were given likewise with it, and Sea- [p. 77] scurvie-grass.[88] To kill lice, boil the roots of *Hellebore* in milk, and anoint the hair of the head therewith or other places.

Mandrake, is a very rare plant, the *Indians* know it not, it is found in the woods about *Pascataway*, they do in plain terms stink, therefore *Reubens*-Flowers that he brought home were not *Mandrakes*, Gen. 30.14, 15, 16. *They are rendered in the Latine* Amabiles flores, *the same word say our Divines is used in* Canticles, 7.4. Amabiles istos flores edentes odorem, & secundum ostia nostra omnes pretiosos fructus, recentes simul ac veteres, dilecte mi, repono tibi. *So that the right translation is,* Reuben *brought home amiable and sweet smelling Flowers; this in the* Canticles *(say they) expounding the other.*[89]

Calamus Aromaticus, or the sweet smelling reed, it Flowers in *July*; see *New-Englands* rarities.[90]

87. This paean to tobacco is one of the most frequently reprinted passages in Josselyn's work. But, as the italics indicate, it probably comes from a lost or untraced source.

88. Orpine is a succulent herb, *Sedum telephium*. Sorrel: various species of dock, genus *Rumex*, naturalized from Europe. Sea scurvy grass or convolvulus, known today as bindweed or morning glory, was also used in Josselyn's time to concoct a medicated ale.

89. Mandrake includes all members of the genus *Mandragora*, the malodorous roots of which were thought to resemble the human body; thus arose the belief that the plant enhances fertility or acts as an aphrodisiac. So it appears in the story of Leah and Rachel, Genesis 30. The Latin passage is not identical with but is clearly parallel to Song of Solomon (Canticles) 7.13: "The mandrakes give a smell, and at our gates are all manner of pleasant fruits, new and old, which I have laid up for thee, O my beloved."

90. Josselyn discusses the sweet flag (*Acorus calamus*) in *Rarities* (53). Though widely used for its scent and supposed medical properties, the plant now is classed as carcinogenic.

Sarsaparilla or roughbind-weed (as some describe it) the leaves and whole bind set with thorns, of this there is store growing upon the banks of Ponds. See the rarities of *New-England*. The leaves of the *Sarsaparilla* there described pounded with Hogs grease and boiled to an unguent, is excellent in the curing of wounds.[91]

Live for ever,[92] it is a kind of *Cud-weed*, [p. 78] flourisheth all summer long till cold weather comes in, it growes now plentifully in our *English* Gardens, it is good for cough of the lungs, and to cleanse the breast taken as you do Tobacco; and for pain in the head the decoction, or the juice strained and drunk in Bear, Wine, or Aqua vitæ, killeth worms. The Fishermen when they want Tobacco take this herb being cut and dryed.

Lysimachus or Loose-strife:[93] there are several kinds, but the most noted is the yellow *Lysimachus* of *Virginia*, the root is longish and white, as thick as ones thumb, the stalkes of an overworn colour, and a little hairie, the middle vein of the leaf whitish, the Flower yellow and like Primroses, and therefore called Tree-primrose, growes upon seedie vessels, &c. The first year it grows not up to a stalke, but sends up many large leaves handsomely lying one upon another, Rose fashion, flowers in *June*, the seed is ripe in *August*, this as I have said is taken by the *English* for Scabious.

St. *John's* wort, it preserveth Cheese made up in it, at Sea. Spurge or Wolfes milch there are several sorts.[94]

Avens, or herb-bennet; you have an account of it in *New-Englands* rarities; but one [p. 79] thing more I shall add, that you may plainly perceive a more masculine quality in the plants growing in *New-England*. A neighbour of mine in Hay-time, having overheat himself, and melted his grease, with striving to outmowe another man, fell dangerously sick, not being able to turn himself in his bed, his stomach gon, and his heart fainting

91. True sarsaparilla is native only to Central and South America. The author undoubtedly had in view *Aralia nudicalis*, which yields a substitute.

92. Everlasting, genus *Antennaria*.

93. Our species of *Lysimachia*, with the exception of *vulgaris*, are indigenous; Tuckerman appears to have erred in naming this plant (192n) which Josselyn discusses in *Rarities* (56).

94. Saint John's wort is *Hypericum perforatum*, today patented for use as a

ever and anon; to whom I administred the decoction of *Avens*-Roots[95] and leaves in water and wine, sweetning it with Syrup of Clove-Gilliflowers, in one weeks time it recovered him, so that he was able to perform his daily work, being a poor planter or husbandman as we call them.

Red-Lilly growes all over the Countrey amongst the bushes. Mr. *Johnson* upon *Gerard* takes the Tulip to be the Lilly of the field mentioned by our Saviour, Matth[ew]. 6.28, 29. *Ac de vestitu quid soliciti estis? discite quomodo lilia agrorum augescant: non fatigantur, neque nent, sed dico vobis, ne Solomonem quidem cum universa gloria sic amictum fuisse ut unum ex istis.* Solomon *in all his Royalty was not like one of them. His reasons are, first from the shape, like a lilly; The second, because those places where our Saviour was conversant they grow wild in the fields. Third, the infinite variety of the co-* [p. 80] *lours. The fourth and last reason, the wondrous beautie and mixture of these Flowers.*[96]

Water-lillys; the black roots dryed and pulverized, are wondrous effectual in the stopping of all manner of fluxes of the belly, drunk with wine or water.

Herba-paris, one berry, herb true love, or four-leaved nightshade, the leaves are good to be laid upon hot tumours.[97]

Umbilicus veneris, or *New-England* daisie, it is good for hot humours, *Erisipelas*, St. *Anthonie's* fire, all inflammations.[98]

Glass-wort,[99] a little quantity of this plant you may take for the

---

food preservative. Spurge in America, genus *Euphorbia*, is frequently poisonous, always acrid in taste; elsewhere it is cultivated for its oil.

95. Avens or herb bennet is genus *Geum*, treated briefly in *Rarities* (45).

96. Again Josselyn reveals his debt to Johnson's edition of Gerard. The passages from Matthew read: "And why take ye thought for raiment? Consider the lilies of the field, how they grow; they toil not, neither do they spin: / And yet I say unto you, That even Solomon in all his glory was not arrayed like one of these."

97. In *Rarities* Josselyn sketches this plant, which, as Tuckerman writes, "is doubtless *Cornus canadensis*" (214), cornel or bunchberry, related to the dogwood.

98. The daisy may be one of our native saxifrages. Erysipelas is an epidermal streptococcal disease that became epidemic in France in 1089; sufferers were cured miraculously by one Saint Anthony.

99. *Salicornia*, a genus of plant high in alkali.

Dropsie, but be very careful that you take not too much, for it worketh impetuously.

Water-plantane,[100] called in *New-England* water Suck-leaves, and Scurvie-leaves, you must lay them whole to the leggs to draw out water between the skin and the flesh.

Rosa-solis, or Sun-dew,[101] moor-grass, this plant I have seen more of, than ever I saw in my whole life before in *England*, a man may gather upon some marish-grounds an incredible quantity in a short time; towards the middle of *June* it is in its season, for then its spear is shot out to its length, of which they take hold and pull the whole plant up by the roots from the moss with ease.

[p. 81] *Amber-greese*[102] I take to be a Mushroom, see the rarities of *New-England*. Monardus *writeth that* Amber-*greese riseth out of a certain clammy and bituminous earth under the Seas, and by the Sea-side, the billows casting up part of it a land, and fish devour the rest; some say it is the feed of a Whale, others, that it springeth from fountains as pitch doth, which fishes swallow down; the air congealeth it.* And sometimes it is found in the crevises and corners of Rocks.

Fuss-balls, *Mullipuffes* called by the Fishermen Wolves-farts,[103] are to be found plentifully, and those bigger by much than any I have seen in *England*.

Coraline[104] there is infinite store of it cast upon the shore, and another plant that is more spinie, of a Red colour, and as hard as Corral. *Coraline* laid to the gout easeth the pain.

Sea-Oake or wreach, or Sea-weed, the black pouches of Oar-weed dryed and pulverized, and drunk with White-wine, is an excellent remedy for the stone.

I will finish this part of my relation concerning plants, with an admirable plant for the curing and taking away of Corns, which many times sore troubleth the Traveller: it is not above a handful high; the little branches are woodie, the leaves like [p. 82] the leaves of Box, but broader and much thicker, hard, and of deep

100. Water plantain (*Alisma plantago-aquatica*), related to the arrowheads.

101. The insectivorous *Drosera*, still called sundew.

102. Ambergris, a waxy substance secreted by whales.

103. Fungi known generically as puffballs today. *Lycoperdon*, a specific genus, means "flatulence of a wolf."

104. A popular term for various seaweeds.

grass-green colour; this bruised or champt in the mouth and laid upon the Corn will take it away clean in one night. And observe all *Indian* Trees and plants, their Roots are but of small depth, and so they must be set.

Of Beasts of the earth there be scarce 120 several kinds, and not much more of the Fowls of the Air, is the opinion of some Naturalists; there are not many kinds of Beasts in *New-England*, they may be divided into Beasts of the Chase of the stinking foot, as *Roes, Foxes, Jaccals, Wolves, Wild cats, Raccons, Porcupines, Squncks, Musquashes, Squirrels, Sables,* and *Mattrises*; and Beasts of the Chase of the sweet foot, *Buck, Red Dear,* Rain-*Dear, Elke, Marouse, Maccarib, Bear, Beaver, Otter, Marten, Hare.*[105]

The *Roe* a kind of Deer, and the fleetest Beast upon earth is here to be found, and is good venison, but not over fat.

The *Fox*, the male is called a dog fox, the female a bitch-fox, they go a clicketing the beginning of the spring, and bring forth their cubs in *May* and *June*. There are two or three kinds of them; one a great yellow *Fox*, another grey, who will climb up into Trees; the black *Fox* is of much esteem. *Foxes* and *Wolves* are usually hunted [p. 83] in *England* from *Holy-Rood* day, till the *Annunciation.* In *New-England* they make best sport in the depth of winter: they lay a sledg-load of Cods-heads on the other side of a paled fence when the moon shines, and about nine or ten of the clock the *Foxes* come to it, sometime two or three, or half a dozen, and more; these they shoot, and by that time they have cased them, there will be as many; So they continue shooting and killing of *Foxes* as long as the moon shineth: I have known half a score kill'd in one night. Their pisles are bonie like a doggs, their

105. Some of these animal names present special problems. Compounded of earlier European accounts, American Indian nomenclature, and oral lore inherited from earlier settlers, Josselyn's terminology sometimes is misleading and his descriptions frequently fantastic. The coyote (*Canis latrans*), though larger than a fox, has long been known as the American jackal. The musquash is certainly the muskrat (*Ondatra zibethieus*), while the "*Mattrise*" is perhaps the wolverine (*Gulo luscus luscus*), which is now extirpated from New England; like the wolverine today, it is "esteemed good furr" (87) and is said to scavenge at moose carcasses (140). "*Maccarib*," as *Rarities* makes clear (20–21), is another designation for the eastern woodland caribou (*Rangifer tarandus*), also now extirpated from the region; Tuckerman argues (155n) that the "*marouse*" is the same creature yet again.

fat liquified and put into the ears easeth the pain, their tails or bushes are very fair ones and of good use, but their skins are so thin (yet thick set with deep furr) that they will hardly hold the dressing.[106]

Jaccals there be abundance, which is a Creature much like a *Fox*, but smaller, they are very frequent in *Palestina*, or the *Holy-land*.

The *Wolf* seeketh his mate and goes a clicketing at the same season with *Foxes*, and bring forth their whelps as they do, but their kennels are under thick bushes by great Trees in remote places by the swamps, he is to be hunted as the *Fox* from *Holy-rood* day till the *Annunciation*. But there [p. 84] they have a quicker way to destroy them. See *New-Englands* rarities.[107] They commonly go in routs, a rout of *Wolves* is 12 or more, sometimes by couples. In 1664. we found a *Wolf* asleep in a small dry swamp under an Oake, a great mastiff which we had with us seized upon him, and held him till we had a rope about his neck, by which we brought him home, and tying of him to a stake we bated him with smaller Doggs, and had excellent sport; but his hinder legg being broken, they knockt out his brains. Sometime before this we had an excellent course after a single *Wolf* upon the hard sands by the Sea-side at low water for a mile or two, at last we lost our doggs, it being (as the *Lancashire* people phrase it) twi-light, that is almost dark, and went beyond them, for the mastiff-bitch had seized upon the *Wolf* being gotten into the Sea, and there held him till one went in and led him out, the bitch keeping her hold till they had tyed his leggs, and so carried him home like a Calf upon a staff between two men; being brought into the house they unbound him and set him upon his leggs, he not offering in the least to bite, or so much as to shew his teeth, but clapping his stern betwixt his leggs, and leering towards the door would willingly have had his liber- [p. 85] ty, but they served him as they did the other, knockt his brains out, for our doggs were not then in a condition to bate him; their eyes shine by

106. Clicketing: mating. From *Holy-Rood* day, till the Annunciation: from 14 September to 25 March. Cased: skinned. Pisle: penis.

107. The quicker way to destroy wolves, detailed in *Rarities* (15–16), is to imbed fishhooks in balls of tallow bait.

night as a Lanthorn: the Fangs of a *Wolf* hung about childrens necks keep them from frighting, and are very good to rub their gums with when they are breeding of Teeth, the gall of a *Wolf* is soveraign for swelling of the sinews; the fiants or dung of a *Wolf* drunk with white-wine helpeth the *Collick*.[108]

The *Wild-cat, Lusern* or *luceret*, or Ounce as some call it, is not inferiour to Lamb, their grease is very soveraign for lameness upon taking cold.[109]

The *Racoon* or *Rattoon* is of two sorts, gray *Rattoons*, and black *Rattoons*, their grease is soveraign for wounds with bruises, aches, streins, bruises; and to anoint after broken bones and dislocations.

The *Squnck* is almost as big as a *Racoon*, perfect black and white or pye-bald, with a bush-tail like a *Fox*, an offensive Carion; The Urine of this Creature is of so strong a scent, that if it light upon any thing, there is no abiding of it, it will make a man smell, though he were of *Alexanders* complexion; and so sharp that if he do but whisk his bush which he pisseth upon in the face of a dogg hunting of him, and that [p. 86] any of it light in his eyes it will make him almost mad with the smart thereof.

The *Musquashes* is a small Beast that lives in shallow ponds, where they build them houses of earth and sticks in shape like mole-hills, and feed upon *Calamus Aromaticus*: in *May* they scent very strong of Muske; their furr is of no great esteem; their stones[110] wrapt in Cotten-wool will continue a long time, and are good to lay amongst cloths to give them a grateful smell.

The *Squirril*, of which there are three sorts, the mouse-squirril, the gray squirril, the flying squirril, called by the *Indian Assapanick*.[111] The mouse-squirril is hardly so big as a Rat, streak'd

108. Here we have several instances of Josselyn's adherence to the pseudo-scientific Doctrine of Signatures, which held that "Everything in nature, whether plant, animal, or mineral . . . exhibited by its properties its specific curative powers" (Stearns 15). The practice of ingesting animal excrement, which continued into the nineteenth century, is known as isopathy.

109. *Wild-cat*: lynx or the bobcat (*Lynx canadensis* and *L. rufus*). Soveraign: efficacious or potent to a superlative degree.

110. Testicles.

111. The "mouse-squirril" is the chipmunk or American ground squirrel, genus *Tamias*; the gray squirrel is *Sciurus carolinensis pennsylvanicus*; and the

on both sides with black and red streaks, they are mischievous vermine destroying abundance of Corn both in the fields and in the house, where they will gnaw holes into Chests, and tear clothes both linnen and wollen, and are notable nut-gatherers in *August*; when hasel and filbert nuts are ripe you may see upon every Nut-tree as many mouse-squirrils as leaves; So that the nuts are gone in a trice, which they convey to their Drays[112] or Nests. The gray squirril is pretty large, almost as big as a Conie,[113] and are very good meat: in some parts of the Countrie there are many of them. The flying squirril is so called, be- [p. 87] cause (his skin being loose and large) he spreads it on both sides like wings when he passeth from one Tree to another at great distance. I cannot call it flying nor leaping, for it is both.

The *Mattrise* is a Creature whose head and fore parts is shaped somewhat like a Lyons, not altogether so big as a house-cat, they are innumerable up in the Countrey, and are esteemed good furr.[114]

The *Sable* is much of the size of a *Mattrise* perfect black, but what store there is of them I cannot tell, I never saw but two of them in Eight years space.

The *Martin* is as ours are in *England*, but blacker, they breed in holes which they make in the earth like Conies, and are innumerable, their skins or furr are in much request.

The *Buck*, *Stag*, and *Rain-Dear* are Creatures that will live in the coldest climates, here they are innumerable, bringing forth three *Fawns* or *Calves* at a time, which they hide a mile asunder to prevent their destruction by the *Wolves*, wild-*Cats*, *Bears*, and *Mequans*:[115] when they are in season they will be very fat; there

---

northern flying squirrel is *Glaucomys sabrinus macrotis*. John Smith likewise terms the flying squirrel "*Assapanick*" (1:154–55).

112. A term applied to nests of squirrels exclusively.

113. Rabbit.

114. Probably the wolverine, given its attraction to carrion (140). The word is unrecorded in contemporary writings or in dictionaries (see my note, "John Josselyn's New England Neologisms," forthcoming in *Seventeenth-Century News*).

115. Eagles or, as he calls them elsewhere, "pilhannaws" (95; n. 134 below). *Rarities* offers a more detailed description of this fowl much like "an *Indian Ruck*, a monstrous great Bird, a kind of Hawk, some say an Eagle" (8).

are but few slain by the *English*. The *Indians* who shoot them, and take of them with toyls,[116] bring them in [p. 88] with their suet, and the bones that grow upon *Stags-Hearts*.

The *Moose* or *Elke* is a Creature, or rather if you will a Monster of superfluity; a full grown *Moose* is many times bigger than an *English* Oxe, their horns as I have said elsewhere, very big (and brancht out into palms) the tips whereof are sometimes found to be two fathom asunder, (a fathom [p. 89] is six feet from the tip of one finger to the tip of the other, that is four cubits) and in height from the toe of the fore-foot, to the pitch of the shoulder twelve foot, both of which hath been taken by some of my *sceptique* Readers to be monstrous lyes. If you consider the breadth that the beast carrieth, and the magnitude of the horns, you will be easily induced to contribute your belief.

What would you say, if I should tell you that in *Green-land* there are *Does* that have as large horns as *Bucks*, their brow Antlers growing downwards beyond their *Musles*,[117] and broad at the end wherewith they scrape away the snow to the grass, it being impossible for them otherwayes to live in those cold Countries; the head of one of these *Does* was sometime since nailed upon a sign-post in *Charter-house-lane*, and these following verses written upon a board underneath it.

> *Like a* Bucks-*head I stand in open view,*
> *And yet am none; nay, wonder not, 'tis true;*
> *The living Beast that these fair horns did owe*
> *Well known to many, was a* Green-land *Doe.*
> *The proverb old is here fulfill'd in me,*
> *That every like is not the same you see.*

And for their height since I came into *England* I have read Dr. *Scroderns* his Chymical dispensatory by Dr. *Rowland*[118] where he

116. Snares.

117. Muzzles. Reindeer and caribou are the only members of the deer family whose females grow horns.

118. Probably William Rowland (fl. 1625–72), assistant to London physician Nicholas Culpeper. With the help of Rowland and others, Culpeper published translations of many medical treatises, including the *London Dispensatory* (1649, 1654). Under his own name Rowland also issued several tracts, but none matches Josselyn's allusion.

writes *that when he lived in* Finland *under* Gustavus Horns, *he saw an* Elke *that was killed and presented to* Gustavus *his Mother, seventeen spans high.* Law[119] you now Sirs of the Gibing crue, if you have any skill in mensuration, tell me what difference there is between Seventeen spans and twelve foot. There are certain tran-scendentia in every Creature, which are the indelible Characters of God, and which discover God;[120] There's a prudential for you, as *John Rhodes* the Fisherman used to say to his mate, *Kitt Lux.* But to go on with the *Moose*; they are accounted a kind of Deer, and have three *Calves* at a time, which they hide a mile asunder too, as other Deer do, their skins make excellent Coats for Mar-tial men, their sinews which are as [p. 90] big as a mans finger are of perdurable toughness and much used by the *Indians*, the bone that growes upon their heart is an excellent Cordial, their bloud is as thick as an *Asses* or *Bulls* who have the thickest bloud of all others, a man the thinnest. To what age they live I know not, certainly a long time in their proper climate. *Some particular living Creatures cannot live in every particular place or region, espe-cially with the same joy and felicity as it did where it was first bred, for the certain agreement of nature that is between the place and the thing bred in that place: As appeareth by* Elephants, *which being translated or brought out of the Second or Third Climate, though they may live, yet will they never ingender or bring forth young.* So for plants, Birds, &c. Of both these Creatures, some few there are have been brought into *England*, but did not long continue. Sir *R. Baker* in his Chronicle tells us of an *Elephant* in *Henry* the Thirds Raign, which he saith was the first that was ever seen there, which as it seems is an error, unless he restrain it to the *Norman*'s time.[121] For Mr. *Speed* writeth that *Claudius Drusus* Emperour of *Rome* brought in the first in his Army; the bones of which digg'd up since are taken for Gyants bones.[122] As for the

119. An interjection denoting surprise, often at being asked a question.

120. Philip F. Gura has written convincingly that this passage and others influenced the thought of Henry David Thoreau, whose books and journals re-veal a keen appreciation of Josselyn's work. This is the only recorded instance of "transcendentia," and of the proverb as a whole.

121. Sir Richard Baker (1568–1645) wrote *A Chronicle of the Kings of En-gland* (1643), which went through many editions in Josselyn's time.

122. John Speed (1552–1629) was the author of a *History of Great Britaine*

Moose the first that was seen in *England*, [p. 91] was in King *Charles* the First Raign; thus much for these magnals[123] amongst the Creatures of God to be wondered at, the next beast to be mentioned is

The *Marouse*, which is somewhat like a *Moose*, but his horns are but small, and himself about the size of a *Stag*, these are the Deer that the flat-footed *Wolves* hunt after.

The *Maccarib* is a Creature not found that ever I heard yet, but upon *Cape-Sable* near to the *French* plantations.

The *Bear* when he goes to mate is a terrible Creature, they bring forth their Cubs in *March*, hunted with doggs they take a Tree where they shoot them, when he is fat he is excellent Venison, which is in *Acorn* time, and in winter, but then there is none dares to attempt to kill him but the *Indian*. He makes his Denn amongst thick Bushes, thrusting in here and there store of *Moss*, which being covered with snow and melting in the day time with heat of the Sun, in the night is frozen into a thick coat of Ice; the mouth of his Den is very narrow, here they lye single, never two in a Den all winter. The *Indian* as soon as he finds them, creeps in upon all four, seizes with his left hand upon the neck of the sleeping *Bear*, drags him to the mouth of [p. 92] the Den, where with a club or small hatchet in his right hand he knocks out his brains before he can open his eyes to see his enemy. But sometimes they are too quick for the *Indians*, as one amongst them called black *Robin* lighting upon a male-*Bear* had a piece of his buttock torn off before he could fetch his blow: their grease is very soveraign. One Mr. *Purchase* cured himself of the *Sciatica* with *Bears-greese*, keeping some of it continually in his groine.[124]

(1611). On elephants compare Pliny (3:13), who discourses likewise upon their first appearance in Italy.

123. Magnals: great or wonderful things.

124. Undoubtedly Thomas Purchase, who came to New England in 1624 and began his settlement in 1628 at Pejepscot, now Brunswick, Maine. In 1631 he wed Mary Grove, former mistress of the notorious Sir Christopher Gardiner, who scandalized the Massachusetts Puritans. Gardiner was an agent for Gorges, as was Purchase after 1635. James P. Baxter, in *The Trelawny Papers*, affirms the belief that Purchase "lived to the extreme age of a hundred and one years" (106n). On bear lore, see Pliny (3:91), who reports too that bear grease is restorative.

It is good too for swell'd Cheeks upon cold, for Rupture of the hands in winter, for limbs taken suddenly with *Sciatica, Gout,* or other diseases that cannot stand upright nor go, bed-rid; it must be well chaft in, and the same cloth laid on still; it prevents the shedding of the hair occasioned by the coldness of winters weather; and the yard [125] of a *Bear* which as a Doggs or Foxes is bonie, is good for to expell Gravel out of the kidneys and bladder, as I was there told by one Mr. *Abraham Philater* a *Jersey-man.*

The *Beaver* or Pound-dog is an Amphibious Creature, lives upon the land as well as in the water. I suppose they feed upon fish, but am sure that the Bark of Trees is also their food; there is an old proverbial saying, *sic me jubes quotidie, ut fiber salicem*: you love me as the *Beaver* doth the willow; [p. 93] who eateth the Bark and killeth the Tree. [126] They will be tame, witness the *Beaver* that not long since was kept at *Boston* in the *Massachusets-Bay*, and would run up and down the streets, returning home without a call. Their skins are highly valued, and their stones are good for the palsie, trembling, and numbness of the hands, boiling of them in Oyl of *Spike*, [127] and anointing the sinews in the neck. If you take of *Castorium* [128] two drams, of womans hair one dram, and with a little Rozen of the *Pine*-Tree, make it up into pills as big as Filberts and perfume a woman in a fit of the mother with one at a time laid upon coals under her nostrils, it will recover her out of her fit. The grease of a *Beaver* is good for the Nerves, Convulsions, Epilepsies, Apoplexies &c. The tail as I have said in another Treatise, is very fat and of a masculine vertue, as good as *Eringo's* or *Satyrion*-Roots. [129]

The *Otter* or River-*Dog* is Amphibious too, he hunteth for his kind in the spring, and bringeth forth his whelps as the *Beaver*

125. Penis.

126. Josselyn's is the only recorded instance of this proverb. The Latin reads: So you enjoin me every day, just as the beaver does the willow.

127. Spikenard, an oil obtained from the mint lavender (*Lavandula*), valerian, or other plants.

128. *Castoreum*: a substance secreted from glands in beavers.

129. Thomas Morton characteristically wrote likewise that the beaver "is of a masculine virtue for the advancement of Priapus" (205). Eryngo here is the European sea-holly (*Eryngium maritimum*), and satyrion a name given to orchids of the *Orchis* genus. Both reputedly act as aphrodisiacs.

doth, they are generally black, and very numerous, they are hunted in *England* from *Shrovetide* untill *Midsummer*, but in *New-England* they take them when they can. The skin of an *Otter* is worth Ten Shillings, [p. 94] and the gloves made thereof are the best fortification for the hands against wet weather that can be thought of, the furr is excellent for muffs, and is almost as dear as *Beaver*, the grease of an *Otter* will make fish turn up their bellies, and is of rare use for many things.

The *Hare*, I have no more to write of them than that they kindle [130] in hollow Trees. What else concerns him, or any of the fore-mentioned Creatures you may have in my *New-Englands* rarities, to which I refer you.

The *Porcupine* likewise I have treated of, only this I forgot to acquaint you with, that they lay Eggs, and are good meat.

The last kind of Beasts are they that are begot by equivocal generation, as *Mules* and several others, that when the Beasts were brought by the Almighty Creator to *Adam*, who gave them names, were not then in *rerum natura*. [131] Of these there are not many known in *New-England*. I know of but one, and that is the *Indian* dog begotten betwixt a *Wolf* and a *Fox*, or between a *Fox* and a *Wolf*, [132] which they made use of, taming of them, and bringing of them up to hunt with, but since the *English* came amongst them they have gotten store of our dogs, which they bring up and keep in as much subjection as they do their webbs. [133]

[p. 95] Of Birds there are not many more than 120 kinds as our Naturalists have conjectured, but I think they are deceived; they are divided into land-birds and water-birds, the land-birds again into birds of prey, birds for meat, singing-birds and others.

130. Give birth.   131. In the nature of things.

132. On the crossbreeding of foxes and wolves, Josselyn is almost certainly mistaken.

133. Webbs: wives. Josselyn's statements in this paragraph require qualification. Recent studies of the Indians show that women probably were not as subjugated as contemporary observers supposed, and that tribal economies were in fact based upon efficient sexual division of labor (Cronon 44–48). Nonetheless, male European writers of the period tended to object to Indian "webbs" working outside the wigwam, a fact perhaps best captured in lines from a poem in *New Englands Prospect* by William Wood: Upon seashores the squaw must "Daunce many a winters Jigge, / To dive for Cocles, and to digge for Clamms, / Whereby her lazie husbands guts she cramms" (33).

The *Pilhannaw* is the King of the Birds of prey in *New-England*, some take him to be a kind of *Eagle*, others for the *Indian-Ruck* the biggest Bird that is, except the *Ostrich*. One Mr. *Hilton* living at *Pascataway*, had the hap to kill one of them: being by the Sea-side he perceived a great shadow over his head, the Sun shining out clear, casting up his eyes he saw a monstrous Bird soaring aloft in the air, and of a sudden all the *Ducks* and *Geese*, (there being then a great many) dived under water, nothing of them appearing but their heads. Mr. *Hilton* having made readie his piece, shot and brought her down to the ground, how he disposed of her I know not, but had he taken her alive & sent her over into *England*, neither *Bartholomew* nor *Sturbridge*-Fair could have produced such another sight.[134]

Hawkes there are of several kinds, as *Goshawkes*, *Falcons*, *Laniers*, *Sparrow-hawkes*, and a little black *hawke* highly prized by the *Indians* who wear them on their [p. 96] heads, and is accounted of worth sufficient to ransome a *Sagamour*: they are so strangely couragious and hardie, that nothing flyeth in the Air that they will not bind with.[135] I have seen them tower so high, that they have been so small that scarcely could they be taken by the eye. *Hawkes* grease is very good for sore eyes.[136]

The *Osprey* I have treated of. There is a small Ash-colour Bird that is shaped like a *Hawke* with talons and beak that falleth upon *Crowes*, mounting up into the Air after them, and will beat them till they make them cry.

134. The *"pilhannaw"* appears to have been a mythical bird like the roc of Arabian legend, hence *"Indian-Ruck."* Tuckerman concludes it "a confused conception made up from several accounts of large birds" (143n), including the great blue heron and the crested eagle. The Mr. Hilton alleged to have killed one was either William Hilton or his brother Edward, both among the early settlers of Eliot, Maine. According to Clark, the two had come over at the behest of Mason and Gorges in 1623 "with instructions to set up a colony that would send fish back to England" (1970, 17).

135. William Wood (66), Thomas Morton (197), and Roger Williams (116–17) also discuss this fierce little hawk that the Indians held in such esteem. If not a species now extinct, it may be the kingbird (genus *Tyrannus*). *Sagamour:* Indian chieftain.

136. Yet another instance of Josselyn's adherence to the Doctrine of Signatures, this cure is advised presumably because the hawk has such excellent vision.

The *Vulture* or *Geire*, which is spoken of in *Levit[icus]*. 11.
14. and called a *Gripe*, their skins are good to line doublets with,
and the bones of their head hung about the neck helpeth the head-
ach. The *Gripe*; see *New Englands* rarities, and for the *Turkie-
buzzard*.[137]

The *Owl* the most flagging Bird that is, of which there are
three sorts, a great grey *Owl* with ears, a little grey *Owl*, and a
white *Owl*, which is no bigger than a *Thrush*.[138] *Plinie* writes that
the brains of an *Owl* asswageth the pain & inflammation in the
lap of the ear. And that Eggs of an *Owl* put into the liquor that a
tospot useth to be drunk with, will make him loath drunkenness
[p. 97] ever after. But now peradventure some will say, what
doth this man mean to bring *Owls* to *Athens*? Verily Sirs I presume to say, had I brought over of the little white *Owls* they
would have been acceptable, they are good mousers, and pretty
Birds to look upon: the *Athenians*, no question[,] are better imployed than to take notice of my *Owls*, poor ragged Birds they are
and want those glistering golden feathers that *Draiton's Owl* is
adorned with, yet they are somewhat of that nature;[139] if an *Athenian* chance in this season of divertisement to cast an eye upon
them I shall be glad, but more glad if he vouchsafe to prune and
correct their feathers, which I confess are discomposed for want
of Art; plain Birds they are, and fit for none but plain men to
manage. Sirs do not mistake me, there's no man living honours
an *Athenian* more than I do, especially where I perceive great
abilities concomiting with goodness of nature: A good nature
(saith Mr. *Perkins*)[140] is the Character of God, and God is the

137. Leviticus 11:13–14 reads, "And these are they which ye shall have in
abomination among the fowls; they shall not be eaten, they are an abomination:
the eagle, and the ossifrage, and the ospray, / And the vulture, and the kite after
his kind."

138. Flagging: languid. The first owl may be the great horned (*Bubo vir-
ginianus*) or the long-eared (*Asio otus*); the second, the tengmalm's (*Aegolius
funereus*); and the third perhaps the saw-whet (*Aegolius acadius*).

139. An allusion to Michael Drayton's (1563–1631) satirical poem *The
Owl*, which appeared in 1604. Athens was regarded as a center for poetry, philosophy, and science.

140. Presumably the English Puritan theologian William Perkins (1558–
1602).

father of learning, knowledge, and every good gift, and hath condescended to become a School-master to us poor mortals, furnishing of us with Philosophy, Historie, Divinity by his holy Scriptures, which if we diligently learn and practice, we shall in [p. 98] time be brought into his Heavenly Academy, where we shall have fulness and perfection of knowledge eternally. But there are a Generation of men and women in this prophane age that despise Gods learning and his Ushers to the *Athenians*, choosing to wallow in the pleasures of sin for a season. I shall conclude this excursion, with that which a Poet writ sometime since, and then return to the trimming of my *Owl*.

> *Say thou pour'st them Wheat,*
> *And they would Acorns eat;*
> *'Twere simple fury in thee still to wast*
> *Thy self, on them that have no tast;*
> *No, give them draff their fill,*
> *Husks, Grains and swill;*
> *They that love Lees and leave the lustie Wine,*
> *Envy them not, their palats with the Swine.*[141]

The *Raven* is here numerous and Crowes, but *Rooks, Danes, Popinjaes, Megpies* there be none.[142] It is observed that the female of all Birds of prey and Ravin is ever bigger than the male, more venturous, hardy, and watchful: but such Birds as do not live by prey and Ravin, the male is more large than the female. So much for Birds of prey, the next are Birds for the dish, and the first of these is,

[p. 99] The *Turkie*, which is in *New-England* a very large Bird, they breed twice or thrice in a year, if you would preserve the young Chickens alive, you must give them no water, for if they come to have their fill of water they will drop away strangely, and you will never be able to rear any of them: they are excellent meat, especially a *Turkie-Capon* beyond that, for which Eight shillings was given, their Eggs are very wholesome and restore decayed nature exceedingly. But the *French* say they breed the Leprosie; the Indesses make Coats of *Turkie*-feathers woven for their Children.

141. The author of these verses is untraced.
142. *Dane* is untraced; a popinjay is a parrot.

The *Partridge* is larger than ours, white flesht, but very dry[;] they are indeed a sort of *Partridges* called *Grooses*.[143]

The *Pidgeon*, of which there are millions of millions, I have seen a flight of *Pidgeons* in the spring, [and] at *Michaelmas* when they return back to the Southward for four or five miles, that to my thinking had neither beginning nor ending, length nor breadth, and so thick that I could see no Sun, they joyn Nest to Nest, and Tree to Tree by their Nests many miles together in *Pine*-Trees. But of late they are much diminished, the *English* taking them with Nets. I have bought at *Boston* a dozen of *Pidgeons* ready pull'd and garbidgd for three pence.[144] [p. 100] Ring-*Doves* they say are there too, but I could never see any.

The *Snow*-Bird is like a *Chaf-Finch*, go in flocks and are good meat.

The singing Birds are *Thrushes* with red breasts, which will be very fat and are good meat, so are the *Thressels*, *Filladies* are small singing Birds, *Ninmurders* little yellow Birds. *New-England* Nightingales painted with orient colours, black, white, blew, yellow, green and scarlet, and sing sweetly, *Wood-larks*, *Wrens*, *Swallows*, who will sit upon Trees, and *Starlings* black as *Ravens* with scarlet pinions; other sorts of Birds there are, as the *Troculus*, *Wag-tail*, or *Dish-water*, which is here of a brown colour, *Titmouse* two or three sorts, the Dunneck or hedge-*Sparrow* who is starke naked in his winter nest. The golden or yellow hammer, a Bird about the bigness of a *Thrush* that is all over as red as bloud, Wood-*Peckers* of two or three sorts, gloriously set out with variety of glittering colours. The *Colibry*, *Viemalin*, or rising or waking Bird, an emblem of the Resurrection, and the wonder of little Birds.[145]

143. The ruffed grouse (*Bonasa umbellus*).

144. The extinct passenger pigeon (*Ecopistes migratorius*). Josselyn here prophetically notes the decline in their numbers and borrows from William Wood, who wrote that the birds join "nest to nest, and tree to tree by their nests, so that the sunne never sees the ground in that place" (28). On this point William Cronon has noted, "The flights of pigeons actually cycled on an eleven- or twelve-year basis, a fact of which Josselyn was unaware; he had merely hit one of the low points in their cycle on his second journey" (193). Perhaps so, but Josselyn's second journey lasted more than eight years. Pull'd and garbidgd: plucked and gutted.

145. Among the songbirds, Josselyn begins encouragingly by identifying

The water-fowl are these that follow, *Hookers* or wild-*Swans*,
Cranes, *Geese* of three sorts, grey, white, and the brant *Goose*, the
first and last are best meat, the white are [p. 101] lean and tough
and live a long time; whereupon the proverb, Older than a white
Goose; of the skins of the necks of grey *Geese* with their bills the
Indians make Mantles and Coverlets sowing them together and
they shew prettily. There be four sorts of *Ducks*, a black *Duck*, a
brown *Duck* like our wild *Ducks*, a grey *Duck*, and a great black
and white *Duck*, these frequent Rivers and Ponds; but of *Ducks*
there be many more sorts, as *Hounds*, old *Wives*, *Murres*, *Doies*,
Shell-drakes, *Shoulers* or *Shoflers*, *Widgeons*, *Simps*, *Teal*, Blew
wing'd, and green wing'd, Divers or *Didapers*, or *Dipchicks*,
Fenduck, *Duckers* or *Moorhens*, *Coots*, *Pochards*, a water-fowl like
a *Duck*, *Plungeons*, a kind of water-fowl with a long reddish Bill,
Puets, *Plovers*, *Smethes*, *Wilmotes*, a kind of *Teal*, *Godwits*,
Humilities, *Knotes*, *Red-Shankes*, *Wobbles*, *Loones*, *Gulls*, White
Gulls, or Sea-*Cobbs*, *Caudemandies*, *Herons*, grey *Bitterns*, *Ox-
eyes*, *Birds* called *Oxen* and *Keen*, *Petterels*, *Kings fishers*, which
breed in the spring in holes in the Sea-banks, being unapt to
propagate in Summer, by reason of the driness of their bodies,
which becomes more moist when their pores are closed by cold.
Most of these Fowls and Birds are eatable. There are little Birds

---

the American robin (*Turdus migratorius*) as a thrush. Many of the names,
however, derive from British dialect and thus are inappropriate as applied to
American species. Again, some of the birds may now be extinct. "*Thressel*" or
thristle is properly the English thrush but may here signify our wood thrush,
Hylocichla mustelina. "*Filladies*" and "*Ninmurders*" are untraced. The so-called
nightingale can only be our painted bunting (*Passerina ciris*), while the starling
"with scarlet pinions" must be a red-winged blackbird, since starlings were not
introduced till late in the nineteenth century. The "*Troculus*" is certainly the
chimney swift (*Chaetura pelagica*), the only identical spelling of which occurs in
George Sandys' *Travels*, which rehearses the ancient legend of this bird supposed to pick clean crocodiles' teeth. Wagtails (genus *Motacilla*) are kinds of
pipits, the dunnock or hedge sparrow of England is *Prunella modularis*, and the
"yellow hammer" is our gilded flicker (*Colaptes auratus*), so named also by Thoreau in *The Maine Woods*. The bird "red as bloud," of course, is the cardinal.
Finally, by "*Colibry*" the hummingbird is intended, a usage that precedes the
earliest *OED* entry of 1740. Hummingbirds, Josselyn asserts in *Rarities*,
"sleep all Winter, and are not to be seen till the Spring" (7)—a mythic construction that explains their absence during migration and links them ultimately
with Christian resurrection accounts.

that frequent the Sea-shore in flocks called *Sanderlins*, [p. 102] they are about the bigness of a *Sparrow*, and in the fall of the leaf will be all fat; when I was first in the Countrie the *English* cut them into small pieces to put into the Puddings instead of suet, I have known twelve score and above kill'd at two shots.[146] I have not done yet, we must not forget the *Cormorant, Shape* or *Sharke*; though I cannot commend them to our curious[147] palats, the *Indian* will eat them when they are fley'd, they take them prettily, they roost in the night upon some Rock that lyes out in the Sea, thither the *Indian* goes in his Birch-*Canow* when the moon shines clear, and when he is come almost to it, he lets his *Canow* drive on of it self, when he is come under the Rock he shoves his Boat along till he comes just under the *Cormorants* watchman, the rest being asleep, and so soundly do sleep that they will snore like so many Piggs; the *Indian* thrusts up his hand of a sudden, grasping

146. Among the many waterfowl listed here, "*Hooker*" is unrecorded elsewhere as a bird name. The three geese designated are the Canada (*Branta canadensis*), the snow (*Chen caerulescens*), and the brant (*Branta bernicla*). This is the only recorded instance of the goose proverb (Whiting G124). Both the "*Hound*" and the "old *Wife*" denote oldsquaw (*Clangula hyemalis*). The murre, genus *Uria*, includes several species. The "*Doie*" is possibly the dovekie (*Alle alle*), a northerly member of the auk family. The "*Shel-drake*" now is known as shelduck (*Tadorna tadorna*) and the "*Shofler*" as shoveler (*Anas clypeata*). "*Simps*" is untraced, though Morton too uses the term (191). Josselyn's "*Didaper*," still known in some places today as dabchick, is a species of grebe (genus *Podiceps*), and his moorhen is the common gallinule. Genus *Pochard* refers to a category of diving duck that includes the canvasback, redhead, and scaup. "*Plungeon*" applies to members of the loon family (genus *Gavia*), and "*Puet*" or *pewit* to the Charadriidae or plover family. "*Smethe*" in context suggests a sandpiper, to which family belong also the godwits (*Limosa*), the knots (*Calidris*), the redshanks (*Tringa*), the willet (*Cataptrophorus semipalmatus*), and the undetermined "humility" or "simplicity" that several of America's early writers treat. "The wobble," we learn in *Rarities*, is "an ill-shaped fowl" (11) that resembles the penguin and cannot fly; this must be the now extinct great auk (*Pinguinis impennis*). Caudemandie: cawdy-mawdy or curlew. The dunlin (*Calidris alpina*) is nicknamed ox-eyes in some British dialects, while several varieties of sandpipers and plovers also have been termed oxen. "*Keen*" is untraced, and petrels are seabirds belonging to the shearwater family. On the hunting of sanderlings or sandpipers (*Calidris alba*), Josselyn again borrows from William Wood, who writes, "I my selfe have killed twelve score at two shootes" (31), a claim almost believable in view of the birds' dense flock patterns.

147. Particular, discriminating.

the watchman so hard round about his neck that he cannot cry out; as soon as he hath him in his *Canow* fast, he clambreth to the top of the Rock, where walking softly he takes them up as he pleaseth, still wringing off their heads; when he hath slain as many as his *Canow* can carry, he gives a shout [p. 103] which awakens the surviving *Cormorants*, who are gone in an instant.[148]

The next Creatures that you are to take notice of, are they that live in the Element of water. *Pliny* reckons them to be of 177 kinds, but certainly if it be true that there is no Beast upon Earth, which hath not his like in the Sea, and which (perhaps) is not in some part parallel'd in the plants of the Earth; we may by a diligent search find out many more: of the same opinion is the Poet, who saith that it is

> *Affirm'd by some that what on Earth we find,*
> *The Sea can parallell in shape and kind.*

Divine *Dubertus* goes further.

> *You Divine wits of elder Dayes, from whom*
> *The deep invention of rare works hath come,*
> *Took you not pattern of your chiefest Tooles*
> *Out of the lap of* Thetis, *Lakes, and pools?*
> *Which partly in the Waves, part on the edges*
> *Of craggy Rocks, among their ragged sedges,*
> *Bring forth abundance of Pins, Pincers, spokes,*
> *Pikes, piercers, needles, mallets, pipes & yoaks,*
> *Oars, sails & swords, saws, wedges, razors, rammers,*
> *Plumes, cornets, knives, wheels, vices, horns and hammers.*[149]

[p. 104] Psalm 104.25, 26. *In ipso mari magno & spatioso, illic reptilia sunt atque innumera animantia parva cum magnis. Illic navea ambulant; balæna quam formasti ludendo in eo.*[150]

148. This instance of Indian craft is perhaps an embellishment of a hint dropped by Wood, who found the cormorant "a very heavy drowsie creature, so that the *Indians* will goe in their Cannowes in the night, and take them from the Rockes, as easily as women take a Hen from roost" (30).

149. Verses by the French poet Guillaume du Bartas (1544–90), from his *Devine Works and Weekes*, "The fifth Day of the first Weeke," translated 1605–7 by Joshua Sylvester.

150. Psalms 104.25, 26: "So is this great and wide sea, wherein are things creeping innumerable, both small and great beasts. / There go the ships: there is that leviathan, whom thou hast made to play therein."

And as the females amongst Beasts and Birds of prey for form and beautie surpass the males, so do they especially amongst fishes; and those I intend to treat of, I shall divide into salt-water fish, and fresh-water fish.

The Sea that *Piscina mirabilis* affords us the greatest number, of which I shall begin first with the Whale a regal fish, as all fishes of extraordinary size are accounted, of these there are (as I have said in another place) seven kinds, the Ambergreese-*Whale* the chiefest. *Anno Dom.* 1668 the 17 of *July* there was one of them thrown up on the shore between *Winter-harbour* and *Cape-porpus*, about eight mile from the place where I lived, that was five and fifty foot long.[151] They are Creatures of vast magnitude and strength. The Royal Psalmist, in the 148 psalm, and the 7 verse, *makes mention of them. Laudate Jehovam terrestria Cete (Dracones as some translate it) & omnes abyssi. And Moses in his history of* Job, *Job 40.20. An extrahas balænam hamo,* &c. [p. 105] *Whereby the subtlety of the Devil is shewed, as also, the greatness and brutishness of the Devil by the Elephant, in the 10 verse of the foregoing Chapter. In the book of* Jonas *prophecies we read of a great fish,* Jonah 1.117. *Pararat autem Jehova piscem magnum, qui obsorberet Jonam. But whether this were a Whale or not is questioned by some.*[152] *In the head (saith Mr.* Parkinson *the Herbalist) of one only sort of Whale-fish is found that which is called* sperma Cæti, *it lyes in a hole therein, as it were a Well, taken out and prest that the oyl may come out, the substance is that we use for* sperma Cæti, *and hath little or no smell, the oyl smells strong.* See the rarities of *New-England.*[153]

The *Sea-hare* is as big as *Grampus* or *Herrin-hog*, and as white

151. *Piscina mirabilis*: marvelous fish pool. The "chiefest" whale is the sperm whale. Winter Harbor (now Leighton's Point) and Cape Porpoise both are near the mouth of the Saco River, Maine.

152. Psalms 148.7: "Praise the Lord from the earth, ye dragons, and all deeps." From Job 41.1: "Canst thou draw out leviathan with an hook?" No mention of elephants appears in the King James Version; however, Job 41.10 reports of the leviathan, "None is so fierce that dare stir him up: who then is able to stand before me?" Of Jonah 1.17 Josselyn quotes only the first sentence: "Now the Lord had prepared a great fish to swallow up Jonah."

153. This italicized passage is a loose quotation from John Parkinson's *Theatrum Botanicum* (1607). Josselyn discusses "spermaceti," seed of the whale, in *Rarities* (35–36).

as a sheet; [154] There hath been of them in *Black-point*-Harbour, & some way up the river, but we could never take any of them, several have shot sluggs at them, but lost their labour.

The *Sturgeon* is a Regal fish too, I have seen of them that have been sixteen foot in length: of their sounds they make *Isinglass*, which melted in the mouth is excellent to seal letters. [155]

Sharkes there are infinite store, who tear the Fishermens nets to their great loss and hinderance; they are of two sorts, one flat [p. 106] headed, the other long snouted, the pretious stone in their heads (soveraign for the stone in a man) so much coveted by the travelling Chirurgeon is nought else but the brains of the flat-headed *Sharke*. With these we may joyn the Dog-fish or Thorn-hound, who hath two long sharp prickles on his back. [156]

The *Sea-horse* or *Morse* is a kind of monster-fish numerous about the Isle of *Sables*, i.e. The Sandy Isle. An amphibious Creature kill'd for their Teeth and Oyl, never brings forth more than two at a birth; as also doth the Soil and Manate or Cow-fish, which is supposed to be the Sea-monster spoken of by *Jeremy*, *Lament[ations]*. 4.3. *Etiam phocæ præbent mamman, lactant catulos suos; So the Latins render it*, phoca *a Sea-calf or Soil*. [157]

The small *Sword-fish* is very good meat, the *Sea-bat* or *Sea-owl* a kind of flying fish.

154. Evidently the beluga, *Delphinapterus leucas*.

155. As Charles F. Adams has glossed a similar passage in Thomas Morton's book, the sturgeon is regal because it is "reserved for the soveraign" of England (Morton 223n) when caught in certain portions of the Thames. "Sounds" are swim bladders; isinglass, a gelatin used as a clarifier and adhesive.

156. The flat-headed shark appears to be the common hammerhead (*Sphyrna zygaena*), and the long-snouted perhaps the grey (*Carcharhinus plumbeas*). Spiny dogfish (Squalidae) have retained the name. The "pretious stone" shows Josselyn's adherence to the medieval theory of formed stones, perpetuated through the seventeenth century (Stearns, ch. 1).

157. Mammals erroneously classed here as fishes include the "*Morse*," or walrus; the "Soil," seal; the "Cow-fish," either a manatee or a dugong, possibly the Steller's sea cow, which was hunted to extinction by 1768. On the hunting of walruses, John Winthrop wrote in 1641, "This summer the merchants of Boston set out a vessel again to the Isle of Sable, with 12 men, to stay there a year. They sent again in the 8th month, and in three weeks the vessel returned and brought home 400 pair of sea horse teeth, which were esteemed worth £300, and left all the men well, and 12 ton of oil and many skins, which they

Negroes or *Sea-Devils* a very ugly fish, having a black scale, there are three sorts of them, one a hideous fish, another about two foot long; of these I have seen store in *Black-point* Harbour in the water, but never attempted to take any of them.

Squids a soft fish somewhat like a cudgel, their horns like a *Snails*, which sometimes are found to be of an incredible length, [p. 107] this fish is much used for bait to catch a *Cod, Hacke, Polluck*, and the like Sea-fish.

The *Dolphin, Bonito*, or *Dozado*, the ashes of their teeth mixed with honey, is good to asswage the pain of breeding teeth in Children.

The *Sea-bream, Dorado*, or *Amber-fish*, they follow ships as doth the *Dolphin*, and are good meat.

The *Mackarel*, of which there is choicefull plenty all summer long, in the spring they are ordinarily 18 inches long, afterwards there is none taken but what are smaller.

The *Liver-fish* like a *Whiting*.

The *Herrin* which are numerous, they take of them all summer long. In *Anno Dom.* 1670. they were driven into *Black-point* Harbour by other great fish that prey upon them so near the shore, that they threw themselves (it being high water) upon dry land in such infinite numbers that we might have gone up half way the leg amongst them for near a quarter of a mile. We used to qualifie[158] a pickled *Herrin* by boiling of him in milk.

The *Alewife* is like a *herrin*, but has a bigger bellie therefore called an *Alewife*, they come in the end of *April* into fresh [p. 108] Rivers and Ponds; there hath been taken in two hours time by two men without any Weyre at all, saving a few stones to stop the passage of the River, above ten thousand. The *Italian* hath a proverb, that he that hath seen one miracle will easily believe another; but this relation far from a miracle will peranter[159] meet, instead of a belief[,] with an Adulterate construction from

---

could not bring away, being put from the island in a storm" (2:35−36). Lamentations 4.3 reads in part: "Even the sea monsters draw out the breast, they give suck to their young ones."

158. Legal jargon meaning to modify or soften.

159. Obscure variant of *peradventure*: perchance.

those that are somewhat akin to St. *Peters* mockers, such as deny the last judgement.[160] I have known in *England* 9 score and 16 *Pikes* and *Pickarel* taken with three Angles between the hours of three and ten in the morning, in the River *Owse* in the Isle of *Ely*, three quarters of a yard long above half of them; they make red *Alewives* after the same manner as they do *herrins* and are as good.

The *Basse* is a salt water fish too, but most end taken in Rivers where they spawn, there hath been 3000 *Basse* taken at a set, one writes that the fat in the bone of a *Basses head is his braines which is a lye*.

The *Salmon* likewise is a Sea-fish, but as the *Basse* comes into Rivers to spawn, a *Salmon* the first year is a *Salmon-smelt*; The second a *Mort*; The third a *Spraid*; The fourth a *Soar*; The fifth a *Sorrel*; The sixth [p. 109] a *forket tail*; and the seventh year a *Salmon*.[161] There are another sort of *Salmon* frequent in those parts called white *Salmons*.

Capeling is a small fish like a smelt.[162]

The *Turtle* or *Tortoise* is of two sorts Sea-*Turtles* and land-*Turtles*: of Sea-*Turtles* there are five sorts, of land-*Turtles* three sorts, one of which is a right land-*turtle* that seldom or never goes into the water, the other two being the River-*Turtle*, and the pond-*Turtle*: there are many of these in the brooke *Chyson* in the *Holy land*.[163] The ashes of a Sea-*Turtle* mixt with oyl or *Bears*-grease causeth hair to grow: the shell of a land-*Turtle* burnt and the ashes dissolved in white wine and oyl to an unguent healeth chaps and sores of the feet: the flesh burnt and the ashes mixt with wine and oyl healeth sore legs: the ashes of the burnt shell and the whites of eggs compounded together healeth chaps in womens nipples; and the head pulverized with it prevents the falling of

160. In condemning "St. *Peters* mockers," Josselyn alludes to Acts 2.13, where Peter's detractors charge that the Pentecostal gift of tongues is due to surfeit of "new wine."

161. The Atlantic salmon (*Salmo salar*). Stages in the salmon growth cycle have been designated differently among cultures and throughout time; other names include fry, smolt, peal, and pink. Unrecorded in the *OED* are instances of "*Spraid*," "*Soar*," and "*Sorrel*" in this context.

162. Capelin (*Mallotus villosus*), unlike smelt, are purely a marine species.

163. Qishon or Kishon in northern Israel.

the hair, and will heal the Hemorrhoids, first washing of them with white-wine, and then strewing on the powder.

Lobster, which some say is at first a *Whelk*,[164] I have seen a *Lobster* that weighed twenty pound, they cast their shell-coats in the spring, and so do *Crabs*; having underneath a thin red skin which growes thicker and [p. 110] hard in short time. The *Indians* feed much upon this fish, some they rost, and some they dry as they do *Lampres* and *Oysters* which are delicate breakfast meat so ordered, the *Oysters* are long shell'd, I have had of them nine inches long from the joynt to the toe, containing an *Oyster* like those the Latines called *Tridacuan* that were to be cut into three pieces before they could get them into their mouths, very fat and sweet.[165]

The *Muscle* is of two sorts, Sea-*muscles* in which they find Pearl and river-*muscles*. Sea-*muscles* dryed and pulverized and laid upon the sores of the *Piles* and *hemorrhoids* with oyl will perfectly cure them.

The *Whore* is a shell-fish, the shells are called whores-eggs, being fine round white shells in shape like a *Mexico* pompion, but not bigger than a good large Hens-egg; they are wrought down the sides with little knobs and holes very prettily, but are but thin and brittle.

The *Perriwig*[166] is a shell-fish that lyeth in the Sands flat and round as a shovel-board piece and very little thicker; these at a little hole in the middle of the shell thrust out a cap of hair, but upon the least motion of any danger it drawes it in again.

Trouts there be good store in every brook, ordinarily two and twenty inches [p. 111] long, their grease is good for the *Piles* and *clifts*.

The *Eal* is of two sorts, salt-water *Eals* and fresh-water *Eals*; these again are distinguished into yellow bellied *Eals* and silver bellied *Eals*; I never eat better *Eals* in no part of the world that I have been in, than are here. They that have no mind or leasure to take them, may buy of an *Indian* half a dozen silver bellied *Eals*

164. The waved whelk (*Buccinum undatum*) is a marine snail.

165. Compare William Wood, who had written that the New England oyster "without the shell is so big that it must admit of a devision before you can well get it into your mouth" (35).

166. Sea anemone.

as big as those we usually give 8 pence or 12 pence for at *London*, for three pence or a groat. There is several wayes of cooking them, some love them roasted, others baked, and many will have them fryed; but they please my palate best when they are boiled, a common way it is to boil them in half water, half wine with the bottom of a manchet, a fagot of Parsley, and a little winter savory, when they are boiled they take them out and break the bread in the broth, and put to it three or four spoonfuls of yeast, and a piece of sweet butter, this they pour to their *Eals* laid upon sippets and so serve it up.[167] I fancie my way better which is this, after the *Eals* are fley'd and washt I fill their bellies with Nutmeg grated and Cloves a little bruised, and sow them up with a needle and thred, then I stick a Clove here and there in their sides about an inch asunder, [p. 112] making holes for them with a bodkin, this done I wind them up in a wreath and put them into a kettle with half water and half white wine-vinegar, so much as will rise four fingers above the *Eals*; in midst of the *Eals* I put the bottom of a penny white loaf, and a fagot of these herbs following, Parsley one handful, a little sweet Marjoram, Peniroyal[168] and Savory, a branch of Rosemary, bind them up with a thred, and when they are boiled enough take out the *Eals* and pull out the threds that their bellies were sowed up with, turn out the Nutmeg and Cloves, put the *Eals* in a dish with butter and vinegar upon a chafing-dish with coals to keep warm, then put into the broth three or four spoonfuls of good Ale-yeast with the juice of half a Lemmon; but before you put in your yeast beat it in a porringer with some of the broth, then break the crust of bread very small and mingle it well with the other half of the Lemmon, and so serve them up to the Table in two dishes.

The *Frost-fish* is little bigger than a *Gudgeon* and are taken in fresh brooks; when the waters are frozen they make a hole in the Ice about half a yard or yard wide, to which the fish repair in great numbers, where with [p. 113] small nets bound to a hoop about the bigness of a firkin-hoop with a staff fastned to it they

167. Manchet: loaf of fine white bread. Sippet: toast or fried bread used as garnish.

168. Pennyroyal is a European mint (*Mentha pulegium*).

lade them out of the hole.[169] I have not done with the fish yet,
being willing to let you know all of them that are to be seen and
catch'd in the Sea and fresh waters in *New-England*, and because I
will not tire your patience overmuch, having no occasion to en-
large my discourse, I shall only name them and so conclude.[170]

Aleport	*Bull-head*	*Rock-Cod*
Albicore	*Bur-fish*	*Sea-Cod*
Barracha	*Cat-fish*	*divers*
Barracontha	*Cony-fish*	*kinds of*
Blew-fish	*Clam*	*Crabs*

169. The "*Frost-fish*" is the Atlantic tomcod (*Microgadus tomcod*), found today only rarely in fresh water. Firkin: a small wooden tub for butter, lard, etc.

170. As with the birds and mammals, Josselyn's catalog of New England
fishes frequently assigns to American species names from the European. Some
may be identified by cross-reference with the similar list included in *Rarities*,
especially pp. 23–32. Neither book distinguishes between shellfish and finfish.
The term "*Aleport*" is unrecorded in either dialect or standard usage, as are
"*Barracha*," "*Barracontha*," "*Burfish*" (burbot?), "*Flail-fish*," "*Sea-flea*," and
"*Vlatise*." "*Cony-fish*" perhaps here signifies venomous marine gastropods
known as cones, not native to New England. The cusk (*Brosme brosme*) is a
primitive barbed cod. According to the *OED*, the cunner is the blue perch or
burgall (*Ctenolabrus adspersus*) of New England, while "*Javelin*" in the seventeenth century denoted the pilchard (*Sardina pilchardus*). In *Rarities*, Josselyn
writes that bears feed upon "a shell-fish called a *Horse-foot*" (13), presumably
bivalve, likely a cockle (*Hippopus hippopus*?). The "*Hen-fish*" actually is a clam,
Venus gallina, an instance in our century of dialect giving rise to a species name.
The "*Limpin*" is perhaps the limpet, a variety of marine gastropod. "*Lumpe*"
must designate the lumpfish family (Cyclopteridae), whose members are characterized by a powerful suction disc formed from the pelvic fins. "*Maid*" was
previously a dialect name for the young of sundry rays and skates, while the
raylike sharks known as monkfish have retained their name. The "*Nun-fish*" is
an undetermined shellfish described by other early writers as edible. The plaice
(*Pleuronectes platessa*) is today the most marketed flounder species, and the "*Pur-
ple-fish*" is a gastropod family that includes the *Murex* rock shells used since
Roman times to manufacture purple dye (Pliny 3:247–57). "*Porgee*" is a name
given variously to small marine basses, perches, and breams. The sea raven
(*Corvina nigra*) is a species of drum perch.
The "*Spurling*" is an obscure designation for the smelt (genus *Osmerus*).
Sprats (*Sprattus*) are close relatives of herring, which may in fact be intended
here since sprats are not indigenous to New England's coast. The thornback ray
is *Raja clavata*, and the tropical unicorn fish is *Naso unicornis*, so named for the
poisonous blade or horn above its nose.

Sea-Cucum-	Limpin	Scallop
ber	Lumpe	[p. 114]
Cunner	Maid	Scate
Cusk	Monk-fish	Stingray
Sea-Darts	Sea-mullet	Sculpin
or Javelins	Nun-fish	Shadd
Flail-fish	Perch	Sheath-fish
Flounder	Periwincle	Shrimps
or Flowke	Pike	Smelt
Flying-fish	Pilat-fish	Spurlin
several kinds	Plaice	Sprates
Sea-flea	Polluck	Star-fish
Grandpisse	Porgee	Sword-fish
Haddock	Porpisse	Thornback
Hake	Prawne	Turbet
Hallibut	Purple-fish	The Vlatise
Hen-fish	Sea-Raven	or saw-fish
Horse-foot	Remora	Sea-Urchin
Lampre	Sail-fish	Sea-Unichorn

The fish are swum by and the Serpents are creeping on, terrible creatures, carrying stings in their tails. That will smart worse that a *Satyrs* whip, though it were as big as Mr. *Shepperds* the mad Gentleman at *Milton-Mowbrayes Constantinus Lasculus.*[171]

The chief or Captain of these is the Rattle-snake described already in my Journal, in some places of the Countrey there are none as at *Plimouth, New-town, Nahant* and some other places, they will live on one side of the River, and but swimming over and coming into the woods dye immediately.

The fat of a Rattle-snake is very Soveraign for frozen limbs, bruises, lameness by falls, Aches, Sprains. The heart of a Rattle-snake dried and pulverized and drunk with wine or beer is an approved remedy against the biting and venome of a Rattle-snake. Some body will give me thanks for disco- [p. 115] vering these secrets and the rest; *Non omnibus omnia conveniunt.*[172]

The *Snake* of which there are infinite numbers of various col-

171. The source of this allusion is untraced, but there may be some connection with the town of Melton Mowbray in Leicestershire.

172. All things are not suitable for all people.

ours, some black, others painted with red, yellow and white, some again of a grass-green colour powdered all over as it were with silver dust or *Muscovie*-glass.[173] But there is one sort that exceeds all the rest, and that is the Checkquered snake,[174] having as many colours within the checkquers shaddowing one another, as there are in a Rainbow. There are two sorts of snakes, the land-snake and the water-snake; the water-snake will be as big about the belly as the Calf of a mans leg; I never heard of any mischief that snakes did, they kill them sometimes for their skin and bones to make hatbands off, their skins likewise worn as a Garter is an excellent remedie against the cramp. I have found of the skins that they are cast in woods in some quantity, they cast not their very skins, but only the superfluous thin skin that is upon the very skin, for the very skin is basted to the flesh, so Lobsters and Crabs.

The Earth-worm, these are very rare and as small as a horse hair, but there is a Bug that lyes in the earth and eateth the seed, that is somewhat like a Maggot of a white colour with a red head, and is about [p. 116] the bigness of ones finger and an inch or an inch and half long. There is also a dark dunnish Worm or Bug of the bigness of an Oaten-straw, and an inch long, that in the spring lye at the Root of Corn and Garden plants all day, and in the night creep out and devour them; these in some years destroy abundance of *Indian* Corn and Garden plants, and they have but one way to be rid of them, which the *English* have learnt of the *Indians*; And because it is somewhat strange, I shall tell you how it is, they go out into a field or garden with a Birchen-dish, and spudling the earth about the roots, for they lye not deep, they gather their dish full which may contain about a quart or three pints, then they carrie the dish to the Sea-side when it is ebbing-water and set it a swimming, the water carrieth the dish into the Sea and within a day or two if you go into your field you may look your eyes out sooner than find any of them.[175]

173. An early name for mica, a silicate of potassium and aluminum.

174. Probably the milk snake (*Lampropeltis triangulum*), a member of the king snake family.

175. Spudling: turning over. The effectiveness of this Indian practice relies upon what Sir James Frazier in *The Golden Bough* has termed contagious magic, a practice founded "upon the notion that things which have once been conjoined

Sow-bugs or *Millipedes* there be good store, but none of that sort that are blew and turn round as a pea when they are touched; neither are there any *Beetles* nor *Maple-Bugs*, but a stinking black and red *Bug* called a *Cacarooch* or *Cockroach*, and a little black *Bug* like a *Lady-cow* that breeds in skins and furs and will eat them to their [p. 117] utter spoil. Likewise there be infinite numbers of *Tikes* hanging upon the bushes in summer time that will cleave to a mans garments and creep into his Breeches eating themselves in a short time into the very flesh of a man.[176] I have seen the stockins of those that have gone through the woods covered with them. Besides these there is a *Bug*, but whether it be a Native to the Countrie or a stranger I cannot say: Some are of the opinion that they are brought in by the Merchant with Spanish goods, they infest our beds most, all day they hide themselves, but when night comes they will creep to the sleeping wretch and bite him worse than a flea, which raiseth a swelling knub that will itch intolerably, if you scratch it waxeth bigger and growes to a scab; and if you chance to break one of the *Bugs* it will stink odiously: they call them *Chinches* or *Wood-lice*, they are fat, red and in shape like a *Tike* and no bigger.[177] There are also Palmer-worms which is a kind of Catterpiller, these some years will devour the leaves of Trees leaving them as naked almost as in winter, they do much harm in the *English* Orchards. Of *Snails* there are but few, and those very little ones, they lye at the Roots of long grass in moist places, and are no where else to be found. [p. 118] Spiders and Spinners there be many, the last very big and of several colours.

The Pismire or Ant must not be forgotten, accounted the least Creature, and by *Salomon* commended for its wisdom,

---

must remain ever afterwards, even when quite dissevered from each other, in such a sympathetic relation that whatever is done to the one must similarly affect the other" (1:174).

176. The black and red insect resembling the ladybug ("*Lady-cow*") is perhaps the larder beetle (*Dermestes lardarius*). The "Tike," of course, is the tick.

177. This troublesome bug fits descriptions of the sandflea or chigger of the American tropics, a New World pest that devastated the Old World once imported from Española. The "swelling nub" results from the insect laying eggs beneath the skin of its host; the result can be permanent lameness or the entry of serious diseases such as tetanus (Crosby 209).

Prov[erbs]. 30.24, 25. *Quatuor ista parva sunt humilia, tamen sunt sapientia, apprime sapientia: formicæ populus infirmus, quæ comparant æstate cibum suum*, &c.[178] There are two sorts, red Ants and black Ants, both of them are many times found winged; not long since they were poured upon the Sands out of the clouds in a storm betwixt *Black-point* and *Saco*, where the passenger might have walkt up to the Ankles in them.

The Grasshopper is innumerable and bigger by much than ours in *England*, having Tinsel-wings, with help whereof they will flye and skip a great way. Next to these in number are your Crickets, a man can walk no where in the summer but he shall tread upon them; The *Italian* who hath them cryed up and down the streets (*Grille che cantelo*) and buyeth them to put into his Gardens, if he were in *New-England* would gladly be rid of them, they make such a dinn in an Evening. I could never discover the Organ of their voice, they have a little clift in their Crown which opens, and at the same instant they shake their wings.[179]

[p. 119] The Eft or Swift in *New-England* is a most beautiful Creature to look upon, being larger than ours, and painted with glorious colours; but I lik'd him never the better for it.[180]

Frogs too there are in ponds and upon dry land, they chirp like Birds in the spring, and latter end of summer croak like Toads.[181]

It is admirable to consider the generating of these Creatures, first they lay their gelly on the water in ponds and still waters, which comes in time to be full of black spots as broad as the head

178. As far as Josselyn renders it, Proverbs 30.24 reads: "There be four things which are little upon the earth, but they are exceeding wise: / The ants are a people not strong, yet they prepare their meat in the summer."

179. The Italian of the street vendor's cry probably is intended to mean "Crickets that I am crying" (i.e., "selling"). Crickets sing by rubbing together the front and rear legs.

180. Eft: newt or salamander. A number of salamanders are indigenous to New England; Josselyn may intend the colorful red salamander (*Pseudotriton ruber ruber*). In English lore the creatures have long suffered the reputation of being poisonous and bringing bad luck.

181. Josselyn has been criticized for the credulity he displays in this passage (Tyler 1:159). However, William Wood is perhaps originally responsible for the belief that New England frogs "in the *Spring* doe chirpe and whistle like a bird, and at the latter end of summer croake like our English frogges" (46).

of a Ten-penny nail, and round, these separate themselves from
the gleir, and after a while thrust out a tail, then their head comes
forth, after their head springs out their fore-legs, and then their
hinder-legs, then their tail drops off, and growes to have a head
and four legs too, the first proves a frog, the latter a water nuet.
The Herbalist useth to say by way of admiration, *quælibet herba
deum &c.*[182] So God is seen in the production of these small Creatures which are part of the Creation; *Laudate Jehovam cælites,
laudate eum in excelsis, &c. Laudent nomen Jehovæ quæ ipso præci-
piente illico creata sunt &c. Ipsæ bestiæ & omnes jumenta, reptilia
& aves alatæ,* Psal. 148.[183]

The Toad is of two sorts, one that is [p. 120] speckled with
white, and another of a dark earthy colour; there is of them that
will climb up into Trees and sit croaking there; but whether it be
of a third sort, or one of the other, or both, I am not able to
affirm; but this I can testifie that there be Toads of the dark coloured kind that are as big as a groat loaf. Which report will not
swell into the belief of my sceptique Sirs; nor that there is a Hell,
being like *Salomon's* fool, Prov. 27.22. *Sed si contunderes stultum
in mortario cum mola pistillo, non recederet ab eo stultitia ejus.*[184]

Now before I proceed any further, I must (to prevent mis-
constructions) tell you that these following Creatures, though
they be not properly accounted Serpents, yet they are venomous
and pestilent Creatures. As, first the Rat, but he hath been brought
in since the *English* came thither, but the Mouse is a Native, of
which there are several kinds not material to be described; the Bat
or flitter mouse is bigger abundance than any in *England* and
swarm,[185] which brings me to the insects or cut-wasted Creatures

182. The notion of frogs and newts being mutually generated is, of course,
fantastic. Gleir: the jelly mass surrounding the eggs. The Latin reads: "Every
herb manifests God."

183. Portions of Psalms 148.1, 5, 10: "Praise ye the Lord from the heavens: praise him in the heights." "Let them praise the name of the Lord: for he
commanded, and they were created." "Beasts, and all cattle; creepings things,
and flying fowl."

184. The smaller toad described here may be *Bufo americanus*. Proverbs
27.22 reads: "Though thou shouldest bray a fool in a mortar among wheat with
a pestle, yet will not his foolishness depart from him."

185. The rat is undoubtedly the black rat (*Rattus rattus*), introduced by
colonists as early as 1609 but now supplanted in New England by the Norway

again, as first the honey-Bee, which are carried over by the *English* and thrive there exceedingly, in time they may be produced from Bullocks when the wild Beasts are destroyed.[186] But the wasp is com- [p. 121] mon, and they have a sort of wild humble-Bee that breed in little holes in the earth. Near upon twenty years since there lived an old planter at *Black-point*, who on a Sunshine day about one of the clock lying upon a green bank not far from his house, charged his Son, a lad of 12 years of age to awaken him when he had slept two hours, the old man falls asleep and lying upon his back gaped with his mouth wide enough for a Hawke to shit into it; after a little while the lad sitting by spied a humble-Bee creeping out of his Fathers mouth, which taking wing flew quite out of sight, the hour as the lad ghest being come to awaken his Father he jogg'd him and called aloud Father, Father, it is two a clock, but all would not rouse him, at last he sees the humble-Bee returning, who lighted upon the sleepers lip and walked down as the lad conceived into his belly, and presently he awaked.[187]

The Countrey is strangely incommodated with flyes, which the *English* call Musketaes, they are like our gnats, they will sting so fiercely in summer as to make the faces of the *English* swell'd and scabby, as if the small pox for the first year. Likewise there is a

---

rat (*Rattus norvegicus*), which arrived in the region about 1775 (Godin 137–38). Among the several mice mentioned here, the widespread white-footed mouse (*Peromyscus maniculatus*) is a native, whereas the house mouse (*Mus musculus*) arrived with the earliest settlers. The bat called "flitter mouse" is probably the little brown myotis (*Myotis lucifugus*).

186. A variation of an important folk motif concerning bees. See Thompson (B713.1): *Bees born from the carcass of an ox*. The belief that carcasses of oxen may spontaneously generate bees goes back at least as far as Virgil's *Georgica* and is parodied as late as 1797 by American author Royall Tyler in *The Algerine Captive*, where Latin-fed Updike Underhill slays a fat heifer and waits for it to putrify "in order to raise a swarm of bees." The tale has biblical precedent as well. In Judges 14, Samson kills a lion to whose carcass bees swarm and generate honey, an image also underlying American poet Michael Wigglesworth's *Meat out of the Eater* (1670).

187. For this anecdote, another folk motif, again see Thompson (E172.1.1): *Sleeper not to be wakened, since soul is absent*. The old man sleeping in Josselyn's tale apparently cannot be aroused because his soul has departed in the form of a bee; when his soul returns, he wakens. For further variations of this last belief, see also Frazier (3:37ff).

small black fly no bigger than a flea, so numerous up in the Countrey, [p. 122] that a man cannot draw his breath, but he will suck
of them in: they continue about Thirty dayes say some, but I say
three moneths, and are not only a pesterment but a plague to the
Countrey.[188] There is another sort of fly called a Gurnipper that
are like our horse-flyes, and will bite desperately, making the
bloud to spurt out in great quantity; these trouble our *English*
cattle very much, raising swellings as big as an egg in their hides.
The Butterfly is of several sorts and larger than ours; So are their
Dragon-flyes. Glow-worms have here wings, there are multitudes of them insomuch that in the dark evening when I first went
into the Countrey I thought the whole Heavens had been on fire,
seeing so many sparkles flying in the air: about *Mount-Carmel*,
and the valley of *Acree* in the *Holy-land* there be abundance of
them.[189]

These are taken for *Cantharides*.[190] *Cantharides* are green flyes
by day, in the night they pass about like a flying Glow-worm with
fire in their tails.

I have finished now my relation of plants, &c. I have taken
some pains in recollecting of them to memory, and setting of
them down for their benefit from whom I may expect thanks; but
I believe my re- [p. 123] ward will be according to *Ben Johnsons*
proverbs, Whistle to a Jade and he will pay you with a fart, Claw
a churl by the britch and he will shit in your fist.[191]

The people that inhabited this Countrey are judged to be of the
Tartars called *Samonids* that border upon *Moscovia*, and are di-
vided into Tribes; those to the East and North-east are called
Churchers and *Tarentines*, and *Monhegans*. To the South are the
Pequets and *Narragansets*. Westward *Connecticuts* and *Mowhacks*.

188. Native mosquitoes include *Aedes rusticus* and *A. vexans*. The Adiron-
dack black fly, *Prosimilium hirtipes*, still plagues the northeastern states.

189. The "gurnipper" undoubtedly is the biting horse fly (*Stomyx cal-
citrans*). The "glow-worm," of course, is a firefly (family Lampyridae); Mount
Carmel and the seaport city of Acre are both near the Qishon River in northern
Israel.

190. The insect family Cantharidae contains the carnivorous soldier and
sailor beetles.

191. From Ben Jonson's 1621 court masque *The Gypsies Metamorphosed*, ll.
776–78: "Why, well said, Clawe a Churle by the arse / and hee'l shite in yor.
fist." / "I, or whistle to a Iade, and heel pay you wth. a fart."

To the Northward *Aberginians* which consist of *Mattachusets*, *Wippanaps* and *Tarrentines*. The *Pocanakets* live to the Westward of *Plimouth*. Not long before the *English* came into the Countrey, happened a great mortality amongst them, especially where the *English* afterwards planted, the East and Northern parts were sore smitten with the Contagion; first by the plague, afterwards when the *English* came by the small pox, the three Kingdoms or *Sagamorships* of the *Mattachusets* were very populous, having under them seven Dukedoms or petti-*Sagamorships*, but by the plague were brought from 30000 to 300. There are not many now to the Eastward, the *Pequots* were destroyed by the *English*: the *Mowhacks* are about five hundred: Their speech a dialect of the *Tar-* [p. 124] *tars*, (as also is the *Turkish* tongue).[192] There is difference between Tongues and Languages, the division of speech at *Babel* is most commonly called Languages, the rest Tongues.

As for their persons they are tall and handsome timber'd people, out-wristed, pale and lean *Tartarian* visag'd, black eyed which is accounted the strongest for sight,[193] and generally black hair'd, both smooth and curl'd wearing of it long. No beards, or very rarely, their Teeth are very white, short and even, they ac-

192. The tribes referred to here belonged to the Algonquian language family. Their numbers were greatly diminished following the undetermined epidemic of 1616–17, and the Pequot tribe of Connecticut was all but exterminated by war with the settlers in 1637. The names "Churcher" and "Wippanap" remain untraced, though William Wood likewise uses the former term. The Aberginians most often were referred to as the Pawtuckets, while the Tarrentines have been explained both as the Abnakis (Vaughan 52) and the Micmacs (Salisbury 120). More commonly known as the Wampanoags (King Philip's tribe), the Pokanakets sometimes also were identified with their principal headquarters at Pokanoket (now Bristol), Rhode Island.

Josselyn's confident conjecture that the Indian language is related to the Turkish concurs with Roger Williams' *Key into the Language*: "*Wise* and *Judicious* men, with whom I have discoursed, maintain their *Originall* to be *Northward* from *Tartaria*" (1:23). Many of the New England divines—including Mayhew, Eliot, and Mather—maintained the natives were of Jewish origin; others believed they had descended from the Greeks and Romans. These various theories culminated in James Adair's *History of the American Indians* (1775), which argues exhaustively that the Indians are remnants of the scattered tribes of Israel.

193. Compare Thomas Morton: "Their eies indeede are black as iett; and that coler is accounted strongest for sight" (165).

count them the most necessary and best parts of a man; And as the *Austreans* are known by their great lips, the *Bavarians* by their pokes under their chins, the *Jews* by their goggle eyes, so the *Indians* by their flat noses, yet they are not so much deprest as they are to the Southward.

The *Indesses* that are young, are some of them very comely, having good features, their faces plump and round, and generally plump of their Bodies, as are the men likewise, and as soft and smooth as a mole-skin, of reasonable good complexions, but that they dye themselves tawnie, many pretty Brownetto's and spider finger'd Lasses may be seen amongst them. The *Vetula's* or old women are lean and uglie, all of them are of a modest demeanor, considering their [p. 125] Savage breeding; and indeed do shame our *English* rusticks whose rudeness in many things exceedeth theirs.[194]

Of disposition very inconstant, crafty, timorous, quick of apprehension, and very ingenious, soon angry, and so malicious that they seldom forget an injury, and barbarously cruel, witness their direful revenges upon one another. Prone to injurious violence and slaughter, by reason of their bloud dryed up with overmuch fire, very lecherous proceeding from choller adust[195] and melancholy, a salt and sharp humour; very fingurative or theevish, and bold importunate beggars, both Men and Women guilty of Misoxenie or hatred to strangers, a quality appropriated to the old Brittains, all of them Cannibals, eaters of humane flesh. And so were formerly the Heathen-*Irish*, who used to feed upon the Buttocks of Boyes and Womens Paps; it seems it is natural to Savage people so to do. I have read in Relations of the *Indians* amongst the *Spaniards* that they would not eat a *Spaniard* till they had kept him two or three dayes to wax tender, because their flesh

194. The belief was prevalent that Indians dyed their skins from infancy, and some writers held that this treatment resulted in impermeability. See the Adams edition of Morton (147n) which treats such beliefs as held by Thomas Lechford, John Smith, and William Strachey. Other contemporary writers and modern scholars corroborate Josselyn's view of the natives' modesty, and *Rarities* reveals in greater detail Josselyn's responsiveness to the native women. See especially pp. 99–102 for his fine verses praising them.

195. A favorite term of medical writers from the middle ages, meaning "burnt" or "dry."

was hard. At *Martins* vinyard, an Island that lyes South to *Plimouth* in the way to *Virginia*, certain *Indians* (whilst I was in the Countrey) seised upon a Boat that put in- [p. 126] to a By-*Cove*, kill'd the men and eat them up in a short time before they were discovered.[196]

Their houses which they call *Wigwams*, are built with Poles pitcht into the ground of a round form for most part, sometimes square, they bind down the tops of their poles, leaving a hole for smoak to go out at, the rest they cover with the bark of Trees, and line the inside of their *Wigwams* with mats made of Rushes painted with several colours, one good post they set up in the middle that reaches to the hole in the top, with a staff a cross before it at a convenient height, they knock in a pin on which they hang their Kettle, beneath that they set up a broad stone for a back which keepeth the post from burning; round by the walls they spread their mats and skins where the men sleep whilst their women dress their victuals, they have commonly two doors, one opening to the South, the other to the North, and according as the wind sits, they close up one door with bark and hang a *Dears* skin or the like before the other. Towns they have none, being alwayes removing from one place to another for conveniency of food, sometimes to those places where one sort of fish is most plentiful, other whiles where others are. I have seen half [p. 127] a hundred of their *Wigwams* together in a piece of ground and they shew prettily, within a day or two, or a week they have been all dispersed. They live for the most part by the Sea-side, especially in the spring and summer quarters, in winter they are gone up into the Countrie to hunt *Deer* and *Beaver*, the younger webbs going with them. Tame Cattle they have none, excepting Lice, and Doggs of a wild breed that they bring up to hunt with.

Wives they have two or three, according to the ability of their bodies and strength of their concupiscence, who have the easiest

196. In addition to the comments on cannibalism here, Josselyn displays the racial prejudices and stereotypes he had inherited on such issues as infanticide, parricide, devil worship, scalping, and torture as practiced by the Indians. Cultural bias among the colonists has been the subject of recent studies by Nicholas P. Canny, Francis Jennings, James Axtell and William Sturtevant, and William S. Simmons (see "Works Consulted"). For the onomastic history of Martha's Vineyard see Banks 201–4.

labours of any women in the world; they will go out when their time is come alone, carrying a board with them two foot long, and a foot and half broad, bor'd full of holes on each side, having a foot beneath like a Jack that we pull Boots off with, on the top of the board a broad strap of leather which they put over their fore-head, the board hanging at their back; when they are come to a Bush or a Tree that they fancy they lay them down and are deliv-ered in a trice, not so much as groaning for it, they wrap the child up in a young *Beaver*-skin with his heels close to his britch, leav-ing a little hole if it be a Boy for his Cock to peep out at; and lace him down to the [p. 128] board upon his back, his knees resting upon the foot beneath, then putting the strap of leather upon their fore-head with the infant hanging at their back home they trudge;[197] What other ceremonies they use more than dying of them with a liquor of boiled *Hemlock*-Bark, and their throwing of them into the water if they suspect the Child to be gotten by any other Nation, to see if he will swim, if he swim they acknowl-edge him for their own, their names they give them when they are men grown, and covet much to be called after our *English* manner, *Robin, Harry, Phillip* and the like, very indulgent they are to their Children, and their children sometimes to their Par-ents, but if they live so long that they become a burden to them, they will either starve them or bury them alive, as it was sup-posed an *Indian* did his Mother at *Casco* in 1669.

Their Apparel before the *English* came amongst them, was the skins of wild Beasts with the hair on, Buskins of *Deers*-skin or *Moose* drest and drawn with lines into several works, the lines being coloured with yellow, blew or red, Pumps too they have, made of tough skins without soles. In the winter when the snow will bear them, they fasten to their feet their snow shooes which are made like a large Racket we play at [p. 129] *Tennis* with, lacing them with *Deers*-guts and the like, under their belly they wear a square piece of leather and the like upon their posteriors, both fastened to a string tyed about them to hide their secrets; on

197. Roger Williams writes similarly that Indians "count it a shame for a Woman in Travell to make complaint, and many of them are scarcely heard to groane. I have often knowne in one Quarter of an houre a Woman merry in the House, and delivered and merry againe" (1:197).

their heads they ware nothing: But since they have had to do with the English they purchase of them a sort of Cloth called trading cloth of which they make Mantles, Coats with short sleeves, and caps for their heads which the women use, but the men continue their old fashion going bare-headed, excepting some old men amongst them. They are very proud as appeareth by their setting themselves out with white and blew Beads of their own making, and painting of their faces with the above mentioned colours, they weave sometimes curious Coats with *Turkie* feathers for their Children.

Their Diet is Fish and Fowl, Bear, Wild-cat, Rattoon and Deer; dryed Oysters, *Lobsters* rosted or dryed in the smoak, *Lampres* and dry'd *Moose*-tongues, which they esteem a dish for a *Sagamor*; hard eggs boiled and made small and dryed to thicken their broth with, salt they have not the use of, nor bread, their *Indian* Corn and Kidney beans they boil, and sometimes eat their Corn parcht or roasted in the ear against the fire; they feed like-wise upon earth-nuts, [p. 130] or ground-nuts, roots of water-Lillies, Ches-nuts, and divers sorts of Berries. They beat their Corn to powder and put it up into bags, which they make use of when stormie weather or the like will not suffer them to look out for their food. *Pompions* and water-*Mellons* too they have good store; they have prodigious stomachs, devouring a great deal, meer *voragoes*, never giving over eating as long as they have it, between meals spending their time in sleep till the next kettlefull is boiled, when all is gone they satisfie themselves with a small quantity of the meal, making it serve as the frugal bit amongst the old *Britains*, which taken to the mountenance of a Bean would satisfie both thirst and hunger. If they have none of this, as some-times it falleth out (being a very careless people not providing against the storms of want and tempest of necessity) they make use of Sir *Francis Drake's* remedy for hunger, go to sleep.[198]

They live long, even to an hundred years of age, if they be not cut off by their Children, war, and the plague, which together with the small pox hath taken away abundance of them. *Pliny*

198. *Voragoes*: chasms. Narratives of Drake's expeditions appear throughout the collections of Hakluyt and Purchas, with both of which Josselyn was no doubt familiar.

reckons up but 300 Diseases in and about man, latter writers Six thousand, 236 belonging to the eyes. There are not so many Diseases raign- [p. 131] ing amongst them as our *Europeans*. The great pox is proper to them, by reason (as some do deem) that they are *Man-eaters*, which Disease was brought amongst our *Europeans* first by the *Spaniards* that went with *Christopher Columbus* who brought it to *Naples* with their *Indian*-women, with whom the *Italians* and *French* conversed *Anno Dom.* 1493. *Paracelsus* saith it hapned in the year 1478 and 1480.[199] But all agree that it was not known in *Europe* before *Columbus* his voyage to *America*. It hath continued amongst us above two hundred and three score years. There are Diseases that are proper to certain climates, as the Leprosie to *Ægypt*, swelling of the Throat or *Mentegra* to *Asia*, the sweating sickness to the Inhabitants of the North; to the *Portugals* the Phthisick, to *Savoy* the mumps; So the *West-Indies* the Pox, but this does not exclude other Diseases. Feavers, Plague, Black-pox, Consumption of the Lungs, Falling-sickness, Kings-evil, and a Disease called by the *Spaniard* the Plague in the back, with us *Empyema*,[200] their Physicians are the *Powaws* or *Indian* Priests who cure sometimes by charms and medicine, but in a general infection they seldom come amongst them, [p. 132] therefore they use their own remedies, which is sweating, *&c.* Their manner is when they have plague or small pox amongst them to cover their *Wigwams* with Bark so close that no Air can enter in, lining them (as I said before) within, and making a great fire they remain there in a stewing heat till they are in a top sweat, and then run out into the Sea or River, and presently after they are come into their Hutts again they either

199. The great pox or French pox were common names for syphilis, upon the conjectural origins of which see Crosby (122–64). Paracelsus was Theophrastus von Hohenhein (1493–1541), Swiss alchemist and physician famous for his isolation of diseases generally and congenital syphilis specifically. The most popular edition of his work in Josselyn's time was *Paracelsus His Dispensatory* (1654), issued and probably translated by William Dugard.

200. Among the maladies listed here, *mentagra* is an eruption, tetter, or "lichen" on the chin; so called by Pliny (7:265). Black pox is perhaps pinta, a contagious skin disease of tropical America; king's evil, scrofula or tuberculosis of the lymph glands; and empyema, a condition characterized by an accumulation of pus in the body cavity. On the exchange of illnesses between the Old World and the New, again see Crosby.

recover or give up the Ghost; they dye patiently both men and women, not knowing of a Hell to scare them, nor a Conscience to terrifie them. In times of general Mortality they omit the Ceremonies of burying, exposing their dead Carkases to the Beasts of prey. But at other times they dig a Pit and set the diseased therein upon his breech upright, and throwing in the earth, cover it with the sods and bind them down with sticks, driving in two stakes at each end; their mournings are somewhat like the howlings of the *Irish*, seldom at the grave but in the *Wigwam* where the party dyed, blaming the Devil for his hard-heartedness, and concluding with rude prayers to him to afflict them no further.[201]

They acknowledge a God who they call *Squantam*, but worship him they do not, [p. 133] because (they say) he will do them no harm. But *Abbamocho* or *Cheepie* many times smites them with incurable Diseases, scares them with his Apparitions and panick Terrours, by reason whereof they live in a wretched consternation worshipping the Devil for fear.[202] One black *Robin* an *Indian* sitting down in a Corn field belonging to the house where I resided, ran out of his *Wigwam* frighted with the apparition of two infernal spirits in the shape of *Mohawkes*. Another time two *Indians* and an *Indess*, came running into our house crying out they should all dye, *Cheepie* was gone over the field gliding in the Air with a long rope hanging from one of his legs: we askt them what he was like, they said all wone *Englishman*, clothed with hat and coat, shooes and stockins, *&c.* They have a remarkable observation of a flame that appears before the death of an *Indian* or *En-*

201. Evidence that the devastation of American natives by European contagion continued well past the massive epidemic period of 1616–17. On the Indians' upright burial, compare the American poet Philip Freneau's "Lines occasioned by a Visit to an old Indian Burying Ground" (1788), which praises the practice. James Fenimore Cooper likewise has Natty Bumppo so positioned at his death in the final chapter of *The Prairie* (1827). James Axtell has argued that although Indian corpses indeed were buried in a "flexed position," they were normally placed on their sides (113).

202. The secondary literature treating supposed Indian worship of the devil is voluminous; a good recent study is Neal Salisbury, *Manitou and Providence* (3–4, 137–38, 139, 221, 224). As James Axtell has expressed it, "much to the chagrin of the missionaries, most of the Indians' religious worship seemed to center on attempts to deflect the malificences of this [evil] deity instead of praising the benefactions of the Creator" (75).

glish upon their *Wigwams* in the dead of the night: the first time that I did see it, I was call'd out by some of them about twelve of the clock, it being a very dark night, I perceived it plainly mounting into the Air over our Church, which was built upon a plain little more than half a quarter of a mile from our dwelling house, on the Northside of the Church: look on [p. 134] what side of a house it appears; from that Coast respectively you shall hear of a Coarse[203] within two or three days.

They worship the Devil (as I said)[;] their Priests are called *Powaws* and are little better than Witches, for they have familiar conference with him, who makes them invulnerable, that is shot-free and stick-free. Craftie Rogues, abusing the rest at their pleasure, having power over them by reason of their Diabolical Art in curing of Diseases, which is performed with rude Ceremonies; they place the sick upon the ground sitting, and dance in an Antick manner round about him, beating their naked breasts with a strong hand, and making hideous faces, sometimes calling upon the Devil for his help, mingling their prayers with horrid and barbarous charms; if the sick recover, they send rich gifts, their Bowes and Arrowes, *Wompompers, Mohacks, Beaver-skins,* or other rich Furs to the Eastward, where there is a vast Rock not far from the shore, having a hole in it of an unsearchable profundity, into which they throw them.[204]

Their Theologie is not much, but questionless they acknowledge a God and a Devil, and some small light they have of the Souls immortality; for ask them whi- [p. 135] ther they go when they dye, they will tell you pointing with their finger to Heaven beyond the white mountains, and do hint at *Noah*'s Floud, as may be conceived by a story they have received from Father to Son, time out of mind, that a great while agon their Countrey was drowned, and all the People and other Creatures in it, only one *Powaw* and his *Webb* foreseeing the Flood fled to the white mountains carrying a hare along with them and so escaped; after a

203. Corpse.
204. *Rarities* discusses in some detail a kind of clam or "*Coccle,* of whose Shell the *Indians* make their Beads called *Wompampeag* and Mohaicks" (36), highly prized accouterments corresponding to the "rich gifts" listed here. The fur trade transformed wampum strings from sacred objects to a form of New England currency measured by the fathom (Salisbury 148–50).

while the *Powaw* sent the *Hare* away, who not returning emboldned thereby they descended, and lived many years after, and had many Children, from whom the Countrie was filled again with *Indians*.[205] Some of them tell another story of the *Beaver*, saying that he was their Father.

Their learning is very little or none, Poets they are as may be ghessed by their formal speeches, sometimes an hour long, the last word of a line riming with the last word of the following line, and the whole doth *Constare ex pedibus*.[206] Musical too they be, having many pretty odd barbarous tunes which they make use of vocally at marriages and feastings; but Instruments they had none before the *English* came amongst them, since they have imitated them and will make out Kitts and string them as neat- [p. 136] ly and as Artificially as the best Fiddle-maker amongst us; and will play our plain lessons[207] very exactly: the only Fidler that was in the Province of *Meyn*, when I was there, was an *Indian* called *Scozway*, whom the Fishermen and planters when they had a mind to be merry made use of.

Arithmetick they skill not, reckoning to ten upon their fingers, and if more doubling of it by holding their fingers up, their age they reckon by Moons, and their actions by sleeps, as, if they go a journie, or are to do any other business they will say, three sleeps me walk, or two or three sleeps me do such a thing, that is in two or three days. Astronomie too they have no knowledge of, seldom or never taking observation of the Stars, Eclipses, or Comets that I could perceive; but they will Prognosticate shrewdly what weather will fall out. They are generally excellent *Zenagogues*[208] or guides through the Countrie.

Their exercises are hunting and fishing, in both they will take

205. This story confutes contemporary historian Francis Jennings' argument that the European observed no likeness "between his own theologically certified miracles and mysteries of Christianity and the traditionally certified myths of the Indians" (48).

206. Stand firm in (metrical) feet. See the similar account in *Rarities*: "Their Speeches in their Assemblies are very gravely delivered, commonly in perfect *Hexamiter* Verse, with great silence and attention, and answered again *ex tempore* after the same manner" (5).

207. Descants often performed to accompany biblical verses.

208. Xenagogue (from the Greek): one who conducts or guides strangers.

abundance of pains. When the snow will bear them, the young
and lustie *Indians,* (leaving their papouses and old people at
home) go forth to hunt *Moose, Deere, Bear* and *Beaver,* Thirty or
forty miles up into the Countrey; when they light upon a *Moose*
they run him down, [p. 137] which is sometimes in half a day,
sometimes a whole day, but never give him over till they have
tyred him, the snow being usually four foot deep, and the Beast
very heavie he sinks every step, and as he runs sometimes bears
down Arms of Trees that hang in his way, with his horns, as big
as a mans thigh; other whiles, if any of their dogs (which are but
small) come near, yerking out his heels (for he strikes like a
horse)[,] if a small Tree be in the way he breaks it quite asunder
with one stroak, at last they get up to him on each side and trans-
pierce him with their Lances, which formerly were no other but
a staff of a yard and a half pointed with a Fishes bone made sharp
at the end, but since they put on pieces of sword-blades which
they purchase of the *French,* and having a strap of leather fastned
to the but end of the staff which they bring down to the midst of
it, they dart it into his sides, *hæret latere lethalis arundo,*[209] the
poor Creature groans, and walks on heavily, for a space, then
sinks and falls down like a ruined building, making the Earth to
quake; then presently in come the Victors, who having cut the
throat of the slain take off his skin, their young webbs by this
time are walking towards them with heavie bags and kettles at
their [p. 138] backs, who laying down their burdens fall to work
upon the Carkass, take out the heart, and from that the bone, cut
off the left foot behind, draw out the sinews, and cut out his
tongue, *&c.* and as much of the Venison as will serve to satiate
the hungry mawes of the Company: mean while the men pitch
upon a place near some spring, and with their snow shoos shovel
the snow away to the bare Earth in a circle, making round about a
wall of snow; in the midst they make their *Vulcan* or fire near to a
great Tree, upon the snags whereof they hang their kettles fil'd
with the Venison; whilst that boils, the men after they have refresht themselves with a pipe of Tobacco dispose themselves to
sleep. The women tend the Cookerie, some of them scrape the
slime and fat from the skin, cleanse the sinews, and stretch them

209. *Harundo* in Virgil (*Aeneid* 4.73): The lethal reed sticks fast in [her]
side.

and the like, when the venison is boiled the men awake, and opening of their bags take out as much *Indian* meal as will serve their turns for the present; they eat their broth with spoons, and their flesh they divide into gobbets, eating now and then with it as much meal as they can hold betwixt three fingers, their drink they fetch from the spring, and were not acquainted with other, untill the *French* and *English* traded with that cursed liquor [p. 139] called *Rum, Rum-bullion*, or kill-Devil, which is stronger than spirit of Wine, and is drawn from the dross of Sugar and Sugar Canes, this they love dearly, and will part with all they have to their bare skins for it, being perpetually drunk with it, as long as it is to be had, it hath killed many of them, especially old women who have dyed when dead drunk. Thus instead of bringing of them to the knowledge of Christianitie, we have taught them to commit the beastly and crying sins of our Nation, for a little profit. When the *Indians* have stuft their paunches, if it be fair weather and about midday they venture forth again, if it be foul and far spent, they betake themselves to their field-bed at the sign of the Star, expecting the opening of the Eastern window, which if it promise serenity, they truss up their fardles, and away for another *Moose*, this course they continue for six weeks or two moneths, making their *Webbs* their *Mules* to carry their luggage, they do not trouble themselves with the horns of *Moose* or other *Deer*, unless it be near an *English* plantation; because they are weighty and cumbersome. If the *English* could procure them to bring them in, they would be worth the pains and charge, being sold in *England* after the rate of forty or fifty [p. 140] pounds a Tun; the red heads of *Deer* are the fairest and fullest of marrow, and lightest; the black heads are heavie and have less marrow; the white are the worst, and the worst nourished.[210] When the *Indians* are gone, there gathers to the Carkass of the *Moose* thousands of *Mattrises*, of which there are but few or none near the Sea-coasts to be seen, these devour the remainder in a quarter of the time that they were hunting of it.

Their fishing followes in the spring, summer and fall of the

210. Antlers were sold in the Orient as aphrodisiac, but *Rarities* notes that they were used as well "for Physick" (19), that is, for medicine. See also Josselyn's prescription of "*Harts-horn* pulverized" as part of a cure for pleurisy (*Two Voyages* 184).

leaf. First for *Lobsters, Clams, Flouke, Lumps* or *Podles,* and *Ale-wives*; afterwards for *Bass, Cod, Rock, Blew-fish, Salmon* and *Lampres,* &c.

The *Lobsters* they take in large Bays when it is low water, the wind still, going out in their *Birchen-Canows* with a staff two or three yards long, made small and sharpen'd at one end, and nick'd with deep nicks to take hold. When they spye the *Lobster* crawling upon the Sand in two fathom water, more or less, they stick him towards the head and bring him up. I have known thirty *Lobsters* taken by an *Indian* lad in an hour and a half, thus they take *Flouke* and *Lumps; Clams* they dig out of the *Clam-banks* upon the flats and in creeks when it is low water, where they are bedded some- [p. 141] times a yard deep one upon another, the beds a quarter of a mile in length, and less, the *Alewives* they take with Nets like a pursenet put upon a round hoop'd stick with a handle in fresh ponds where they come to spawn. The *Bass* and *Blew-fish* they take in harbours, and at the mouth of barr'd Rivers being in their *Canows,* striking them with a fisgig, a kind of dart or staff, to the lower end whereof they fasten a sharp jagged bone (since they make them of Iron) with a string fastened to it, as soon as the fish is struck they pull away the staff, leaving the bony head in the fishes body and fasten the other end of the string to the *Canow:* Thus they will hale after them to shore half a dozen or half a score great fishes: this way they take *Sturgeon;* and in dark evenings when they are upon the fishing ground near a Bar of Sand (where the *Sturgeon* feeds upon small fishes (like *Eals*) that are called Lances sucking them out of the Sands where they lye hid, with their hollow Trunks, for other mouth they have none) the *Indian* lights a piece of dry *Birch-Bark* which breaks out into flame & holds it over the side of his *Canow,* the *Sturgeon* seeing this glaring light mounts to the Surface of the water where he is slain and taken with a fisgig. *Salmons* and *Lampres* [p. 142] are catch'd at the falls of Rivers. All the Rivers of note in the Coun-trey have two or three desperate falls distant one from another for some miles, for it being rising ground from the Sea and moun-tainous within land, the Rivers having their Originals from great lakes, and hastning to the Sea, in their passage meeting with Rocks that are not so easily worn away, as the loose earthie mould beneath the Rock, makes a fall of the water in some Rivers as high as a house: you would think it strange to see, yea admire if you saw the bold *Barbarians* in their light *Canows* rush down the swift and headlong stream with desperate speed, but with excellent dexterity, guiding his *Canow* that seldom or never it shoots under water or overturns, if it do they can swim naturally, striking their pawes under their throat like a dog, and not spreading their Arms as we do; they turn their *Canow* again and go into it in the water.[211]

Their Merchandize are their beads, which are their money, of these there are two sorts, blew Beads and white Beads, the first is their Gold, the last their Silver, these they work out of certain shells so cunningly that neither *Jew* nor Devil can counterfeit, they dril them and string them, and make many curious works with them to a- [p. 143] dorn the persons of their *Sagamours* and principal men and young women, as Belts, Girdles, Tablets, Borders for their womens hair, Bracelets, Necklaces, and links to hang in their ears. Prince *Phillip*[212] a little before I came for *England* coming to *Boston* had a Coat on and Buskins set thick with these Beads in pleasant wild works and a broad Belt of the same, his Accoutrements were valued at Twenty pounds. The *English* Merchant giveth them ten shillings a fathom for their white, and as much more or near upon for their blew Beads. Delicate sweet dishes too they make of *Birch-Bark* sowed with threads drawn from *Spruse* or white *Cedar-Roots*, and garnished on the out-side with flourisht works, and on the brims with glistering quills taken from the *Porcupine*, and dyed, some black, others red, the white are natural, these they make of all sizes from a dram cup to a dish containing a pottle, likewise Buckets to carry water or the

211. Another echo of Roger Williams, who noted in 1643 that "It is wonderful to see how they will venture in those Canoes, and how (being oft overset as I myself have been with them) they will swim a mile, yea two or more safe to Land" (1:134). Josselyn's natives build birch-bark canoes—paper birch (*Betula papyrifera*) stretched over a frame of northern white cedar (*Thuja occidentalis*)—whereas the Indians among whom Roger Williams resided in Rhode Island built canoes by hollowing out "a Pine or Oake, or Chesnut-tree" (131), since the paper birch was not readily available in southern New England. See Josselyn's descriptions elsewhere of the construction of the "*Indian*-Pinnace" (27) and of the canoe (144).

212. Chief of the Wampanoags, King Philip (or Metacomet) was killed in 1676 during the final skirmish in the war named after him.

like, large Boxes too of the same materials, dishes, spoons and trayes wrought very smooth and neatly out of the knots of wood, baskets, bags, and matts woven with *Sparke*,[213] barke of the *Line-Tree* and *Rushes* of several kinds, dyed as before, some black, blew, red, yellow, bags of *Porcupine* quills woven and dyed also; Coats woven of [p. 144] *Turkie*-feathers for their Children, Tobacco pipes of stone with Imagerie upon them, Kettles of *Birchen-bark* which they used before they traded with the *French* for Copper Kettles, by all which you may apparently see that necessity was at first the mother of all inventions. The women are the workers of most of these, and are now, here and there one excellent needle woman, and will milk a Cow neatly, their richest trade are Furs of divers sorts, Black *Fox, Beaver, Otter, Bear, Sables, Mattrices, Fox, Wild-Cat, Rattoons, Martins, Musquash, Moose-skins.*

Ships they have none, but do prettily imitate ours in their *Birchen-pinnaces*, their *Canows* are made of *Birch*, they shape them with flat Ribbs of white *Cedar*, and cover them with large sheets of *Birch-bark*, sowing them through with strong threds of *Spruse-Roots* or white *Cedar*, and pitch them with a mixture of *Turpentine* and the hard rosen that is dryed with the Air on the out-side of the Bark of *Firr-Trees*. These will carry half a dozen or three or four men and a considerable fraight, in these they swim to Sea twenty, nay forty miles, keeping from the shore a league or two, sometimes to shorten their voyage when they are to double a Cape they will put to shore, and [p. 145] two of them taking up the *Canow* carry it cross the Cape or neck of land to the other side, and to Sea again; they will indure an incredible great Sea, mounting upon the working billowes like a piece of Corke; but they require skilful hands to guide them in rough weather, none but the *Indians* scarce dare to undertake it, such like Vessels the Ancient *Brittains* used, as *Lucan* relates.

> *Primum cana salix, madefacto vimine, parvam*
> *Texitur in puppim, cæsoque induta juvenco,*
> *Vectoris patiens tumidum super emicat amnem.*
> *Sic Venetus stagnante Pado, fusoque Britanus*
> *Navigat oceano———*

213. Pottle: half gallon. *Sparke*: also *spart*, the English name for various rushes.

When Sicoris *to his own banks restor'd*
Had left the field, of twigs, and willow boord
They made small Boats, cover'd with Bullocks hide,
In which they reacht the Rivers further side.
So sail the Veneti if Padus *flow,*
The Brittains sail on their calm ocean so:
So the Ægyptians sail with woven Boats
Of paper rushes in their Nilus *Floats.*[214]

[p. 146] Their Government is monarchical, the Patrueius[215] or they that descend from the eldest proceeding from his loyns, is the Roytelet[216] of the Tribe, and if he have Daughters, his Son dying without a Son, the Government descends to his Daughters Son: after the same manner, their lands descend. *Cheetadaback*[217] was the chief *Sachem* or *Roytelet* of the *Massachusets*, when the *English* first set down there. *Massasoit*, the great *Sachem* of the *Plimouth Indians*, his dwelling was at a place called *Sowans*, about four miles distant from New-Plimouth.[218] Sasasacus was the chief *Sachem* of the *Pequots*, and *Mientoniack* of the *Narragansets*. The chief *Roytelet* amongst the *Mohawks* now living, is a *Dutchmans* Bastard, and the *Roytelet* now of the *Pocanakets*, that is the *Plimouth-Indians*, is Prince *Philip* alias *Metacon*, the Grandson of *Massasoit*. Amongst the Eastern *Indians*, *Summersant* formerly was a famous *Sachem*. The now living *Sachems* of note are *Sabaccaman*, *Terrumkin* and *Robinhood*.

Their Wars are with Neighbouring Tribes, but the *Mowhawks* are enemies to all the other *Indians*, their weapons of Defence and Offence are Bowes and Arrowes, of late he is a poor *Indian* that is

214. From Thomas May's translation of the *Pharsalia* (F5) of Lucan (A.D. 39–65). The source in Lucan is 4.131–36.

215. Latin *patruelis*: one descended from a father's brother. Commenting on Josselyn's and Roger Williams' identical observations that Indian governments are monarchical, William Cronon has written that "comparison might more aptly have been made to the relations between lords and retainers in the early Middle Ages of Europe" (59). Other historians have also recently emphasized the relatively fluid nature of Indian polity.

216. Petty king.

217. Cheetadaback was more commonly known as Chickatawbut.

218. The place names in this passage are especially subject to the uninhibited orthography of the period. Sowans or Sowams was part of the present site of Warren, Rhode Island.

not ma- [p. 147] ster of two Guns, which they purchase of the *French*, and powder and shot, they are generally excellent marks men; their other weapons are *Tamahawks* which are staves two foot and a half long with a knob at the end as round as a bowl, and as big as that we call the Jack or Mistriss.[219] Lances too they have made (as I have said before) with broken sword blades, likewise they have Hatchets and knives; but these are weapons of a latter date. They colour their faces red all over, supposing that it makes them the more terrible, they are lusty Souldiers to see to and very strong, meer *Hercules Rusticuses*, their fights are by Ambush-ments and Surprises, coming upon one another unawares. They will march a hundred miles through thick woods and swamps to the *Mohawks* Countrey, and the *Mohawks* into their Countrey, meeting sometimes in the woods, or when they come into an *Ene-mies* Countrey build a rude fort with *Pallizadoes*,[220] having loop-holes out of which they shoot their Arrowes, and fire their Guns, pelting at one another a week or moneth together; If any of them step out of the Fort they are in danger to be taken prisoners by the one side or the other; that side that gets the victory excoriats the hair-scalp of the principal slain Enemies which [p. 148] they bear away in Triumph, their prisoners they bring home, the old men and women they knock in the head, the young women they keep, and the men of war they torture to death, as the Eastern *Indians* did two *Mowhawks* whilst I was there, they bind him to a Tree and make a great fire before him, then with sharp knives they cut off the first joynts of his fingers and toes, then clap upon them hot Embers to sear the vains; so they cut him a pieces joynt after joynt, still applying hot Embers to the place to stanch the bloud, making the poor wretch to sing all the while: when Arms and Legs are gone, they flay off the skin of their Heads, and presently put on a Cap of burning Embers, then they open his breast and take out his heart, which while it is yet living in a manner they give to their old Squaes, who are every one to have a bite at it. These Barbarous Customs were used amongst them more frequently before the *English* came; but since by the great mercy of the Almighty they are in a way to be Civilized and con-

219. In the game of bowls, the dish or bowl aimed at.
220. Palisades: stout, tall stakes set close together for defense.

verted to Christianity; there being three Churches of *Indians*
gathered together by the pains of Mr. *John Eliot* and his Son,
who Preaches to them in their Native language, and hath rendered
the Bible in that Language for the benefit of [p. 149] the *Indians*.[221] These go clothed like the *English*, live in framed houses,
have stocks of Corn and Cattle about them, which when they are
fat they bring to the *English* Markets, the Hogs that they rear are
counted the best in *New-England*. Some of their Sons have been
brought up Scholars in *Harvard* Colledge, and I was told that
there was but two Fellowes in that Colledge, and one of them was
an *Indian*; some few of these Christian *Indians* have of late Apos-
tatized and fallen back to their old Superstition and course of
life.[222]

Thus much shall suffice concerning *New-England*, as it was
when the *Indians* solely possest it. I will now proceed to give you
an accompt of it, as it is under the management of the *English*;
but methinks I hear my sceptick Readers muttering out of their
scuttle mouths, what will accrew to us by this rambling *Logodiarce?* You do but bring straw into *Egypt*, a Countrey abounding with Corn. Thus by these *Famacides* who are so minutely curious, I am dejected from my hopes, whilst they challenge the
freedom of *David's* Ruffins, Our tongues are our own, whoshall
controll us.[223] I have done what I can to please you, I have piped
and you will not dance.[224] I have told you as strange things as ever
you or your Fathers [p. 150] have heard. The *Italian* saith *Chi
vide un miraculo facilmente ne crede un altro*, he that hath seen one

221. Apostle to the Indians John Eliot (1604–90) translated into the Algonquian language both a catechism (1654) and the first Bible (1661–63) to be
printed in New England. Among the fourteen "praying towns" he had helped
found for the Massachusetts Bay Indians by 1674, only Natick and Hassawesitt
(now Grafton) included churches officially recognized by the colony's religious
leaders (Vaughan 293).

222. The so-called Indian College, part of Harvard, was erected by 1654
but had failed by 1692. During this period several Indians attended, but only
one, Caleb Cheeshahtequmuck, graduated.

223. A logodiarrhe is a flux or flow of words, while "*Famacides*" is unrecorded in the *OED* but evidently is intended to denote those who kill by defamation, those who, as it were, murder fame. The allusion to "*David's* Ruffins"
remains untraced.

224. A metaphor attributed originally to King James (Adams 1:129).

miracle will easilie believe another, *miranda canunt sed non cred-enda poete.*[225] Oh I see the pad, you never heard nor saw the like, therefore you do not believe me; well Sirs I shall not strain your belief any further, the following Relation I hope will be more tolerable, yet I could (it is possible) insert as wonderful things as any my pen hath yet gone over, and may, but it must be upon condition you will not put me to the proof of it. *Nemo tenetur ad impossibilia*, no man is obliged to do more than is in his power, is a rule in law. To be short; if you cannot with the Bee gather the honey, with the Spider suck out the poyson, as Sir *John Davis* hath it.

> *The Bee and Spider by a divers power*
> *Suck honey and poyson from the self-same flower.*[226]

I am confident you will get but little poyson here, no 'tis the poyson of *Asps* under your tongue that swells you: truly, I do take you rather to be Spider catchers than Spiders, such as will not laudably imploy themselves, nor suffer others; you may well say *non amo hominem, sed no pos-* [p. 151] *sum dicere quare*, unless it be because I am a Veronessa, no Romancer.[227] To conclude; if with your mother wit, you can mend the matter, take pen in hand and fall to work, do your Countrey some service as I have done according to my Talent. Henceforth you are to expect no more Relations from me. I am now return'd into my Native Countrey, and by the providence of the Almighty, and the bounty of my Royal Soveraigness am disposed to a holy quiet of study and meditation for the good of my soul;[228] and being blessed with a trans-mentation or change of mind, and weaned from the world, may

225. Josselyn accurately translates the Italian. The Latin phrase reads: Poets sing of things to be wondered at but not of things to be believed.

226. Wyatt, Lyly, Florio, and Jonson are among the numerous English writers whose works bear variations of this common proverb. The lines are not, however, part of the extant corpus of the English jurist and poet Sir John Davies (1596–1626). See Whiting (S367) where the only American instance of this proverb dates from 1796.

227. The Latin phrase reads: I do not like the man, but I can not say why. "Veronessa" is untraced but is possibly meant to denote one who adheres to ver-ities or truths.

228. Evidence that Josselyn enjoyed court patronage.

take up for my word, *non est mortale quod opto.*[229] If what I have done is thought uprears for the approvement of those to whom it is intended, I shall be more than meanly contented.

New-England was first discovered by *John Cabota* and his son *Sebastian* in *Anno Dom.* 1514.[230] A further discovery afterwards was made by the honourable Sir *Walter Rawleigh* Knight in *Anno* 1584. when as *Virginia* was discovered, which together with *Maryland, New-England, Nova Scotia* was known by one common name to the *Indians, Wingandicoa,* and by Sir *Walter Rawleigh* in honour of our Virgin Queen, in whose name he took possession of it, *Virginia.* In [p. 152] King *James* his Reign it was divided into Provinces as is before named. In 1602. these north parts were further discovered by Capt. *Bartholomew Gosnold.* The first *English* that planted there, set down not far from the *Narragansets-Bay,* and called their Colony *Plimouth,* since old *Plimouth, An. Dom.* 1602. Sir *John Popham* Lord chief Justice authorized by his Majesty, King *James,* sent a Colony of *English* to *Sagadehock, An.* 1606. *Newfound-land* was discovered by one *Andrew Thorn* an English man in *Anno* 1527. Sir *Humphrey Gilbert* a west Countrey Knight took possession of it in the Queens name, *Anno* 1582. The two first Colonies in *New-England* failing, there was a fresh supply of *English* who set down in other parts of the Countrey, and have continued in a flourishing condition to this day.[231]

The whole Countrey now is divided into Colonies, and for

229. What I desire is not mortal.

230. John (1450–98) and Sebastian Cabot (c. 1477–1557) landed at Cape Breton Island in 1497; traditionally they have received credit for the discovery of North America.

231. The two failed colonies of New England were Gosnold's on Cuttyhunk Island (1602), and Popham's at Sagadahoc (1607). The voyage of Gosnold (d. 1607) aboard the *Concord* was reported by his shipmate John Brereton in his *Relation of the Discoverie of the North Part of Virginia* (1602). Popham's (c. 1531–1607) explorers of 1606 were captured by a Spanish fleet. In 1607, under his dispatch, the *Gift of God* and the *Mary and John* set down the Sagadahoc colony of 120 on the west side of the inlet now called Atkins Bay in Maine. Gilbert (c. 1539–83) failed in his first attempt of 1578 but in 1583 founded the first British colony in North America at Saint John's, Newfoundland. Andrew Thorn: an error for Robert Thorne (see p. 232 and "Chronological Observations," n. 41).

your better understanding observe, a Colony is a sort of people that come to inhabit a place before not inhabited, or *Colonus quasi*, because they should be Tillers of the Earth.²³² From hence by an usual figure the Countrey where they sit down is called a Colony or Plantation.

The first of these that I shall relate of, though last in possession of the *English*, is now our most Southerly Colony, and next [p. 153] adjoyning to *Mary-land*, *scil*. the *Manadaes* or *Man-ahanent*²³³ lying upon the great River *Mohegan*, which was first discovered by Mr. *Hudson*, and sold presently by him to the *Dutch* without Authority from his Soveraign the King of *England, Anno* 1608.²³⁴ The *Dutch* in 1614 began to plant there, and call'd it *New-Netherlands*, but Sir *Samuel Argal* Governour of *Virginia* routed them,²³⁵ the *Dutch* after this got leave of King *James* to put in there for fresh water in their passage to *Brasile*, and did not offer to plant until a good while after the *English* were settled in the Countrey. In *Anno* 1664 his Majestie *Charles* the Second sent over four worthie Gentlemen Commissioners to reduce the Colonies into their bounds, who had before incroached upon one another, who marching with Three hundred red-Coats to *Manadaes* or *Manhataes* took from the *Dutch* their chief town then called *New-Amsterdam*, now *New York*; the Twenty ninth of *August* turn'd out their Governour with a silver leg, and all but those that were willing to acknowledge subjection to the King of *England*, suffering them to enjoy their houses and estates as before. Thirteen days after Sir *Robert Carr* took the Fort and Town of *Auravia* now called *Albany*; and Twelve days after that, the Fort and Town [p. 154] of *Awsapha*, then *De-la-ware* Castle, man'd with *Dutch* and *Sweeds*. So now the *English* are masters of

232. *Colonus quasi*: as (though a) husbandman.

233. *Scil.*: a Latin abbreviation for *scilicet*, "namely." Manahanent: Manhattan.

234. In 1609, Henry Hudson discovered the river now named for him, and by 1633, Dutch traders in this New Netherland were competing commercially with the colonists of Virginia and New England.

235. Argall (c. 1572–1626) captured Pocahontas and routed the French from Maine in 1613. However, he played no certain part in skirmishes against the Dutch. For a discussion of the "alleged Argall incursion" into New Netherland, an incident reported by several contemporary writers, see "Chronological Observations" for 1614 and Winsor (4:427, 432).

three handsome Towns, three strong Forts and a Castle, not losing one man. The first Governour of these parts for the King of *England* was Colonel *Nicols*, a noble Gentleman, and one of his Majesties Commissioners, who coming for *England* in *Anno Dom.* 1668 as I take it, surrendered the Government to Colonel *Lovelace*.[236]

The Countrey here is bless'd with the richest soil in all *New-England*, I have heard it reported from men of Judgement and Integrity, that one Bushel of *European Wheat* hath yielded a hundred in one year. Their other Commodities are Furs, and the like.

New-York is situated at the mouth of the great River *Mohegan*, and is built with *Dutch* Brick *alla-moderna*, the meanest house therein being valued at One hundred pounds, to the Landward it is compassed with a Wall of good thickness; at the entrance of the River is an Island well fortified, and hath command of any Ship that shall attempt to pass without their leave.

Albany is situated upon the same River on the West-side, and is due North from *New-York* somewhat above Fifty miles.

[p. 155] Along the Sea-side Eastward are many *English*-Towns, as first *Westchester*, a Sea-Town about Twenty miles from *New-York*; to the Eastward of this is *Greenwich*, another Sea-Town much about the same distance; then *Chichester*, *Fairfield*, *Stratford*, *Milford*, all Sea-Towns twenty and thirty mile distant from one another, twenty miles Eastward of *Milford* is *Newhaven* the Metropolis of the Colony begun in 1637. One Mr. *Eaton* being there Governour: it is near to the shoals of *Cape Cod*, and is one of the four united Colonies.[237]

The next Sea-Town Eastward of *Newhaven* is called *Guilford* about ten mile, and I think belonging to that Colony.

236. Peter Stuyvesant (1592–1672), the "Governour with a silver leg," surrendered New Netherland to the English in September 1664; his leg actually was made of wood with silver bands. Sir Robert Carr (c. 1590–1645) completed the English conquest of the Dutch settlements; Richard Nicolls (1624–72) was first governor of New York; and Francis Lovelace (c. 1618–75) served as his successor in 1668.

237. Otherwise known as the New England Confederation, the four united colonies of Plymouth, Massachusetts Bay, Connecticut, and New Haven came together on 19 May 1643. In 1639, Theophilus Eaton (1590–1658) was chosen first governor of the colony he established at New Haven.

From *Gilford* to *Connecticut-River*, is near upon twenty miles, the fresh River *Connecticut* bears the name of another Colony begun in the year 1636 and is also one of the four united Colonies. Upon this River are situated 13 Towns, within two, three & four miles off one another. At the mouth of the River, on the West-side is the *Lord-Say*, and *Brooks fort*, called *Saybrook-fort*. Beyond this Northward is the Town of *Windsor*, then *Northampton*, then *Pinsers-house*.[238] On the Eastside of the River, *Hartford*, about it low land well stored with meadow and very fertile. *Wethersfield* is [p. 156] also situated upon *Connecticut* River and *Springfield*; but this town although here seated, is in the jurisdiction of the *Mattachusets*, and hath been infamous by reason of Witches therein. *Hadley* lyes to the Northward of *Springfield*. *New London* which I take to be in the jurisdiction of this Coloney is situated to the Eastward of *Connecticut*-River by a small River, and is not far from the Sea. From *Connecticut*-River *long-Island* stretcheth it self to *Mohegan* one hundred and twenty miles, but it is but narrow and about sixteen miles from the main; the considerablest Town upon it is *Southampton* built on the Southside of the Island towards the Eastern end: opposite to this on the Northernside is *Feversham*, Westward is *Ashford*, *Huntingdon*, &c. The Island is well stored with Sheep and other Cattle, and Corn, and is reasonable populous. Between this Island and the mouth of *Connecticut*-River lyeth three small Islands, *Shelter-Island*, *Fishers-Island*, and the Isle of *Wight*.[239] Over against *New-London* full South lyeth *Block-Island*.

The next place of note on the Main is *Narragansets-Bay*, within which Bay is *Rhode-Island* a Harbour for the *Shunamitish* Brethren, as the Saints Errant, the Quakers who are rather to be esteemed Vagabonds, than Religious persons, &c.

[p. 157] At the further end of the *Bay* by the mouth of *Narragansets*-River, on the South-side thereof was old *Plimouth* plantation *Anno* 1602. Twenty mile out to Sea, South of *Rhode-Island*, lyeth *Martins* vineyard in the way to *Virginia*, this Island is governed by a discreet Gentleman Mr. *Mayhew* by name. To

238. *"Pinsers-house"* can only be Deerfield, Massachusetts.

239. Now called Gardiners Island, since its purchase by Lion Gardiner after the Pequot War of 1637.

the Eastward of *Martin's* vineyard lyeth *Nantocket-Island*, and further Eastward *Elizabeths-Island*, these Islands are twenty or thirty mile asunder, and now we are come to *Cape-Cod*.[240]

Cape-Cod was so called at the first by Captain *Gosnold* and his Company *Anno Dom.* 1602, because they took much of that fish there; and afterward was called *Cape-James* by Captain *Smith*: the point of the *Cape* is called *Point-Cave* and *Tuckers* Terror, and by the *French* and *Dutch Mallacar*, by reason of the perillous shoals. The first place to be taken notice of on the South-side of the *Cape* is *Wests*-Harbour, the first Sea-Town *Sandwich* formerly called *Duxbury* in the Jurisdiction of *New-Plimouth*. Doubling the *Cape* we come into the great *Bay*, on the West whereof is *New-Plimouth-Bay*, on the Southwest-end of this *Bay* is situated *New-Plimouth*, the first *English*-Colony that took firm possession in this Countrey, which was in 1620, and the first Town built [p. 158] therein, whose longitude is 315 degrees, in latitude 41 degrees and 37 minutes, it was built nine years before any other Town, from the beginning of it to 1669 is just forty years, in which time there hath been an increasing of forty Churches in this Colony (but many more in the rest) and Towns in all *New-England* one hundred and twenty, for the most part along the Sea-Coasts, (as being wholsomest) for somewhat more than two hundred miles: onely on *Connecticut*-River (as I have said) is thirteen Towns not far off one another.

The other Towns of note in this Colony are *Green-Harbour* to the Eastward of *Plimouth* towards the point of the *Cape*, & therefore somewhat unaccessible by land, here is excellent Timber for shipping; then *Marshfield, Yarmouth, Rehoboth, Bridgwater, Warwick, Taunton, Eastham*, by the *Indians* called *Namset*.

The first Town Northeast from *Green-harbour* is *Sittuate* in the jurisdiction of the *Mattachusets*-Colony, more Northward of *Sittuate* is *Conchusset* and *Hull* a little Burg lying open to the Sea,

240. Cuttyhunk was the site of "old *Plimouth* plantation," as Josselyn calls it, Bartholomew Gosnold's abortive colony of 1602. Thomas Mayhew, Sr. (1593–1682) and his son Thomas (c. 1621–57) became patentees in 1641 to Martha's Vineyard, Nantucket, and the Elizabeth Islands. Nantucket Island is closer to fifteen miles south and east of Martha's Vineyard; The Elizabeth Islands lie some four miles north and west.

from thence we came to *Merton-point* over against which is *Pullin-point*. Upon *Merton-point* (which is on the Larboard-side) is a Town called *Nantascot*, which is two Leagues from *Boston*, where [p. 159] Ships commonly cast Anchor.[241] *Pullin-point* is so called, because the Boats are by the seasing or Roads haled against the Tide which is very strong, it is the usual Channel for Boats to pass into *Mattachusets-Bay*.

There is an Island on the South-side of the passage containing eight Acres of ground. Upon a rising hill within this Island is mounted a Castle commanding the entrance, no stately Edifice, nor strong; built with Brick and Stone, kept by a Captain, under whom is a master-Gunner and others.

The *Bay* is large, made by many Islands, the chief *Deere*-Island, which is within a slight shot of *Pullin-point*, great store of *Deere* were wont to swim thither from the Main; then *Bird*-Island, *Glass*-Island, *Slate*-Island, the Governours Garden, where the first Apple-Trees in the Countrey were planted, and a vinyard; then *Round*-Island, and *Noddles*-Island not far from *Charles*-Town: most of these Islands lye on the North-side of the *Bay*.

The next Town to *Nantascot* on the South-side of the *Bay* is *Wissaguset* a small Village, about three miles from *Mount-wolleston*, about this Town the soil is very fertile.[242]

Within sight of this is *Mount-wolleston* or *Merry-mount*, called *Massachusets*-fields, [p. 160] where *Chicatabat* the greatest *Saga-more* of the Countrey lived before the plague: here the Town of *Braintree* is seated, no Boat nor Ship can come near to it, here is an Iron mill: to the West of this Town is *Naponset*-River.[243]

Six miles beyond *Braintree* lyeth *Dorchester*, a frontire Town pleasantly seated, and of large extent into the main land, well watered with two small Rivers, her body and wings filled some-what thick with houses to the number of two hundred and more, beautified with fair Orchards and Gardens, having also plenty of

241. Conchusset is now Cohasset, Pullen Point is Point Shirley, and Nantasket is part of Hull.

242. Wessagusset has been absorbed by Weymouth; Mount Wallaston is now Quincy.

243. Neponset River.

Corn-land, and store of Cattle, counted the greatest Town heretofore in *New-England*, but now gives way to *Boston*, it hath a Harbour to the North for Ships.

A mile from *Dorchester* is the Town of *Roxbury*,[244] a fair and handsome Countrey Town, the streets large, the Inhabitants rich, replenished with Orchards and Gardens, well watered with springs and small freshets, a brook runs through it called *Smelt-*River, a quarter of a mile to the North-side of the Town runs stony River: it is seated in the bottom of a shallow *Bay*, but hath no harbour for shipping. Boats come to it, it hath store of Land and Cattle.

Two miles Northeast from *Roxbury*, and [p. 161] Forty miles from *New-Plimouth*, in the latitude of 42 or 43 degrees and 10 minutes, in the bottom of *Massachusets-Bay* is *Boston* (whose longitude is 315 degrees, or as others will 322 degrees and 30 seconds). So called from a Town in *Lincolnshire*, which in the *Saxons* time bare the name of St. *Botolph* and is the Metropolis of this Colony, or rather of the whole Countrey, situated upon a *Peninsula*, about four miles in compass, almost square, and invironed with the Sea, saving one small *Isthmus* which gives access to other Towns by land on the South-side. The Town hath two hills of equal height on the frontire part thereof next the Sea, the one well fortified on the superficies with some Artillery mounted, commanding any Ship as she sails into the Harbour within the still *Bay*; the other hill hath a very strong battery built of whole Timber and fill'd with earth, at the descent of the hill in the extreamest part thereof, betwixt these two strong Arms, lyes a large *Cove* or *Bay*, on which the chiefest part of the Town is built, to the Northwest is a high mountain that out-tops all, with its three little rising hills on the summit called *Tramount*,[245] this is furnished with a Beacon and great Guns, from hence you may over-[p. 162] look all the Islands in the *Bay*, and descry such Ships as are upon the Coast; the houses are for the most part raised on the Sea-banks and wharfed out with great industry and cost, many of

244. Both Dorchester, above, and Roxbury are now suburbs of south Boston.

245. Trimount, the hill that served to name Boston before 1630 (Adams 1:288).

them standing upon piles, close together on each side the streets as in *London*, and furnished with many fair shops, their materials are Brick, Stone, Lime, handsomely contrived, with three meeting Houses or Churches, and a Town-house built upon pillars where the Merchants may confer, in the Chambers above they keep their monethly Courts. Their streets are many and large, paved with pebble stone, and the South-side adorned with Gardens and Orchards. The Town is rich and very populous, much frequented by strangers, here is the dwelling of their Governour. On the North-west and North-east two constant Fairs are kept for daily Traffick thereunto. On the South there is a small, but pleasant Common where the Gallants a little before Sun-set walk with their *Marmalet*-Madams, as we do in *Morefields*, &c. till the nine a clock Bell rings them home to their respective habitations, when presently the Constables walk their rounds to see good orders kept, and to take up loose people.[246] Two miles from the town, [p. 163] at a place called *Muddy-River*,[247] the Inhabitants have Farms, to which belong rich arable grounds and meadows where they keep their Cattle in the Summer, and bring them to *Boston* in the Winter; the Harbour before the Town is filled with Ships and other Vessels for most part of the year.

Hingham is a Town situated upon the Sea-coasts, South-east of *Charles-River*: here is great store of Timber, deal-boards, masts for Ships, white-Cedar, and fish is here to be had.

Dedham an inland-town ten miles from *Boston* in the County of *Suffolk* well watered with many pleasant streams, and abounding with Garden fruit; the Inhabitants are Husband-men, somewhat more than one hundred Families, having store of Cattle and Corn.

The Town of *Waymouth* lyes open to the Sea, on the East Rocks and Swamps, to the South-ward good store of *Deer*, arable land and meadows.

On the North-side of *Boston* flows *Charles-River*, which is about six fathom deep, many small Islands lye to the Bayward,

246. Marmalade-madam: strumpet, according to the *OED*, in which this is the only citation. Actually, Josselyn appears to have had a milder meaning in mind. On the detail of the bell, see Goss (46–52).

247. The town of Muddy River has become Brookline.

and hills on either side the River, a very good harbour, here may forty Ships ride, the passage from *Boston* to *Charles-Town* is by a Ferry worth forty or fifty pounds a [p. 164] year, and is a quarter of a mile over. The River *Mystick* runs through the right side of the Town, and by its near approach to *Charles-River* in one place makes a very narrow neck, where stands most part of the Town, the market place not far from the waterside is surrounded with houses, forth of which issue two streets orderly built and beautified with Orchards and Gardens, their meeting-house stands on the North-side of the market, having a little hill behind it; there belongs to this Town one thousand and two hundred Acres of arable, four hundred head of Cattle, and as many Sheep, these also provide themselves Farms in the Country.

Up higher in *Charles-River* west-ward is a broad Bay two miles over, into which runs *Stony-River* and *Muddy-River*.

Towards the South-west in the middle of the *Bay* is a great Oyster-bank, towards the North-west is a Creek; upon the shore is situated the village of *Medford*, it is a mile and half from *Charles-town*.

At the bottom of the *Bay* the River begins to be narrower, half a quarter of a mile broad; by the North-side of the River is *New-town*, three miles from *Charles-town*, a league and half by water, it was first in- [p. 165] tended for a City, the neatest and best compacted Town, having many fair structures and handsom contrived streets; the Inhabitants rich, they have many hundred Acres of land paled with one common fence a mile and half long, and store of Cattle; it is now called *Cambridge* where is a Colledge for Students of late; it stretcheth from *Charles-River* to the Southern part of *Merrimach-River*.

Half a mile thence on the same side of the River is *Water-town* built upon one of the branches of *Charles-River*, very fruitful and of large extent, watered with many pleasant springs and small Rivulets, the Inhabitants live scatteringly. Within half a mile is a great pond divided between the two Towns, a mile and half from the Town is a fall of fresh waters which conveigh themselves into the Ocean through *Charles-River*, a little below the fall of waters they have a wair to catch fish, wherein they take store of *Basse*, *Shades*, *Alwives*, *Frost fish* and *Smelts*, in two tides they have gotten one hundred thousand of these fishes.[248] They have store of Cattle and Sheep, and near upon two thousand Acres of arable land, Ships of small burden may come up to these Towns.

[p. 166] We will now return to *Charles-Town* again, where the River *Mystick* runs on the North-side of the Town (that is the right side as beforesaid) where on the Northwest-side of the River is the Town of *Mystick*,[249] three miles from *Charles-town*, a league and half by water, a scattered village; at the head of this River are great and spacious ponds, full of *Alewives* in the spring-time, the notedst place for this sort of fish. On the West of this River is Merchant *Craddock's* plantation, where he impaled a park.[250]

Upon the same River and on the North-side is the Town of *Malden*.

The next Town is *Winnisimet*[251] a mile from *Charles-Town*, the River only parting them, this is the last Town in the still bay of *Massachusets*.

Without *Pullin-point*, six miles North-east from *Winnisimet* is *Cawgust*, or *Sagust*, or *Sangut* now called *Linn*, situated at the bottom of a *Bay* near a River, which upon the breaking up of winter with a furious Torrent vents it self into the Sea, the Town consists of more than one hundred dwelling-houses, their Church being built on a level undefended from the North-west wind is made with steps descending [p. 167] into the Earth, their streets are straight and but thin of houses, the people most husbandmen. At the end of the *Sandy beach* is a neck of land called *Nahant*, it is six miles in circumference. Black *William* an *Indian* Duke out of his generosity gave this to the *English*. At the mouth of the River

248. Weir, a screen trap. American Indians used fish weirs on a grand scale. As Neal Salisbury has observed, "the Boylston Street Fishweir, built about 2500 B.C. in what is now Boston, covered approximately two acres and consisted of some 65,000 stakes between which brush was inserted to trap fish" (17).

249. Mystic is now Somerville, a suburb of south Boston.

250. Matthew Cradock, Puritan merchant of London and temporary governor of the Massachusetts Bay Colony before John Endecott took over. Cradock never came to the colony but did maintain several plantations there. Impaled: fenced or staked in.

251. Chelsea.

runs a great Creek into a great marsh called *Rumney-marsh*, which is four miles long, and a mile broad, this Town hath the benefit of minerals of divers kinds, Iron, Lead, one Iron mill, store of Cattle, Arable land and meadow.[252]

To the North-ward of *Linn* is *Marvil* or *Marble-head*, a small Harbour, the shore rockie, upon which the Town is built, consisting of a few scattered houses; here they have stages for fishermen, Orchards and Gardens, half a mile within land good pastures and Arable land.

Four miles North of *Marble-head* is situated *New-Salem* (whose longitude is 315 degrees, and latitude 42 degrees 35 minutes) upon a plain, having a River on the South, and another on the North, it hath two Harbours, Winter Harbour and Summer Harbour which lyeth within *Darbie's* fort, they have store of Meadow and Arable, in this Town are some very rich Merchants.

[p. 168] Upon the Northern Cape of the *Massachusets*, that is *Cape-Ann*[,] a place of fishing is situated, the Town of *Glocester* where the *Massachusets* Colony first set down, but *Salem* was the first Town built in that Colony, here is a Harbour for Ships.

To the North-ward of *Cape-Ann* is *Wonasquam*,[253] a dangerous place to sail by in stormie weather, by reason of the many Rocks and foaming breakers.

The next Town that presents it self to view is *Ipswich* situated by a fair River, whose first rise is from a Lake or Pond twenty mile up, betaking its course through a hideous *Swamp* for many miles, a Harbour for *Bears*, it issueth forth into a large *Bay*, (where they fish for *Whales*) due East over against the Islands of *Sholes* a great place for fishing, the mouth of that River is barr'd; it is a good haven-town, their meeting-house or Church is beautifully built, store of Orchards and Gardens, land for husbandry and Cattle.[254]

252. Rumney Marsh is now Revere. The "one Iron mill" is the famous Saugus Iron Works, in "Sangut," as Josselyn designates the town a few lines earlier.

253. Annisquam.

254. This paragraph certifies that Josselyn knew and borrowed from Johnson's *Wonder-Working Providence* (1654). The river near Ipswich, Johnson writes, "betakes its course through a most hideous swamp of large extent, even for many miles, being a great Harbour for Beares" (96). Indeed, for much of his information on the Massachusetts towns, Josselyn borrows, frequently ver-

Wenham is an inland Town very well watered, lying between *Salem* and *Ipswich*, consisteth most of men of judgment and experience in *re rustica*, well stored with Cattle. At the first rise of *Ipswich*-River in the highest part of the land near the head [p. 169] springs of many considerable Rivers; *Shashin* one of the most considerable branches of *Merrimach* River, and also at the rise of *Mistick* River, and ponds full of pleasant springs, is situated *Wooburn* an inland-Town four miles square beginning at the end of *Charles-town* bounds.[255]

Six miles from *Ipswich* North-east is *Rowley*, most of the Inhabitants have been Clothiers.

Nine miles from *Salem* to the North is *Agowamine*,[256] the best and spaciousest place for a plantation, being twenty leagues to the Northward of *New-Plimouth*.

Beyond *Agowamin* is situated *Hampton* near the Sea-coasts not far from *Merrimach*-River, this Town is like a *Flower-deluce*, having two broad streets of houses wheeling off from the main body thereof, they have great store of salt Marshes and Cattle, the land is fertil, but full of Swamps and Rocks.[257]

Eight miles beyond *Agowamin* runneth the delightful River *Merrimach* or *Monumach*, it is navigable for twenty miles, and

---

batim, from Johnson's famous book. The Isles of Shoals, eight barren islands, lie some ten miles southeast of Portsmouth harbor between Maine and New Hampshire.

255. In *re rustica*: in country matters. "*Shashin*" is Shawsheen, and "*Wooburn*" is Woburn, of which Edward Johnson was a founder in 1640. This paragraph too derives from Johnson, who assessed Woburn's "scituation" thus: "as the first rise of Ipswitch river, and the rise of Shashin, one of the most considerable branches of Merrimeck, as also the first rise of Mistick river and ponds, it is very full of pleasant springs, and great variety of very good water" (214). Clearly Johnson was an authority on the area, and J. Franklin Jameson has called his chapter on Woburn "a *locus classicus* for the genesis of the Massachusetts towns and churches, or at least for the procedure followed after the General Court and the people had settled down to a regular course of action" (Johnson 212n).

256. Josselyn evidently is confused here, for Agawam was an Indian village located on the site of modern Ipswich.

257. On the town of Hampton, Johnson once again serves as source: "it is like a Flower-de-luce, two streets of houses wheeling off from the main body thereof, the land is fertile, but filled with swamps, and some store of rocks" (189).

well stored with fish, upon the banks grow stately Oaks, excellent Ship timber, not inferiour to our *English*.

On the South-side of *Merrimach*-River [p. 170] twelve miles from *Ipswich*, and near upon the wide venting streams thereof is situated *Newberrie*, the houses are scattering, well stored with meadow, upland, and Arable, and about four hundred head of Cattle.

Over against *Newberrie* lyes the Town of *Salisbury*, where a constant Ferry is kept, the River being here half a mile broad, the Town scatteringly built.

Hard upon the River of *Shashin* where *Merrimach* receives this and the other branch into its body, is seated *Andover*, stored with land and Cattle.

Beyond this Town by the branch of *Merrimach*-River called *Shashin*, lyeth *Haverhill*, a Town of large extent about ten miles in length, the inhabitants Husbandmen, this Town is not far from *Salisbury*.

Over against *Haverhill* lyeth the Town of *Malden*,[258] which I have already mentioned.

In a low level upon a fresh River a branch of *Merrimach* is seated *Concord*, the first inland Town in *Massachusets* patent,[259] well stored with fish, *Salmon, Dace, Alewive, Shade*, &c. abundance of fresh marsh and Cattle, this place is subject to bitter storms.

[p. 171] The next Town is *Sudbury* built upon the same River where *Concord* is, but further up; to this Town likewise belongs great store of fresh marshes, and Arable land, and they have many Cattle, it lyeth low, by reason whereof it is much indammaged with flouds.

In the Centre of the Countrey by a great pond side, and not far from *Woeburn*, is situated *Reading*, it hath two mills, a saw-mill and a Corn-mill, and is well stockt with Cattle.

The Colony is divided into four counties, the first is *Suffolk*, to which belongs *Dorchester, Roxbury, Waymouth, Hingham, Dedham, Braintre, Sittuate, Hull, Nantascot, Wisagusset*. The second County is *Middlesex*, to this belongs *Charles-town, Water-town,*

258. An error. Malden lies five miles north of Boston.
259. Concord was founded in 1636.

*Cambridge, Concord, Sudbury, Woeburn, Reading, Malden, Mis-
tick, Medford, Winnisimet* and *Marble-head.* To the third County
which is *Essex,* belongs *New-Salem, Linn, Ipswich, New-Berry,
Rowley, Glocester, Wenham,* and *Andover.* The fourth County is
Northfolk, to this belongs *Salisbury, Hampton* and *Haverhill.*[260]

In the year of our Lord 1628, Mr. *John Endicot* with a number of *English* people set down by *Cape-Ann* at that place called
[p. 172] afterwards *Gloster,* but their abiding-place was at
Salem, where they built a Town in 1629. and there they gathered
their first Church, consisting but of Seventy persons; but afterwards increased to forty three Churches in joynt Communion
with one another, and in those Churches were about Seven thousand, seven hundred and fifty Souls, Mr. *Endicot* was chosen
their first Governour.[261]

The Twelfth of *July Anno. Dom.* 1630. *John Wenthorp* Esq;
and the assistants, arrived with the Patent for the *Massachusets,*
the passage of the people that came along with him in ten Vessels
came to 95000 pound: the Swine, Goats, Sheep, Neat,[262] Horses
cost to transport 12000 pound, besides the price they cost them;
getting food for the people till they could clear the ground of
wood amounted to 45000 pound: Nails, Glass, and other Iron
work for their meeting and dwelling houses 13000 pound; Arms,
Powder, Bullet, and Match, together with their Artillery 22000
pound, the whole sum amounts unto One hundred ninety two
thousand pounds.[263] They set down first upon *Noddles-Island,* afterwards they began to build upon the main. In 1637. there were
not many houses in the Town of [p. 173] *Boston,* amongst which
were two houses of entertainment called Ordinaries, into which if
a stranger went, he was presently followed by one appointed to
that Office, who would thrust himself into his company uninvited,

260. By 1643 the Massachusetts Bay Colony had grown so large that it was
divided along the lines here described. Today, of course, the county divisions
are much different.
261. John Endecott (1588–1665) was first acting governor for the Massachusetts Bay Colony, at Salem, from 1628 till Winthrop's arrival in 1630.
262. Ox, cow or steer.
263. This catalog of goods and costs comes more or less verbatim from
Johnson's exposition of the Winthrop fleet of 1630; the "13000 pound" should
be 18,000.

and if he called for more drink than the Officer thought in his judgment he could soberly bear away, he would presently countermand it, and appoint the proportion, beyond which he could not get one drop.

The Patent was granted to Sir *Henry Rosewell*, Sir *John Young* Knight, *Thomas Southcoat, John Humphrey, John Endicot* and *Simon Whitecomb*, and to their Heirs, Assigns, and Associats for ever. These took to them other Associats, as Sir *Richard Saltonstall, Isaac Johnson, Samuel Aldersey, Jo. Ven, Matth. Craddock, George Harwood, Increase Nowell, Rich. Perry, Rich. Bellingham, Nathaniel Wright, Samuel Vasell, Theophilus Eaton, Thomas Goffe, Thomas Adams, Jo. Brown, Samuel Brown, Thomas Hutchins, Will. Vasell, Will. Pinchon* and *George Foxcroft. Matth. Craddock* was ordained and constituted Governour by Patent, and *Thomas Goffe* Deputy Governour of the said Company, the rest Assistants.[264]

That part of *New-England* granted to [p. 174] these forementioned Gentlemen lyeth and extendeth between a great River called *Monumach*, alias *Merrimach*, and the often frequented *Charles-River*, being in the bottom of a *Bay* called *Massachusets*, alias *Mattachusetts*, alias *Massatusets-bay*; and also those lands within the space of three *English* miles, on the South part of the said *Charles-River*, or any or every part, and all the lands within three miles to South-ward part of the *Massachusets-bay*, and all those lands which lye within the space of three *English* miles to the North-ward of the River *Merrimach*, or to the North-ward of any and every part thereof, and all lands whatsoever within the limits aforesaid, North and South, in latitude, and in breadth and length and longitude of and within all the main land there, from the *Atlantick* and the Western-Sea and Ocean on the East-part, to the South-Sea on the West-part, and all lands and grounds, place and places, soils, woods and wood-groves, Havens, Ports, Rivers,

---

264. On 19 March 1627 the Council for New England issued to Endecott and his associates a grant for all that territory lying west between the Merrimack and the Charles rivers, along with three miles to the north and south respectively of those boundaries. Among the councilors or assistants named, dissension soon developed over issues of commerce and religion. When, for example, Endecott discovered Joseph and Samuel Browne attempting to perpetuate Anglican liturgy at the Bay, he sent them speedily back to England.

Waters, fishings and Hereditaments whatsoever lying within the aforesaid lands and limits, and every part and parcel thereof, and also all Islands lying in *America* aforesaid in the said Seas, or either of them on the Western or Eastern [p. 175] Coasts or parts of the said tracts of lands. Also all mines and minerals as well Royal of Gold, Silver, as others *&c.* With power to rule and govern both Sea and land, holden of the East manner of *Greenwich* in *Com. Kent*, in free and common soccage, yielding and paying to the King the fifth part of the Oar of Gold and Silver which shall be found at any time.[265]

This Colony is a body Corporated and Politick in fact by the name of the Governour and Company of the *Mattachusets-bay* in *New-England.* That there shall be one Governour, and Deputy-Governour, and Eighteen Assistants of the same Company from time to time.

That the Governour and Deputy-Governour, Assistants and all other Officers to be chosen from amongst the freemen, the last *Wednesday* in *Easter*-term yearly in the general Court.

The Governour to take his Corporal Oath to be true and faithful to the Government, and to give the same Oath to the other Officers.

[p. 176] To hold a Court once a month, and any seven to be a sufficient Court.

And that there shall be four general Courts kept in Term time, and one great general and solemn Assembly to make Laws and Ordinances; So they be not contrary and repugnant to the Laws and Statutes of the Realm of *England.* Their form of Government and what their Laws concern, you may see in the ensuing Table.

265. This paragraph is a patchwork of portions of the Massachusetts Bay Company's charter. Socage is land tenure. More specifically, free and common socage "conceived of land simply as property carrying an economic rent, a rent which was often negligible. In Massachusetts, the Crown's only claim was to receive one-fifth of all the gold and silver found there" (Cronon 71).

What follows are extracts from the tenets of the Bay government and the body of laws of 1646.

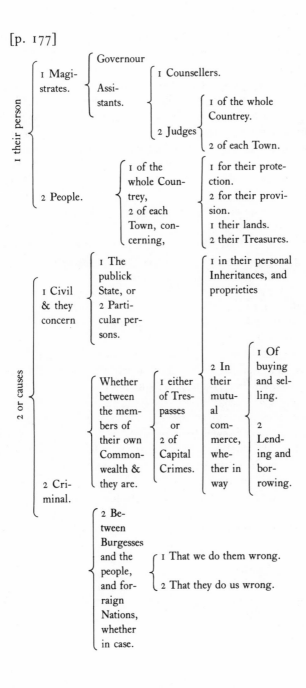

1 their person

1 Magistrates.
  Governour
  Assistants.
    1 Counsellers.
    2 Judges
      1 of the whole Countrey.
      2 of each Town.

2 People.
  1 of the whole Countrey,
  2 of each Town, concerning,
    1 for their protection.
    2 for their provision.
    1 their lands.
    2 their Treasures.

2 or causes

1 Civil & they concern
  1 The publick State, or
  2 Particular persons.
    1 in their personal Inheritances, and proprieties

2 Criminal.
  Whether between the members of their own Commonwealth & they are.
    1 either of Trespasses or
    2 of Capital Crimes.
      2 In their mutual commerce, whether in way
        1 Of buying and selling.
        2 Lending and borrowing.

  2 Between Burgesses and the people, and forraign Nations, whether in case.
    1 That we do them wrong.
    2 That they do us wrong.

[p. 178] *Anno. Dom.* 1646. they drew up a body of their Laws for the well ordering of their Commonwealth, as they not long since termed it.

The military part of their Commonwealth is governed by one Major-General, and three Serjeant Majors; to the Major-General belongeth particularly the Town of *Boston*, to the three Serjeant Majors belong the four Counties, but with submission to the Major-General. The first Serjeant Major chosen for the County of *Suffolk* was Major *Gibbons*. For the County of *Middlesex* Major *Sedgwick*. For the County of *Essex* and *Northfolk* Major *Denison*.[266]

Every Town sends two Burgesses to their great and solemn general Court.

For being drunk, they either whip or impose a fine of Five shillings; so for swearing and cursing, or boring through the tongue with a hot Iron.

For kissing a woman in the street, though in way of civil salute, whipping or a fine.

For single fornication whipping or a fine.

For Adultery, put to death, and so for Witchcraft.

An *English* woman suffering an *Indian* to have carnal knowledge of her, had an *Indian* cut out exactly in red cloth sewed [p. 179] upon her right Arm, and injoyned to wear it twelve moneths.

Scolds they gag and set them at their doors for certain hours, for all comers and goers by to gaze at.

Stealing is punished with restoring four fould, if able; if not, they are sold for some years, and so are poor debtors.

If you desire a further inspection of their Laws, I must refer you to them being in print, too many for to be inserted in this Relation.

The Governments of their Churches are Independent and

266. Edward Gibbons (d. 1652) succeeded Endecott as major general in 1649. He was allegedly first one of Thomas Morton's followers, then a buccaneer, and finally a landowner and solid citizen of Boston. Major Robert Sedgwick (d. 1656) also eventually attained the position of major general, under Cromwell, in Jamaica, where he died. Daniel Denison (c. 1612–82) was an early settler of Ipswich and an active participant in local politics.

Presbyterial, every Church (for so they call their particular Congregations) have one Pastor, one Teacher, Ruling Elders and
Deacons.

They that are members of their Churches have the Sacraments
administred to them, the rest that are out of the pale as they phrase
it, are denied it. Many hundred Souls there be amongst them
grown up to men & womens estate that were never Christened.

They judge every man and woman to pay Five shillings *per*
day, who comes not to their Assemblies,[267] and impose fines of
forty shillings and fifty shillings on such as meet together to worship God.

[p. 180] Quakers they whip, banish, and hang if they return
again.

Anabaptists they imprison, fine and weary out.

The Government both Civil and Ecclesiastical is in the hands
of the thorow-pac'd Independents and rigid Presbyterians.

The grose *Goddons*, or great masters, as also some of their
Merchants are damnable rich; generally all of their judgement,
inexplicably covetous and proud, they receive your gifts but as an
homage or tribute due to their transcendency, which is a fault
their Clergie are also guilty of, whose living is upon the bounty
of their hearers. On Sundays in the afternoon when Sermon is
ended the people in the Galleries come down and march two a
breast up one Ile and down the other, until they come before the
desk, for Pulpit they have none: before the desk is a long pue
where the Elders and Deacons sit, one of them with a mony box
in his hand, into which the people as they pass put their offering,
some a shilling, some two shillings, half a Crown, five shillings
according to their ability and good will, after this they conclude
with a Psalm; but this by the way.

The chiefest objects of discipline, Religi- [p. 181] on and mo-
rality they want, some are of a *Linsie-woolsie* disposition, of several professions in Religion, all like *Æthiopians* white in the
Teeth only, full of ludification[268] and injurious dealing, and

267. As Josselyn knew firsthand. At least three times he was presented and
fined for non-attendance of church meetings.

268. Linsie-woolsie: Strangely mixed, confused. Compare Edward
Johnson's use of this phrase (240) to describe the 1646 petition to the General
Court by Samuel Maverick and others who sought admission for Anglicans

cruelty the extreamest of all vices. The chiefest cause of *Noah*'s floud, Prov. 27.26. *Agni erant ad vestitum tuum*,[269] is a frequent text among them, no trading for a stranger with them, but with a *Græcian* faith, which is not to part with your ware without ready money, for they are generally in their payments recusant and slow, great Syndics, or censors, or controllers of other mens manners, and savagely factious amongst themselves.[270]

There are many strange women too, (in *Salomon's* sence) more the pitty, when a woman hath lost her Chastity, she hath no more to lose.

But mistake me not to general speeches, none but the guilty take exceptions, there are many sincere and religious people amongst them, descryed by their charity and humility (the true Characters of Christianity)[,] by their Zenodochie or hospitality, by their hearty submission to their Soveraign the King of *England*, by their diligent and honest labour in their callings, amongst these we may account the Royalists, who are lookt upon with an evil eye, and [p. 182] tongue boulted or punished if they chance to lash out, the tame *Indian* (for so they call those that are born in the Countrey) are pretty honest too, and may in good time be known for honest Kings men.

They have store of Children, and are well accommodated with Servants; many hands make light work, many hands make a full fraught, but many mouths eat up all, as some old planters have experimented; of these some are *English*, others *Negroes*: of the *English* there are can eat till they sweat, and work till they freeze; & the females that are like Mrs. *Winters* paddocks,[271] very tender fingerd in cold weather.

There are none that beg in the Countrey, but there be Witches

---

and Presbyterians to the New England churches. Ludification: mocking or deception.

269. Proverbs 27.26 reads: "The lambs are for thy clothing, and the goats are the price of the field."

270. This passage contains another echo of George Sandys' *Travels*, which advances the "Proverb, *To trade with Grecian trust*, which is not to part with their wares without money" (61). Recusant: dissenting from an established church or refusing to acknowledge authority.

271. *Paddy*, an Irish servant, may be intended by "paddock." If so, this antedates the earliest *OED* example of 1780.

too many, bottle-bellied Witches amongst the Quakers,[272] and others that produce many strange apparitions if you will believe report, of a *Shallop* at Sea man'd with women, of a Ship and a great red Horse standing by the main-mast, the Ship being in a small *Cove* to the Eastward vanished of a suddain. Of a Witch that appeared aboard of a Ship twenty leagues to Sea to a Mariner who took up the Carpenters broad Axe and cleft her head with it, the Witch dying of the wound at home, with such like bugbears and *Terriculamentæs.*[273]

[p. 183] It is published in print, that there are not much less than Ten hundred thousand souls *English, Scotch* and *Irish* in *New-England.*

Most of their Magistrates are dead, not above two left in the *Massachusets,* but one at *Plimouth,* one at *Connecticut,* and one at *New-haven,* they having done their generation work are laid asleep in their beds of rest till the day of doom, there and then to receive their reward according as they have done be it good or evil. Things of great indurance we see come to ruine, and alter, as great Flouds and Seas dryed up; mighty hills and mountains sunk into hollow bottoms: marvel not then that man is mortal, since his nature is unconstant and transitory.

The Diseases that the *English* are afflicted with, are the same that they have in *England,* with some proper to *New-England,* griping of the belly (accompanied with Feaver and Ague) which turns to the bloudy-flux,[274] a common disease in the Countrey, which together with the small pox hath carried away abundance of their children, for this the common medicines amongst the poorer sort are Pills of Cotton swallowed, or Sugar and Sallet-oyl

272. John Greenleaf Whittier, an American Quaker, used this observation as an epigraph in his *Supernaturalism in New England* (1847) but wrongly attributed it to Josselyn's *Rarities.*

273. Sources or objects of needless dread. Among the marvels and prodigies described in this paragraph, the great red horse may have its source in Revelation 6.4: "And there went out another horse that was red: and power was given to him that sat thereon to take peace from the earth, and that they should kill one another: and there was given unto him a great sword." The ship "vanished of a suddain" probably was Captain George Lamberton's, which left New Haven in 1646 and was not seen again till it returned as a phantom some months later, then finally disappeared (Andrews 1:176–77).

274. Severe dysentery.

boiled thick and made into Pills, Alloes pulverized [p. 184] and taken in the pap of an Apple. I helped many of them with a sweating medicine only.

Also they are troubled with a disease in the mouth or throat which hath proved mortal to some in a very short time, Quinsies, and Impostumations of the Almonds, with great distempers of cold. Some of our *New-England* writers affirm that the *English* are never or very rarely heard to sneeze or cough, as ordinarily they do in *England*, which is not true.[275] For a cough or stitch upon cold, Wormwood, Sage, Marygolds, and Crabs-claws boiled in posset-drink and drunk off very warm, is a soveraign medicine.

Pleurisies and Empyemas are frequent there, both cured after one and the same way; but the last is a desperate disease and kills many. For the Pleurisie I have given *Coriander*-seed prepared, *Carduus* seed, and *Harts-horn* pulverized with good success, the dose one dram in a cup of Wine.

The Stone terribly afflicts many, and the Gout, and Sciatica, for which take Onions roasted, peeled and stampt, then boil them with neats-feet oyl and Rhum to a Plaister, and apply it to the hip.

Head-aches are frequent, Palsies, Dropsies, Worms, Noli-me-tangeres,[276] Cancers, [p. 185] pestilent Feavers. Scurvies, the body corrupted with Sea-diet, Beef and Pork tainted, Butter and Cheese corrupted, fish rotten, a long voyage, coming into the searching sharpness of a purer climate, causeth death and sickness amongst them.

Men and women keep their complexions, but lose their Teeth: the Women are pittifully Tooth-shaken; whether through the coldness of the climate, or by sweet-meats of which they have store, I am not able to affirm, for the Toothach I have found the

275. Quinsies: tonsillitis or inflammation of the throat. Almonds: tonsils, which are subject to "Impostumations" or abscesses. Distempers of cold: influenza. Among the New England writers alluded to here, foremost in view perhaps was William Wood, who wrote: "In publike assemblies it is strange to heare a man sneeze or cough as ordinarily they doe in old *England*" (5).

276. Chancres or ulcers of the face. "'The whole nose is frequently destroyed by the progressive ravages of this peculiar disorder, which sometimes cannot be stopped or retarded by any treatment, external or internal'" (Felter 41n).

following medicine very available, Brimstone and Gunpowder compounded with butter, rub the mandible with it, the outside being first warm'd.

For falling of the hair occasioned by the coldness of the climate, and to make it curl, take of the strong water called Rhum and wash or bath your head therewith, it is an admirable remedie.

For kibed[277] heels, to heal them take the yellowest part of Rozen, pulverize it and work it in the palm of your hand with the tallow of a candle to a salve, and lay of it to the sore.

For frozen limbs, a plaister framed with Soap, Bay-salt, and Molosses is sure, or Cow-dung boiled in milk and applyed.

For Warts and Corns, bathe them with Sea-water.

[p. 186] There was in the Countrey not long since living two men that voided worms seven times their length. Likewise a young maid that was troubled with a sore pricking at her heart, still as she lean'd her body or stept down with her foot to the one side or the other; this maid during her distemper voided worms of the length of a finger all hairy with black heads; it so fell out that the maid dyed; her friends desirous to discover the cause of the distemper of her heart, had her open'd, and found two crooked bones growing upon the top of the heart, which as she bowed her body to the right or left side would job their points into one and the same place, till they had worn a hole quite through. At *Cape-Porpus* lived an honest poor planter of middle-age, and strong of body, but so extreamly troubled with two lumps (or wens as I conjectured) within him, on each side one, that he could not rest for the day nor night, being of great weight, and swagging to the one side or the other, according to the motion or posture of his body; at last he dyed in *Anno* 1668 as I think, or thereabouts. Some Chirurgeons there were that profferred to open him, but his wife would not assent to it, and so his disease was hidden in the Grave.

[p. 187] It is the opinion of many men, that the blackness of the *Negroes* proceeded from the curse upon *Cham*'s posterity,[278]

277. Chapped.
278. Cham or Ham was the youngest son of Noah and father to the land of Canaan. His name in Egyptian means "black." In Genesis 9.25 he incurred his father's curse: "And he said, Cursed be Canaan; a servant of servants shall he be

others again will have it to be the property of the climate where they live. I pass by other Philosophical reasons and skill, only render you my experimental knowledge: having a *Barbarie-moor* under cure, whose finger (prickt with the bone of a fish) was Impostumated, after I had lanc'd it and let out the Corruption the skin began to rise with proud flesh under it; this I wore away, and having made a sound bottom I incarnated it, and then laid on my skinning plaister, then I perceived that the *Moor* had one skin more than *Englishmen*; the skin that is basted to the flesh is bloudy and of the same Azure colour with the veins, but deeper than the colour of our *European* veins. Over this is an other skin of a tawny colour and upon that *Epidermis* or *Cuticula*, the flower of the skin (which is that Snakes cast) and this is tawny also, the colour of the blew skin mingling with the tawny makes them appear black. I do not peremptorily affirm this to be the cause, but submit to better judgment.[279] More rarities of this nature I could make known unto you, but I hasten to an end; only a word or two of our *English* Creatures, and then to Sea again.

[p. 188] I have given you an Account of such plants as prosper there, and of such as do not; but so briefly, that I conceive it necessary to afford you some what more of them. *Plantain* I told you sprang up in the Countrey after the *English* came, but it is but one sort, and that is broad-leaved plantain.

Gilliflowers thrive exceedingly there and are very large, the Collibuy or humming-Bird is much pleased with them. Our *English* dames make Syrup of them without fire, they steep them in Wine till it be of a deep colour, and then they put to it spirit of *Vitriol*,[280] it will keep as long as the other.

Eglantine or sweet *Bryer* is best sowen with *Juniper-berries*, two

---

unto his brethren." This passage and the curse continued to be used to defend slavery up till emancipation.

279. This study of the Moor is couched in language suggesting an appeal to the Royal Society, which had noncommittally reviewed *Rarities* in its *Philosophical Transactions* of 15 July 1672. On Josselyn's theory of skin color, Tuckerman has remarked: "Dr. Mitchell, the botanist of Virginia, has a paper on the same topic,—the cause of the negro's color,—in the Philosophical Transactions; but this appears less in accordance with more recent researches . . . than Josselyn's observations" (114n).

280. Sulfuric acid.

or three to one *Eglantine-berry* put into a hole made with a stick, the next year separate and remove them to your banks, in three years time they will make a hedge as high as a man, which you may keep thick and handsome with cutting.

Our *English Clover-grass* sowen thrives very well.

Radishes I have seen there as big as a mans Arm.

Flax and *Hemp* flourish gallantly.

Our *Wheat* i.e. summer *Wheat* many [p. 189] times changeth into *Rye*, and is subject to be blasted, some say with a vapour breaking out of the earth, others, with a wind North-east or North-west, at such time as it flowereth, others again say it is with lightning. I have observed, that when a land of *Wheat* hath been smitten with a blast at one Corner, it hath infected the rest in a weeks time, it begins at the stem (which will be spotted) and goes upwards to the ear making it fruitless:[281] in 1669 the pond that lyeth between *Water-town* and *Cambridge*, cast its fish dead upon the shore, forc't by mineral vapour as was conjectured.

Our fruit-Trees prosper abundantly, *Apple-trees*, *Pear-trees*, *Quince-trees*, *Cherry-trees*, *Plum-trees*, *Barberry-trees*. I have observed with admiration, that the Kernels sown or the Succors planted produce as fair & good fruit, without graffing, as the Tree from whence they were taken: the Countrey is replenished with fair and large Orchards. It was affirmed by one Mr. *Woolcut* (a magistrate in *Connecticut* Colony) at the Captains Messe (of which I was) aboard the Ship I came home in, that he made Five hundred Hogsheads of *Syder* out of his own Orchard in one year. *Syder* is very plentiful in the Countrey, ordinarily sold for Ten shillings a Hogshead. At the tap- [p. 190] houses in *Boston* I have had an Ale-quart spic'd and sweetned with Sugar for a groat, but I shall insert a more delicate mixture of it. Take of *Maligo-Raisons*, stamp them and put milk to them, and put them in an *Hippocras*-bag and let it drain out of it self, put a quantity of this with a spoonful or two of Syrup of *Clove-Gilliflowers* into every bottle, when you bottle your *Syder*, and your *Planter* will have a liquor that exceeds *passada*, the Nectar of the Countrey.[282]

281. Wheat blast, or black stem rust, is an Old World fungus that first appeared in New England in the 1660s. Imported barberries were the hosts that supported one phase of the rust's life cycle.

282. The "Succors" Josselyn suggests planting are suckers or shoots arising

The *Quinces, Cherries, Damsons*, set the Dames a work, *Marmalad* and preserved *Damsons* is to be met with in every house. It was not long before I left the Countrey that I made *Cherry-wine*, and so may others, for there are good store of them both red and black.

Their fruit-trees are subject to two diseases, the *Meazels*, which is when they are burned and scorched with the Sun, and lowsiness, when the wood-peckers job holes in their bark: the way to cure them when they are lowsie is to bore a hole into the main root with an Augur, and pour in a quantity of Brandie or Rhum, and then stop it up with a pin made of the same Tree.

The first Neat carried thither was to [p. 191] *New-Plimouth Anno* 1624. These thrive and increase exceedingly, but grow less in body than those they are bred of yearly.

Horses there are numerous, and here and there a good one, they let them run all the year abroad, and in the winter seldom provide any fother for them, (except it be Magistrates, great Masters and Troopers Horses) which brings them very low in flesh till the spring, and so crest fallen, that their crests never rise again. Here I first met with that excrescence called *Hippomanes*, which by some is said to grow on the forehead of a foal new cast,[283] and that the Mare bites it off as soon as foaled; but this is but a fable. A neighbor at *Black point* having a Mare with foal tyed her up in his Barn, the next day she foaled, and the man standing by spied a thing like a foals tongue to drop out of the foals mouth, which he took up and presented me with it, telling me withal, that he heard many wonderful things reported of it, and that it was rank poyson. I accepted of it gladly and brought it home with me, when it was dry it lookt like Glew, but of a dark brown colour; to omit all other uses for it, this I can assure you that a piece of it soakt in warm water or cold, will take the spots out of wollen Clothes being rub'd thereon.

---

from the base of the tree; his spelling may point to a folk etymology, whereby the parent tree "succors" the infant shoot. Hippocras was a cordial drink of wine flavored with spices and strained through a fine-mesh "*Hippocras* bag." *Passada* may be a variant of *posset*: spiced milk curdled with ale, wine, or vinegar.

283. "*Hippomanes*" is a fleshy substance, reputedly aphrodisiac, said by Pliny to be found upon the forehead of newborn foals (3:115).

[p. 192] *Goats* were the first small Cattle they had in the Countrey, he was counted no body that had not a Trip or Flock of *Goats*: a hee-*Goat* gelt at *Michaelmas* and turn'd out to feed will be fat in a moneths time, & is as good meat as a weather.[284] I was taught by a *Barbary Negro* a medicine which before I proceed any further I will impart unto you, and that was for a swelling under the throat. Take *Goats* hair and clay and boil them in fair water to a poultis, and apply it very warm.

Hoggs are here innumerable, every planter hath a Heard, when they feed upon shell-fish and the like, as they do that are kept near the Sea and by the fishers stages,[285] they tast fishie and rank; but fed with white Oak-Acorns, or *Indian*-Corn and Pease there is not better Pork in the whole world: besides they sometimes have the *Meazels*, which is known when their hinder legs are shorter than ordinary.

Catts and *Dogs* are as common as in *England*, but our *Dogs* in time degenerate; yet they have gallant *Dogs* both for fowl & wild Beasts all over the Countrey: the *Indians* store themselves with them, being much [p. 193] better for their turns, than their breed of wild dogs, which are (as I conceive) like to the *Tasso-canes* or mountain dogs in *Italy*.

Of *English* Poultry too there is good store, they have commonly three broods in a year; the hens by that time they are three years old have spurs like the Cock, but not altogether so big, but as long, they use to crow often, which is so rare a thing in other Countries, that they have a proverb *Gallina recinit* a Hen crowes. And in *England* it is accounted ominous; therefore our Farmers wives as soon as they hear a Hen crow wring off her neck, and so they serve their spur'd Hens, because they should not break their Eggs with their spurs when they sit. In the year 1637.[286] which was when I went my first Voyage to *New-England* a good woman brought aboard with her a lusty Cock and Hen that had horns like spurs growing out on each side of their Combs, but she spoiled the breed, killing of them at Sea, to feed upon, for she loved a fresh bit.

284. Gelt: gelded. Wether: a castrated sheep.
285. Platforms used to dry split fish.
286. In fact, 1638, on 26 April.

In *Anno* 1647/8.[287] certain *Indians* coming to our house clad in *Deere-skin* coats, desired leave to lodge all night in our kitchin, it being a very rainie season, some of them lay down in the middle of the Room, and others under the Table, in the morning they [p. 194] went away before any of the people were up; the poultry had their breakfast usually in cold weather in the kitchin, and because they should not hinder the passing of the people too and again, it was thrown under the Table; in the afternoon they began to hang the wing, in the night the sickest dropt dead from the perch, and the next day most of them dyed; we could not of a sudden ghess at the cause, but thought the *Indians* had either bewitched, or poysoned them: it came at last into my head, seeing their Crops very full, or rather much swell'd, to open them, where I found as much *Deers* hair as Corn, they that pickt up none of the hair lived and did well.

In the year 1667. *October* the 7th amongst our poultry we had one white game Cock of the *French* kind, a bird of high price, when he was three years old he drooped and his spirit was quite gone; one of our *Negro* maids finding him in the yard dead brought him into the house and acquainted me with it. I caused her to draw him, when his guts were all drawn out she put in her hand again and felt a lump in his body as big as a half-penny loaf, strongly fastned to his back, and much ado she had to pull it out; I found it to be a tuff bag, containing stuff like liver, and very heavie, at one end [p. 195] of the bag, another little bag filled with a fatty matter, his gizard, liver, and heart wasted. The Pipe or Roupe is a common disease amongst their poultry infecting one another with it. I conceive it cometh of a cold moisture of the brain, they will be very sleepie with it, the best cure for it is *Garlick*, and smoaking of them with dryed *Hysope*.[288]

In *September* following my Arrivage in the *Massachusets* about the twelfth hour of the eight day, I shipt my self and goods in a Bark bound to the East-ward, meeting as we sailed out the *Dutch* Governour of *New-Netherlands*, who was received and entertained at *Boston* by the Governour and Magistrates with great sol-

287. Evidently a misprint for 1667/8.
288. Roup is a poultry disease characterized by swellings of the rump. In Leviticus 14.1−7 the aromatic herb hyssop figures in a cure for leprosy.

emnity.[289] About nine of the clock at night we came to *Salem* and lay aboard all night.

The Ninth day we went ashore to view the Town which is a mile long, and lay that night at a Merchants house.

The Tenth day we came from *Salem* about twelve of the clock back to *Marble-head*: here we went ashore and recreated our selves with Musick and a cup of Sack and saw the Town, about ten at night we returned to our Bark and lay aboard.

The Eleventh being Saturday, and the wind contrary, we came to *Charles-town*, [p. 196] again about twelve of the clock we took store of *Mackarel*.

The Thirteenth being Monday, we went aboard again about nine of the clock in the morning and out to Sea, about Sun going down we took store of *Mackarel*. The wind was scanty all along, and in the night time we durst not bear much sail, because of the Rocks and foaming breakers that lay in our way.

The Fourteenth day we came up with *Pascataway*, or *Pascatique*, where there is a large River and a fair harbour, within here is seated a Colony, properly belonging to the Heirs of Captain *Mason* sometime since of *London*; but taken into the Colony of *Massachusets*, by what right I will not here discuss.[290]

The chiefest places of note are the *Bay* or *Harbour* North from *Boston*, on the West-side of the Harbour are built many fair houses, and so in another part called *Strawberry-bank*.

By the harbour is an Island which of late days is filled with buildings; besides there are two Towns more seated up higher upon the River, the one called *Dover*; the River-banks are clothed with stately Timber, and here are two miles meadow land and arable enough; the other Town is called *Excester*.[291]

[p. 197] At the River *Pascataway* begins the Province of *Main*: having pleased our selves with the sight of *Pascataway* at a distance we sailed on, and came to *Black-point*.

The Fifteenth day, about eight of the clock at night, where the

289. Peter Stuyvesant surrendered New Netherland to the British in 1664 and lived on his farm on the Bowery till his death in 1672.

290. John Mason (1586–1635) founded a settlement on the Piscataqua River. Massachusetts Bay annexed the region in 1652.

291. Dover and Exeter are now part of New Hampshire.

next day I was shrewdly pinched with a great frost, but having two or three bottles of excellent *Passada*, and good cheer bestowed upon me I made shift to bear it out, and now we are in the Province of *Main*.

The Province of *Main*, (or the Countrey of the *Traquoes*) heretofore called *Laconia* or *New-Summersetshire*, is a Colony belonging to the Grandson of Sir *Ferdinando Gorges* of *Ashton Phillips* in the County of *Sommerset*, the said Sir *Ferdinando Gorges* did expend in planting several parts of *New-England* above Twenty thousand pounds *sterling*, and when he was between three and four score years of age did personally engage in our Royal Martyrs service; and particularly in the Seige of *Bristow*, and was plundered and imprisoned several times, by reason whereof he was discountenanced by the pretended Commissioners for forraign plantations, and his Province incroached upon by the *Massachusets* Colony, who assumed the Government thereof.[292] His Majestie that now Reigneth sent over his Com- [p. 198] missioners to reduce them within their bounds, and to put Mr. *Gorges* again into possession. But there falling out a contest about it, the Commissioners settled it in the Kings name (until the business should be determined before his Majestie) and gave Commissions to the Judge of their Courts, and the Justices to Govern and Act according to the Laws of *England*, & by such Laws of their own as were not repugnant to them: But as soon as the Commissioners were returned for *England*, the *Massachusets* enter the province in a hostile manner with a Troop of Horse and Foot and turn'd the Judge and his Assistants off the Bench, Imprisoned the Major or Commander of the Militia, threatned the Judge, and some others that were faithful to Mr. *Gorges* interests. I could discover many other foul proceedings, but for some reasons which might be given, I conceive it not convenient to make report thereof to vulgar ears; & *quæ supra nos nihil ad nos.*[293] Onely this

292. Ferdinando Gorges (c. 1566–1647) has been called the father of American colonization. Knighted for military service in 1591, he was a founding member of the Plymouth Company (1606) and the Council for New England (1620). Ashton Phillips was the Gorges estate in Somerset. The siege of Bristol, in which Gorges played some small part, was a 1643 Civil War battle won by Royalists.

293. Those things above are nothing to us.

I could wish, that there might be some consideration of the great losses, charge and labour, which hath been sustained by the Judge, and some others for above thirty years in upholding the rights of Mr. *Gorge* and his Sacred Majesties Dominion against a many stubborn and elusive people.

[p. 199] *Anno. Dom.* 1623. Mr. *Robert Gorge*, Sir *Ferdinando Gorges* brother[294] had for his good service granted him by Patent from the Council of *Plimouth* all that part of the Land commonly called *Massachusiack*, situated on the North-side of the Bay of *Massachusets*.

Not long after this Sir *Ferdinando Gorges* had granted to him by Patent from the middest of *Merrimack*-River to the great River *Sagadehock*, then called *Laconia*.

In 1635. Capt. *William Gorge*, Sir *Ferdinando's* Nephew, was sent over Governour of the Province of *Main*, then called *New-Sumersetshire*.

Sir *Ferdinando Gorge* received a Charter-Royal from King *Charles* the first the third of *April* in the Fifteenth of his Raign, granting to him all that part and portion of *New-England*, lying and being between the River of *Pascataway*, that is, beginning at the entrance of *Pascataway-harbour*, and so to pass up the same into the River of *Newichawanoe* or *Neqhechewanck*,[295] and through the same into the farthest head thereof aforesaid, North-eastward along the Seacoasts, for Sixty miles to *Sagadehoc*-River to *Kenebeck*, even as far as the head thereof, and up into the main land North-westward for the space of one hundred and twenty [p. 200] miles.[296] To these Territories are adjoyned the North half-Isle of *Sholes*, with several other Islands, it lyeth between 44 degrees and 45 of Northerly latitude. The River *Canada* on the North-east the Sea coast South, amongst many large Royalties, Jurisdictions and Immunities was also granted to the said Sir *Fer-*

---

294. In fact, his son.

295. Newichawannock is now Berwick, Maine.

296. Gorges received his patent for the province of Maine in 1639. As James P. Baxter has written in *The Trelawny Papers*, "The extraordinary Charter of King Charles to Gorges of the Province of Maine . . . made him, his heirs and associates, absolute Lords Proprietors of the province, excepting only 'the faith and alleageaunce and the supreme dominion' due to the Crown" (316n). See also Andrews (1:419–23).

dinando Gorge, the same Royalties, priviledges and franchises as are, or of right ought to be enjoyed by the Bishop of *Durham* in the County Palatine of *Durham*; the planters to pay for every hundred Acres of land yearly, two shillings six pence, that is such land as is given to them and their Heirs for ever.

The Officers by Patent are a Deputy Governour, a Chancellor, a Treasurer, a Marshall for Souldiers, an Admiraltie for Sea affairs, and a Judge of the Admiraltie, a Master of Ordinance, a Secretary, *&c.*

Towns there are not many in this province. *Kittery* situated not far from *Pascataway* is the most populous.

Next to that Eastward is seated by a River near the Sea *Gorgiana*,[297] a Majoraltie, and the Metropolitan of the province.

Further to the Eastward is the Town of *Wells*.

Cape-Porpus Eastward of that, where there is a Town by the Sea side of the same name, [p. 201] the houses scatteringly built, all these Towns have store of salt and fresh marsh with arable land, and are well stockt with Cattle.

About eight or nine mile to the Eastward of *Cape-Porpus*, is *Winter-harbour*,[298] a noted place for Fishers, here they have many stages.

Saco adjoyns to this, and both make one scattering Town of large extent, well stored with Cattle, arable land and marshes, and a Saw-mill.

Six mile to the Eastward of *Saco* & forty mile from *Gorgiana* is seated the Town of *Black point*, consisting of about fifty dwelling houses, and a Magazine or *Doganne*, scatteringly built, they have store of neat and horses, of sheep near upon Seven or Eight hundred, much arable and marsh salt and fresh, and a Corn-mill.[299]

To the Southward of the *point* (upon which are stages for fishermen) lye two small Islands beyond the *point*, North-eastward runs the River *Spurwinch*.

Four miles from *Black-point*, one mile from *Spurwinch*-River

297. Now York, Maine.
298. The present Winter Harbor, Maine is much further east, near Bar Harbor. Josselyn must intend the site of present-day Camp Ellis.
299. Black Point now is Scarborough. *Doganne*: Italian *dogana*, custom house.

Eastward lyeth *Richmans-Island*, whose longitude is 317 degrees 30 seconds, and latitude 43 degrees and 34 minutes, it is three mile in circumference, and hath a passable and gravelly ford on the [p. 202] North-side, between the main and the Sea at low-water: here are found excellent Whetstones, and here likewise are stages for fishermen.

Nine mile Eastward of *Black-point* lyeth scatteringly the Town of *Casco* upon a large Bay, stored with Cattle, Sheep, Swine, abundance of marsh and Arable land, a Corn-mill or two, with stages for fishermen.

Further Eastward is the Town of *Kenebeck* seated upon the River.

Further yet East-ward is *Sagadehock*, where there are many houses scattering, and all along stages for fishermen, these too are stored with Cattle and Corn lands.

The mountains and hills that are to be taken notice of, are first *Acomenticus* hills, between *Kettery* and *Gorgiana*, the high hills of *Ossapey* to the West-ward of *Saco* River, where the princely *Pilhanaw* Ayries, the white mountains, to the North-ward of *Black-point*, the highest *Terrasse* in *New-England*, you have the description of it in my Treatise of the rarities of *New-England*.

A Neighbour of mine rashly wandering out after some stray'd Cattle, lost his way, and coming as we conceived by his Relation near to the head spring of some of the branches of *Black-point* River or *Saco*-River, [p. 203] light into a Tract of land for God knowes how many miles full of delfes and dingles,[300] and dangerous precipices, Rocks and inextricable difficulties which did justly daunt, yea quite deter him from endeavoring to pass any further: many such like places are to be met with in *New-England*.

The ponds or lakes in this province are very large and many, out of which the great Rivers have their original; we read of the lake *Balsena* that is thirty miles about, here are that come very near to it, stored with all sorts of fresh water fish; and if you will believe report, in one of them huge fishes like Whales are to be seen, and some of them have fair Islands in them. Twelve mile from *Casco-bay*, and passable for men and horses, is a lake called

---

300. Valleys or clefts between hills. The *OED* contains no citation for this exact use of *delf*, which ordinarily denotes a hollow delved or dug by hand.

by the *Indians Sebug*,[301] on the brink thereof at one end is the famous Rock shap'd like a *Moose-Deere* or *Helk*, Diaphanous, and
called the *Moose-Rock*. Here are found stones like Crystal, and
Lapis Specularis or *Muscovia* glass both white and purple.

On the East-side of *Black-point* River upon a plain, close to the
Sea-bank is a pond two mile in compass, fish it produceth, but
those very small and black, and a number of Frogs and Snakes,
and much fre- [p. 204] quented by wild-fowl, *Ducks*, *Teal*, and
wild-*Swans*, and *Geese*, especially spring and fall when they pass
along to the South-ward, and return again to the North-ward
where they breed.

The principal Rivers in the province of *Main*, are *Pascataway*-
River, *York*-River, *Kenibunck*-River, near to this River clay bullets were cast up by a mineral vapour, this River is by the Town
of *Wells*.[302] Then *Saco*-River on the East-side of the Town, the
shore Rockie all along both sides, where musick echoes from several places: seven miles up the River is a great fall where abundance of *Salmon*, and *Lamprons* are taken at the fall; a great way
up, the River runs upon the Rock, *in rupibus desendendo efficit
rivos*,[303] he cutteth out Rivers among the Rocks, saith *Job*, of the
Almighty, *Job* 28.10. A little above the fall is a saw-mill. Then
Black-point-River divided into many branches; this as most of the
Rivers in *New-England*, is bar'd with a bank of Sand, where the
Indians take *Sturgeon* and *Basse*. *Spur-vinck*-River is next, which
by his near approach to *Black-point*-river maketh that neck of
land almost an Island. Further East-ward is *Kenebeck*-river fifty
leagues off of *New-Plimouth* Eastward, and *Pechipscut*[304] famous
[p. 205] for multitudes of mighty large *Sturgeon*. The last river
of the province East-ward is the great river *Sagadehock* where Sir
John Pophams Colony seated themselves.

The chief harbours are *Cape-porpus*, *Winter-harbour*, in which
are some small Islands[,] *Black-point*, *Richmans-Island*, *Casco-
bay* the largest in the province full of Islands.

301. Sebago.
302. For a map and discussion of the confusions attending identification of
Maine's rivers in early accounts, see Winsor (3:189–91).
303. "He cutteth out rivers among the rocks," a portion of Job 28.10.
304. The Black Point River is now the Nonesuch; the Pechipscut, now the
Androscoggin.

From *Sagadehock* to *Nova Scotia* is called the Duke of *Yorkes* province, here *Pemmaquid, Montinicus, Mohegan, Capeanawhagen,* where Capt. *Smith* fisht for *Whales; Muscataquid,* all fill'd with dwelling houses and stages for fishermen, and have plenty of Cattle, arable land and marshes.[305]

Nova Scotia was sold by the Lord *Starling* to the *French,* and is now wholly in their possession.[306]

Now we are come to *New-found-land,* which is over against the gulf of St. *Lawrence,* an Island near as spacious as *Ireland,* and lyeth distant from the Continent as far as *England* is from the nearest part of *France,* and near half the way between *Ireland* and *Virginia,* its longitude is 334 degrees 20 seconds, and North latitude 46 degrees 30 minutes, or as others will 53 minutes. *The longitude of places are uncertainly reported, but in latitudes most agree.* [p. 206] *Longitude is the distance of the meridian of any place from the meridian which passeth over the Isles of* Azores, *where the beginning of longitude is said to be. The meridian is a great circle dividing the Equinoctial at right Angles into two equal parts, passing also through both the Poles, and the Zenith, to which circle the Sun coming twice every* 24 *hours, maketh the middle of the day, and the middle of the night. Every place hath a several meridian, but they all meet in the poles of the world. Latitude is counted from the Equinoctial to the end of* 30 *degrees on each side thereof. The Equinoctial is a great circle imagined in the Heavens, also dividing the heavens into two equal parts, and lying just in the middle betwixt the two poles, being in compass from West to East,* 360 *degrees, every degree thereof on the terrestrial Globe valuing* 20 *English miles, or* 60 *miles.*

Into the Bay of St. *Lawrence* the River of St. *Lawrence* or *Canada* disimbogues[307] it self, a River far exceeding any River in the elder world, thirty or forty mile over at the mouth, and in the

---

305. Pemaquid Point, the Matinicus Islands, Monhegan Island, Cape Anawagen (now Cape Newagen), and Muscongus Island were sites of early settlements in Maine (Burrage 172). There is an account of Captain John Smith's whaling trip (1:323) in the first page of his *Description of New England* (1616).

306. Lord William Alexander was the son of Sir William Alexander, Earl of Stirling. The efforts of the Alexanders to colonize Nova Scotia were undone by the 1632 Treaty of St. Germain-en-Laye, which involved a compensated restoration of all of Canada to France.

307. Discharges or empties.

Channel one hundred fathom deep; it runs on the back-side of *New-England* and *Virginia*: the *French* (it is said) have gone up six weeks voyage in it, and have not yet discovered the spring-head:[308] the longitude is 334 degrees [p. 207] 11 seconds, in 50 degrees 21 minutes of North latitude. This may satisfie a modest Reader, and I hope yield no offence to any. I shall onely speak a word or two of the people in the province of *Main* and the Dukes province, and so conclude.

The people in the province of *Main* may be divided into Magistrates, Husbandmen, or Planters, and fishermen; of the Magistrates some be Royalists, the rest perverse Spirits, the like are the planters and fishers, of which some be planters and fishers both, others meer fishers.

Handicrafts-men there are but few, the Tumelor[309] or Cooper, Smiths and Carpenters are best welcome amongst them, shopkeepers there are none, being supplied by the *Massachusets* Merchants with all things they stand in need of, keeping here and there fair Magazines stored with *English* goods, but they set excessive prices on them, if they do not gain *Cent per Cent*, they cry out that they are losers, hence *English* shooes are sold for Eight and Nine shillings a pair, worsted stockins of Three shillings six pence a pair, for Seven and Eight shillings a pair, Douglass that is sold in *England* for one or two and twenty pence an ell,[310] for four shillings a yard, Serges of two shillings or three shillings a yard, for Six and Seven [p. 208] shillings a yard, and so all sorts of Commodities both for planters and fishermen, as Cables, Cordage, Anchors, Lines, Hooks, Nets, Canvas for Sails, *&c.* Bisket twenty five shillings a hundred, Salt at an excessive rate, pickled-herrin for winter bait Four and five pound a barrel (with which they speed not so well as the waggish lad at *Cape-porpus*, who baited his hooks with the drown'd *Negro*'s buttocks)[,] so for Pork and Beef.

The planters are or should be restless pains takers, providing for their Cattle, planting and sowing of Corn, fencing their

308. The expedition of Jacques Cartier up the Saint Lawrence River occurred in 1535; an account of his voyage appeared in Hakluyt in 1600.

309. No *OED* citation. Possibly related to the French *tonnelier*, "cooper."

310. Douglass: untraced, although probably a woolen fabric. An ell was a measure of length, forty-five inches by English reckoning.

grounds, cutting and bringing home fuel, cleaving of claw-board[311] and pipe-staves, fishing for fresh water fish and fowling takes up most of their time, if not all; the diligent hand maketh rich, but if they be of a droanish disposition as some are, they become wretchedly poor and miserable, scarce able to free themselves and family from importunate famine, especially in the winter for want of bread.[312]

They have a custom of taking Tobacco, sleeping at noon, sitting long at meals sometimes four times in a day, and now and then drinking a dram of the bottle extraordinarily: the smoaking of Tobacco, if moderately used refresheth the weary much, and so doth sleep.

> [p. 209] *A Traveller five hours doth crave*
> *To sleep, a Student seven will have,*
> *And nine sleeps every Idle knave.*[313]

The Physitian allowes but three draughts at a meal, the first for need, the second for pleasure, and the third for sleep; but little observed by them, unless they have no other liquor to drink but water. In some places where the springs are frozen up, or at least the way to their springs made unpassable by reason of the snow and the like, they dress their meat in *Aqua Cælestis*, i.e. melted snow, at others times it is very well cookt, and they feed upon (generally) as good flesh, Beef, Pork, Mutton, Fowl and fish as any in the whole world besides.

Their Servants which are for the most part *English*, when they are out of their time,[314] will not work under half a Crown a day,

311. Claw-board: clapboard.

312. Compare William Wood's less compassionate assessment of the early settlers. Those who disparage New England, he writes, are generally of a "droanish disposition, that would live of the sweate of another mans browes" (48).

313. See the *Epigrams* of Francis Daniel Pastorius (1651–1720), poet and founder of Germantown, Pennsylvania:

> The *hours* for *Sleep* I thus prefix:
> To students five; to Merchants six,
> To gentlemen I do grant seven,
> To sluggards eight, to Fools eleven.
>   (Meserole 487)

314. That is, when their periods of indenture have expired.

although it be for to make hay, and for less I do not see how they can, by reason of the dearness of clothing. If they hire them by the year, they pay them Fourteen or Fifteen pound, yea Twenty pound at the years end in Corn, Cattle and fish: some of these prove excellent fowlers, bringing in as many as will maintain their masters house; besides the profit that accrews by their feathers. [p. 210] They use (when it is to be had) a great round shot, called *Barstable* shot, (which is best for fowl) made of a lead blacker than our common lead, to six pound of shot they allow one pound of powder, Cannon powder is esteemed best.[315]

The fishermen take yearly upon the coasts many hundred kentals of Cod, hake, haddock, polluck &c. which they split, salt and dry at their stages, making three voyages in a year. When they share their fish (which is at the end of every voyage) they separate the best from the worst, the first they call Merchantable fish, being sound, full grown fish and well made up, which is known when it is clear like a Lanthorn horn and without spots; the second sort they call refuse fish, that is such as is salt burnt, spotted, rotten, and carelessly ordered: these they put off to the *Massachusets* Merchants; the merchantable for thirty and two and thirty ryals a kental, (a kental is an hundred and twelve pound weight) the refuse for Nine shillings and Ten shillings a kental, the Merchant sends the merchantable fish to *Lisbonne, Bilbo, Burdeaux, Marsiles, Talloon, Rochel, Roan*, and other Cities of *France*, to the *Canaries* with claw-board and pipe-staves which is there and at the *Charibs* a prime Commodity: the refuse fish they put [p. 211] off at the *Charib-Islands, Barbadoes, Jamaica*, &c. who feed their *Negroes* with it.

To every Shallop belong four fishermen, a Master or Steersman, a Midship-man, and a Foremast-man, and a shore man who washes it out of the salt, and dries it upon hurdles pitcht upon stakes breast high and tends their Cookery; these often get in one voyage Eight or Nine pound a man for their shares, but it doth some of them little good, for the Merchant to increase his gains [begins] by putting off his Commodity in the midst of their voyages, and at the end thereof comes in with a walking

315. Wood writes similarly that, for fowling, "a great round shot called *Bastable*-shot, is the best; being made of a blacker lead than ordinary shot" (52).

Tavern, a Bark laden with the Legitimate bloud of the rich grape, which they bring from *Phial, Madera, Canaries*, with *Brandy, Rhum*, the *Barbadoes strong-water*, and *Tobacco*, coming ashore he gives them a Taster or two, which so charms them, that for no perswasions that their imployers can use will they go out to Sea, although fair and seasonable weather, for two or three days, nay sometimes a whole week till they are wearied with drinking, taking ashore two or three Hogsheads of *Wine* and *Rhum* to drink off when the Merchant is gone. If a man of quality chance to come where they are roystering and gulling in *Wine* with a dear felicity, he must be sociable and *Roly-poly* with them, taking off [p. 212] their liberal cups as freely, or else be gone, which is best for him, for when *Wine* in their guts is at full tide, they quarrel, fight and do one another mischief, which is the conclusion of their drunken compotations.³¹⁶ When the day of payment comes, they may justly complain of their costly sin of drunkenness, for their shares will do no more than pay the reckoning; if they save a Kental or two to buy shooes and stockins, shirts and wastcoats with, 'tis well, otherwayes they must enter into the Merchants books for such things as they stand in need off, becoming thereby the Merchants slaves, & when it riseth to a big sum are constrained to mortgage their plantation if they have any, the Merchant when the time is expired is sure to seize upon their plantation and stock of Cattle, turning them out of house and home, poor Creatures, to look out for a new habitation in some remote place where they begin the world again. The lavish planters have the same fate, partaking with them in the like bad husbandry, of these the Merchant buys Beef, Pork, Pease, Wheat and *Indian* Corn, and sells it again many times to the fishermen. Of the same nature are the people in the Dukes province, who not long before I left the Countrey petitioned the Governour and Magistrates in [p. 213] the *Massachusets* to take them into their Government, Birds of a feather will ralley together.

Anno Dom. 1671. The year being now well spent, and the Government of the province turned topsiturvy, being heartily weary and expecting the approach of winter, I took my leave of my friends at *Black-point*. And on the 28 of *August* being Mon-

316. Roistering: acting in boisterous or blustery fashion; gulling: guzzling.

day I shipt my self and my goods aboard of a shallop bound for *Boston*: towards Sun set, the wind being contrary, we put into *Gibbons* his Island, a small Island in *Winter-harbour* about two leagues from *Black-point* West-ward, here we stayed till the 30. day being Wednesday, about nine of the clock we set sail, and towards Sun-set came up with *Gorgiana*, the 31 day being Thursday we put into *Cape-Ann*-harbour about Sun-set. *September* the 1 being Saturday in the morning before day we set sail and came to *Boston* about three of the clock in the afternoon, where I found the Inhabitants exceedingly afflicted with griping of the guts, and Feaver, and Ague, and bloudy Flux.

The Eight day of *October* being Wednesday, I boarded the new-Supply of *Boston* 120 Tun, a Ship of better sail than defence, her Guns being small, and for salutation only, the Master Capt. *Fairweather*, her [p. 214] sailers 16. and as many passengers. Towards night I returned to *Boston* again, the next day being Thanksgiving day,[317] on Fryday the Tenth day we weighed Anchor and fell down to *Hull*.

The 12 and 13 day about 20 leagues from *Cape-Sable* a bitter storm took us, beginning at seven of the clock at night, which put us in terrible fear of being driven upon the *Cape*, or the Island of *Sables* where many a tall ship hath been wrackt.

November the One and twenty about two of the clock afternoon we saw within kenning before us thick clouds, which put us in hope of land, the *Boson*[318] brings out his purse, into which the passengers put their good will, then presently he nails it to the main-mast, up go the boyes to the main-mast-top sitting there like so many *Crowes*, when after a while one of them cryes out land, which was glad tidings to the wearied passengers, the boyes descend, and the purse being taken from the mast was distributed amongst them, the lad that first descryed land having a double share: about three of the clock *Scilly* was three leagues off.

The Four and twentieth day we came to *Deal*, from thence the 25. to *Lee*, the 26. being Sunday we stemmed the Tide to *Gravesend*, about two of the clock af- [p. 215] ternoon. The 27 we came

317. This is the earliest printed record of *Thanksgiving Day* in the language, according to the *OED*.

318. Bo's'n or boatswain, a petty officer in charge of the crew. Compare this anecdote with "The Quarter-Deck" chapter of Herman Melville's *Moby-Dick*.

up with *Wollich*[319] where I landed and refresht my self for that night, next day I footed it four or five miles to *Bexley* in *Kent* to visit a near kinsman, the next day proved rainie, the 30 day being Fryday my kinsman accommodated me with a Horse and his man to *Greenwich*, where I took a pair of Oars and went aboard our Ship then lying before *Radcliff*, here I lay that night. Next day being Saturday, and the first of *December* I cleared my goods, shot the bridge and landed at the *Temple*[320] about seven of the clock at night, which makes my voyage homeward 7 weeks and four days, and from my first setting out from *London* to my returning to *London* again Eight years Six moneths and odd days.

Now by the merciful providence of the Almighty, having perform'd Two voyages to the North-east parts of the Western-world, I am safely arrived in my Native Countrey; having in part made good the *French* proverb, Travail where thou canst, but dye where thou oughtest, that is, in thine own Countrey.

Finis.[321]

319. Woolwich, a metropolitan borough of east London.

320. One of the four Inns of Court in London. Josselyn apparently rowed a boat from Greenwich, stopped for inspection at the custom house, then passed beneath London Bridge ("shot the bridge") on an incoming tide. What he saw must have startled him, since London was rebuilding after the Great Fire of 1666.

321. All descriptions of the *Two Voyages* record errors in pagination at this point. In my copy text, p. 216 is blank. Next is an unnumbered title leaf for the "Chronological Observations," the verso of which is blank. Three pages comprising "The Preface" follow, the first numbered 223, the other two unnumbered. One blank verso precedes the first leaf of the chronology, which is paginated 224. The second leaf, without any break in the language sense, is paginated 227, 228. The gather/signature pattern is unaffected.

CHRONOLOGICAL
OBSERVATIONS OF AMERICA,

*From the year of the World
to the year of Christ
1673.*

LONDON:
Printed for *Giles Widdowes*, at the *Green-Dragon* in St. *Paul's*-Church-yard, 1674.

[page break]
[p. 223]   THE PREFACE.

The Terrestrial World is by our learned Geographers divided into four parts, Europe, Asia, Africa *and* America *so named from* Americus Vespucius *the* Florentine, *Seven years after* Columbus; *although* Columbus *and* Cabota *deserved rather the honour of being Godfathers to it: notwithstanding by this name it is now known to us, but was utterly unknown to the Ancient* Europeans *before their times, I will not say to the* Africans *and* Asians, *for* Plato *in his* Timeus *relateth of a great Island, called* Atlantis, *and* Philo *the* Jew *in his book* De Mundo, that it was over-flowen with water, by reason of a mighty Earthquake; The like hap- [page break] pened to it 600 years before *Plato:* thus was the *Atlantick* Ocean, caused to be a

148

Sea, *if you will believe the same Philosopher, who flourished* 366 *years before the Birth of our Saviour.*[1]

America *is bounded on the South with the streight of* Magellan, *where there are many Islands distinguished by an interflowing Bay; the West with the pacifique Sea, or* mare-del-zur, *which Sea runs toward the North, separateing it from the East parts of* Asia; *on the East with the* Atlantick, *or our Western Ocean called* mare-del-Nort; *and on the North with the Sea that separateth it from* Groveland,[2] *thorow which Seas the supposed passage to* China *lyeth; these north parts, as yet are but barely discovered by our voyagers.*

The length of this new World between the streights of Anian *and* Magellan *is* 2400 German *miles, in breadth between* Cabo de fortuna *near the* Anian *streights is* 1300 German *miles.*[3] *About* 18 *leagues from* Nombre [page break] de dios, *on the South-Sea lyeth* Panama *(a City having three fair Monasteries in it) where the narrowest part of the Countrey is, it is much less than* Asia, *and far bigger than* Europe, *and as the rest of the world divided into Islands and Continent, the Continent supposed to contain about* 1152400000 *Acres.*

The Native people I have spoken of already: The discoverers and Planters of Colonies, especially in the North-east parts; together with a continuation of the proceedings of the English *in* New-England, *from the first year of their setling there to purpose, to this present year of our Lord* 1673. *with many other things by the way inserted and worth the observing I present unto your view in this ensuing Table.*
[page break]
[page break]

1. Philo Judaeus (fl. 20 B.C.–A.D. 40) was greatly influenced by the *Timaeus* of Plato, who died 347 B.C.

2. Greenland evidently is intended.

3. The ancient German mile varied between three and six English miles. The mythical Strait of Anian was supposed to connect the Atlantic and Pacific oceans; for an interesting study of this belief, see Gordon Speck (235ff). The Anian myth began with the Spaniards but had its greatest impact upon the English when disseminated by Humphrey Gilbert's promotional *Discourse* (1576), which strove to prove the existence of a northwest passage.

Anno Mundi, *3720.*[4]

Britain known to the *Græcians* as appeared by *Polybius* the *Greek* Historian 265 years before the Birth of our Saviour, & after him *Athenæus* a *Greek* Author of good account 170 before Christ, related that *Hiero* sent for a mast for a great Ship that he had built to *Britain*.[5]

3740.

Hanno the *Carthaginian*[6] flourished, who sent to discover the great Island *Atlantis*, i.e. *America*.

3873.

Britain unknown to the *Romans* was first discovered to them by *Julius Cæsar*, 54 years before the Birth of Christ,[7] who took it to be part of the Continent of *France*, and got nothing but the sight of that part called afterwards *England*, which is the South of *Britain*.

Anno Domini, *86.*

Britain discovered to be an Island, and conquered by *Julius Agricola* 136. years after *Julius Cæsars* entrance into it.[8]

99.

[p. 224] The Emperour *Trajan* flourished and stretched the Confines of the *Roman* Empire, unto the remotest Dominions of the *East Indies*, who never before that time had heard of a *Roman*.[9]

---

4. Josselyn is following the biblical timetable from creation, as it is still reckoned at the Jewish New Year.

5. Polybius' (c. 205–125 B.C.) *Histories* recounts Roman history from 266 to 146 B.C.; the work of Athenaeus, his contemporary, is titled *The Deipnosophists*.

6. Navigator of the sixth to fifth centuries B.C. who voyaged down the west coast of Africa.

7. Caesar invaded Britain 55–54 B.C.

8. Father-in-law of Tacitus, Agricola pacified Britain in A.D. 78.

9. Trajan conducted successful wars against the Parthians from A.D. 114 to 116.

745.

Boniface Bishop of *Mens* a City in *Germany*, was accused before Pope *Zachary* in the time of *Ethelred* King of the *East-Angles* for Heresie, *&c.* in that he averred there were Antipodes. St. *Augustine* and *Lactantius* opinion was that there were none.[10]

827.

Egbert the *Saxon* Monarch changed the name of the people in *England*, and called them *English-men*.

844.

The *Turks* or *Scythians* came from thence in the time of *Ethelwolf* King of the *West-Saxons*. If the *Ottoman*-line should fail, the *Chrim Tartar* is to succeed, being both of one Family.

959.

Edgar Sirnamed the Peaceable, the 30 Monarch of the *English*, caused the Wolves to be destroyed by imposing a Tribute upon the Princes of *Wales*; and *Fage* Prince of *North-Wales* paid him yearly 300 Wolves, [p. 227] which continued three years space, in the fourth year there was not a Wolf to be found, and so the Tribute ceased.[11]

1160.

In the Emperours *Frederick Barbarossa's* time,[12] certain *West-Indians* came into *Germany*.

1170.

Madoc the Son of *Owen Gwineth* Prince of *North-Wales* his

---

10. Winifred, an English Benedictine missionary, later Saint Boniface (c. 680–755), became archbishop of Mainz in 748. Antipode: a person representing the diametrical opposite of one's character, frequently figured as inhabiting the opposite side of earth. Firmianus Lactantius wrote Christian tracts during the latter third and early fourth centuries.

11. That is, Edgar (944–75) demanded homage or tribute from his subject prince Fage after becoming the king of united England.

12. Frederick I, king of Sicily (1198–1212) and Holy Roman Emperor.

voyage to the *West-Indies*, he planted a Colony in the Western part
of the Countrey, in our *Henry* the Seconds Raign.[13]

1300.

Flavio of *Malphi* in *Naples*[14] invented the Compass in our
Edward the firsts time.

1330.

The *Canaries* discovered by an *English* Ship.[15]

1337.

In *Edward* the third's time a Comet appeared, continuing 30
days.

1344.

Machan an *English-man* accidentally discovered *Madera-
Island*.[16]

1350.

Estotiland discovered by fishermen of *Freez-land*,[17] in *Edward*
the third's Raign.

1360.

The Franciscan-Fryer *Nicholas de Linno*,[18] [p. 228] who is
said to discover the Pole by his black Art, went thither in the
Raign of *Edward* the Third.

13. Madog ab Owain Gwynedd (1150–c. 1180), legendary Welsh prince
said by his countrymen to have discovered America.

14. Flavio Biondo (1388–1463), Italian historian and antiquary.

15. Reputedly discovered instead by an Italian, Lancelot Malocello, in
1270.

16. The Portuguese navigator Zarco discovered the Madeira island group
in 1420.

17. Mythical land thought to lie near Newfoundland and to host a rich
kingdom. The Italian brothers Nicolo and Antonio Zeno (d. 1406) were responsible for the legends of Frislanda, Engrönland, and Estotiland; their maps
were also very influential.

18. Perhaps Nicholas of Lyra (c. 1270–c. 1390), Franciscan professor at
the Sorbonne.

1372.

Sir *John Mandivel*,[19] the Great Traveller dyed at *Leige* a City in the *Netherland* Provinces in *Edward* the Third's Raign.

1380.

Nicholas and *Antonio Zeni*, two Noble Gentlemen of *Venice* were driven by Tempest upon the Island of *Estotiland* or *Gronland*,[20] in our *Edward* the Third's Raign.

1417.

The *Canaries* Conquered by *Betan-Court* a *Frenchman*.[21]

1420

The Island of *Madera* discovered in our *Henry* the Fifth's time.

1428.

The Island *Puerto Santo*, or *Holy-port* distant from *Madera* 40 miles, discovered by *Portingal* Mariners on *All-hallowes-day*, and therefore called *Holy-port*, it is in compass 150 miles, in *Henry* the Sixth's Raign.

1440.

The Island of *Cape de verd discovered.*[22]

1452.

The *Marine* parts of *Guinea*[23] discovered by the *Portingals* in *Henry* the Sixth's Raign.

19. Mandeville (d. 1372) was a pseudonymous compiler of fantastic travel accounts from the East, which he embellished and published in French between 1357 and 1371.

20. Grönland, or Greenland, was identified in the 1625 Purchas translation with the fabulous kingdom allegedly discovered by the Zenos.

21. Jean de Bethencourt battled successfully for the Canary Islands from 1402 to 1406.

22. Cape Verde Islands, discovered in 1456 for Portugal by the Venetian navigator Ca Da Mosto.

23. West African territory claimed by the Portuguese in 1446.

1478.

[p. 229] *Ferdinando* first Monarch of all *Spain*.[24]

1485.

Henry the Seventh began to Raign.

1486.

The Kingdom of *Angola* and *Congo*, with the Islands of St. *George*, St. *James* and St. *Helens* discovered.[25]

1488.

Christopher Columbus a *Genouese* offered the discovery of the *West-Indies* to *Henry* the Seventh.

1492.

Christopher Columbus sent to discover the *West-Indies* by *Ferdinando* King of *Arragon*, and *Isabella* Queen of *Castile*, who descended from *Edward* the Third King of *England*.

The *Caribby-Islands* the *Antilles* or *Canibal*, or *Camerean-Islands* now discovered by *Christopher Columbus*, who took possession of *Florida* and *Hispaniola*[26] for the King of *Spain*.

1493.

Alexander the Sixt Pope of *Rome* a *Spaniard*,[27] took upon him to divide the world by his Bull, betwixt the *Portingal* and the *Spaniard*, bearing date the fourth of *May*, giving to the one the East, and to the other the *West-Indies*.

[p. 230] St. *Jean Porto Rico* discovered by *Christopher Columbus*, *Cuba* and *Jamaica* discovered by him, this was his second voyage.[28]

24. In 1479 Spain was united by the marriage of Isabella of Castile and Ferdinand II of Aragon.

25. Actually in 1484, by Portuguese navigator Diogo Cam.

26. West Indies island now divided between Haiti and the Dominican Republic.

27. Natal name Rodrigo Lanzal y Borja (c. 1431–1503).

28. Named originally San Juan Bautista, for Saint John the Baptist, Puerto Rico was discovered on 19 November 1493; Cuba on 27 October 1492; Jamaica on 5 May 1492.

1495.

Sebastian Cabota the first that attempted to discover the North-west passage at the charge of *Henry* the Seventh.[29]

1497.

Christopher Columbus his third voyage to the *West-Indies*, and now he discovered the Countreys of *Paria* and *Cumana*, with the Islands of *Cubagua* and *Margarita*.[30]

John Cabota and his Son *Sebastian Cabota* sent by *Henry* the Seventh, to discover the *West-Indies*, which they performed from the *Cape* of *Florida* to the 67 degree and a half of Northerly latitude, being said by some to be the first that discovered *Florida*, *Virginia*, and *New-found-land*.[31]

Vasques de Gama his voyage to *Africa*.[32]

1500.

Christopher Columbus his fourth and last voyage to the *West-Indies*.[33]

Jasper Corteriaglis a *Portugal*, his voyage to discover the North-West passage, he discovered *Greenland*, or *Terra Corteriaglis*, or *Terra di Laborodoro*.[34]

1501.

Americus Vesputius a *Florentine* imployed by the King of *Castile* and *Portingal*, to dis- [p. 231] cover the *West-Indies*, named from him Seven year after *Columbus*, *America*.[35]

29. In fact, Henry sent Sebastian's father, John Cabot, in 1497.

30. The Paria Peninsula and the city of Cumana, both part of Venezuela, were claimed by Columbus on 5 August 1498; Cubagua and Margarita, on 15 August.

31. The English based their right of claim to North America largely upon the Cabots' discoveries there. The Cabots were in fact searching for a route to Asia at this time.

32. Vasco da Gama was searching for a route to India.

33. Columbus' fourth voyage actually began in 1502.

34. Gaspar Corte-Real (c. 1450–c. 1501) voyaged to Newfoundland and Labrador in this year.

35. Few facts of Vespucci's voyages are known, though in 1501 he appears to have accompanied the Portuguese master Coelho sent to survey Brazil.

1506.

Christopher Columbus dyed.

1508.

Henry the Seventh dyed *August* the Two and twentieth.[36]
Henry the Eighth King of *England*.

1514.

Sebastian Cabota, the Son of *John* made further discovery of all
the North-east coasts from *Cape Florida* to *New-found-land*, and
Terra Laborador.[37]

1516.

The voyage of Sir *Thomas Pert* Vice-Admiral of *England*, and
Sebastian Cabota, the Eighth of *Henry* the Eighth to *Brasil*, St.
Domingo, and St. *Juan de puerto rico*.

1520.

Ferdinando Magellano a noble *Portingal* set forth to sail about
the world, but was 1521 unfortunately slain.[38]

1522.

The *Bermuduz-Isle* 400 in number, beginning 500 miles distant from *Virginia*, and 3300 from the City of *London* in the latitude 32 degrees and 30 minutes, discovered now accidentally by
John Bermuduz a *Spaniard*.[39]

1523.

[p. 232] *Stephen Gomez* his voyage to discover the North-west
passage, some will have it in Twenty five.[40]

36. Henry Tudor actually died in 1509.
37. Accounts of the younger Cabot's life at this time are obscure, but there is
no evidence he made this voyage.
38. Magellan left Spain on 20 September 1519.
39. The discovery resulted from the shipwreck of Juan Bermudéz during a
voyage from Spain to Cuba with a cargo of hogs.
40. Esteban Goméz, sponsored by Spain on this voyage, had been a muti-
neer aboard the *San Antonio* of Magellan's fleet of 1520.

1527.

New-found-land discovered by one *Andrew Thorn*,[41] the Southern part but 600 leagues from *England*.
John de Ponce for the *Spaniard* took possession of *Florida*.[42]

1528.

Nevis or *Mevis* planted now according to some writers.[43]

1534.

California questioned, whether Island or Continent, first discovered by the *Spaniard*.[44]
Nova Francia lying between the 40 and 50 degree of the *Arctic-poles Altitude* discovered by *Jaques Carthier* in his first voyage, the first Colony planted in *Canada*.[45]

1536.

The Puritan-Church policy began now in *Geneva*.[46]

1542.

Monsieur du Barvals voyage to *Nova Francia*, sent to inhabit those parts.[47]

41. Evidently an error for Robert Thorne, the younger (d. 1527), who never traveled to Newfoundland. Best known for letters he wrote in 1527 (reprinted in Hakluyt in 1582), Thorne urged exploration for a polar route via Newfoundland to Asia.
42. Juan Ponce de Leon (1474–1521) discovered and named Florida in 1513.
43. Nevis, in the West Indies, was first colonized in 1628.
44. Hernando Cortés (1485–1547) discovered lower California in 1535.
45. Jacques Cartier (c. 1494–1553) discovered the Saint Lawrence River in 1534.
46. John Calvin (1509–64) settled in Geneva at this time and soon established his theocracy.
47. Jean François de la Rocque de Roberval (c. 1500–61), nobleman, pirate, successor of Cartier as governor for Canada, in 1541 sailed up the Saint Lawrence in search of the legendary riches of Saguenay; his abortive colony was located near the mouth of the Rouge River.

1548.

Henry the Eighth dyed.[48]
Edward the Sixth King of *England* began to Raign.
[p. 233] *Sebastian Cabota* made grand Pilot of *England* by *Edward* the Sixth.[49]

1550.

The sweating sickness in *England*.

1553.

Edward the Sixth dyed.
Mary Queen of *England* began to Raign.
Sir *Hugh Willoughby*, and all his men in two Ships in his first attempt to discover the North-east passage, were in *October* frozen to death in the Haven called *Arzima* in *Lapland*.[50]

1558.

Queen *Mary* dyed.
Elizabeth Queen of *England* began to Raign *November* the Seventeenth.

1560.

Salvaterra a Spaniard his voyage to the North-west passage.[51]

1562.

Sir *John Hawkin's* first voyage to the *West-Indies*.[52]

48. Henry VIII actually died in 1547, the same year Edward VI took the throne.

49. Cabot returned to England in 1548 after many years as royal cartographer in Spain; in 1549 Edward granted him a pension.

50. The Northeastern Passage, like the Northwest, was believed to lead to China and India; Willoughby and crew perished in 1554.

51. A confused statement apparently based upon apocrypha recorded in Sir Humphrey Gilbert's *Discourse* (1576), a promotional tract written to prove the existence of the Northwest Passage. Gilbert relates the story, told him by one Salvaterra, of a Spanish friar, Urdaneta, who claimed to have sailed the non-existent Strait of Anian from the Pacific to the Atlantic.

52. Sir John Hawkins (1532–95) in this year entered the slave trade, carrying blacks from Africa to the West Indies and the Spanish Main.

The first expedition of the *French* into *Florida*, undertaken by *John Ribald.*[53]

1565.

Tobacco first brought into *England* by Sir *John Hawkins*, but it was first brought into use by Sir *Walter Rawleigh* many years after.

1566.

The Puritans began to appear in *Eng-* [p. 234] *land.*

1569.

Anthony Jenkinson the first of the *English* that sailed through the *Caspian-*Sea.[54]

1572.

Private Presbyteries now first erected in *England.*
Sir *Francis Drake's* first voyage to the *West-Indies.*[55]

1573.

The *Hollanders* seek for aid from Queen *Elizabeth.*[56]

1576.

Sir *Martin Frobisher* the first in Queen *Elizabeths* days that sought for the North-west passage, or the streight, or passage to *China*, and *meta incognita*,[57] in three several voyages, others will have it in 1577.

1577.

November the 17 Sir *Francis Drake* began his voyage about the world with five Ships, and 164 men setting sail from *Plimouth*,

53. Jean Ribaut (c. 1520–65) set down a French colony in Spanish Florida and was eventually killed by Spaniards.

54. Jenkinson (d. 1611) was the first Englishman to penetrate into central Asia; in 1568–69 he received a coat of arms in recompense for maritime service to his country.

55. Commissioned as a privateer by Queen Elizabeth, Drake first sailed to pillage the West Indies in 1570 and made several voyages thereafter.

56. Spain held Dutch coastal cities in subjection at this time.

57. Name given by Frobisher (c. 1535–94) to Baffin Island.

putting off *Cape de verde*. The beginning of *February*, he saw no
Land till the fifth of *April*, being past the line 30 degrees of latitude, and in the 36 degree entered the River *Plates*[58] whence he
fell with the streight of *Magellan* the 21 of *August*, which with
three of his Ships he passed, having cast off the other two as im-
pediments to him, and the *Marigold* tossed from her General
after [p. 235] passage was no more seen. The other commanded
by Capt. *Winter* shaken off also by Tempest, returned thorow the
Streights and recovered *England*, only the *Pellican*,[59] whereof
himself was Admiral, held on her course to *Chile*, *Coquimbo*,
Cinnama, *Palma*, *Lima*, upon the west of *America*, where he
passed the line 1579 the first day of *March*, and so forth until he
came to the latitude 47. Thinking by those North Seas to have
found passage to *England*, but fogs, frosts and cold winds forced
him to turn his course South-west from thence, and came to Anchor 38 degrees from the line, where the King of that Countrey[60]
presented him his Net-work Crown of many coloured feathers,
and therewith resigned his Scepter of Government unto his Dominion, which Countrey Sir *Francis Drake* took possession of in
the Queens name, and named it *Nova Albion*, which is thought to
be part of the Island of *California*.

Sir *Martin Frobisher's* second voyage.

1578.

Sir *Humphrey Gilbert* a *Devonshire* Knight attempted to discover *Virginia*, but without success.[61]

Sir *Martin Frobisher's* third voyage to *Meta incognita*. *Freeze-
land* now called *West-England*, 25 leagues in length, in the latitude of 57.[62]

58. Rio de la Plata, between Uruguay and Argentina.

59. The *Marigold* of Drake's fleet foundered in a tempest near Cape Horn,
and Captain John Wynter of the *Elizabeth* turned back for England. During
this voyage Drake renamed the *Pelican* the *Golden Hind*.

60. Chief of the Miwok Indians of California.

61. Gilbert's (c. 1539–83) first voyage was aborted by weather and a rebellious crew.

62. Frobisher's third voyage, to mine for ore on Baffin Island, bankrupted
the Company of Cathay; he claimed Friesland, a fictitious island based on reports of Greenland, in the name of the Queen.

[p. 236] Sir *Francis Drake* now passed the Streights of *Magellan* in the Ship called the *Pelican*.

1579.

Sir *Francis Drake* discovered *Nova Albion*[63] in the South Sea. Others will have Sir *Martin Frobisher's* first voyage to discover the North-west passage to be this year.

1580.

From *Nova Albion* he [Drake] fell with *Ternate*, one of the Isles of *Molucco*, being courteously entertained of the King, and from thence he came unto the Isles of *Calebes*, to *Java Major*, to *Cape buona speranza*,[64] and fell with the coasts of *Guinea*, where crossing again the line, he came to the height of the *Azores*, and thence to *England* upon the third of *November* 1580. after three years lacking twelve days, and was Knighted, and his Ship laid up at *Deptford* as a monument of his fame.

1581.

The Provinces of *Holland* again seek for aid to the Queen of *England*.

1582.

Sir *Humphrey Gilbert* took possession of *New-found-land* or *Terra Nova*, in the harbour of St. *John*, for and in the name of [p. 237] Queen *Elizabeth*, it lyeth over against the Gulf of St. *Lawrence*, and is between 46 and 53 degrees of the North-poles Altitude.

1583.

Sir *Walter Rawleigh* in *Ireland*.
Sir *Humphrey Gilbert* attempted a plantation in some remote parts in *New-England*.
He perished in his return from *New-found-land*.[65]

63. Actually the coast of California.
64. Cape of Good Hope.
65. Gilbert's death in a storm at sea followed hard upon his taking formal possession of Newfoundland for England in 1583.

1584.

The woful year of subscription so called by the Brethren, or Disciplinarians.[66]

Sir *Walter Rawleigh* obtained of Queen *Elizabeth* a Patent for the discovery and peopling of unknown Countries, not actually possessed by an Christian Prince. Date *March* 25. in the six and twentieth of her Raign.

April the 27 following, he set forth two Barkes under the Command of Mr. *Philip Amedas* and Mr. *Arthur Barlow*, who arrived on that part of *America*, which that Virgin Queen named *Virginia*, and therof in her Majesties name took possession *July* the Thirteenth.

1585.

Cautionary Towns and Forts in the low-Countreys delivered unto Queen *Elizabeths* hands.[67]

Sir *Richard Greenville* was sent by Sir [p. 238] *Walter Rawleigh April* the Ninth, with a Fleet of 7 sail to *Virginia*, and was stiled the General of *Virginia*. He landed in the Island of St. *John de porto Rico May* the Twelfth, and there fortified themselves and built a *Pinnasse*, &c.[68] In *Virginia* they left 100 men under the Government of Mr. *Ralph Lane*, and others.[69]

Sir *Francis Drake's* voyage to the *West-Indies*, wherein were taken the Cities of St. *Jago*,[70] St. *Domingo*[,] *Cartagena*, and the Town of St. *Augustine* in *Florida*.

66. Subscription: enforced adherence to the Anglican statutes of Supremacy and Uniformity. Puritans of the Elizabethan age, sometimes termed Disciplinarians, grew increasingly subject to new powers conferred upon England's Ecclesiastical Commission in 1583.

67. That is, the queen sent troops to stave off Spanish dominion in the Netherlands.

68. Sir Richard Grenville (c. 1541–91) and his fleet captured Spanish goods in Hispaniola and Puerto Rico. Pinnace: a small boat equipped with sail or oars.

69. The Virginia settlement temporarily governed by Lane (c. 1530–1603) was that of Roanoke Island, whose colonists mysteriously disappeared between 1597 and 1600.

70. Santiago.

Now (say some) Tobacco was first brought into *England* by Mr. *Ralph Lane* out of *Virginia*.

Others will have Tobacco to be first brought into *England* from *Peru*, by Sir *Francis Drake's* Mariners.

Capt. *John Davies* first voyage to discover the North-west passage, encouraged by Sir *Francis Walsingham*, principal Secretary.[71]

1586.

Mr. *Thomas Candish* of *Trimely*, in the County of *Suffolk* Esq. began his voyage in the Ship called the *Desire*, and two ships more to the South-Sea through the Streights of *Magellan* (and from thence round about the circumference of the whole earth)[;] burnt and ransack'd in the entrance of *Chile*, [p. 239] *Peru* and *New-Spain*, near the great Island of *California* in the South-Sea; and returned to *Plimouth* with a pretious booty 1588. *September* the Eighth, being the Third since *Magellan*, that circuited the earth, our *English* voyagers were never out-stript by any.[72]

The Natives of *Virginia* conspired against the *English*.

The same year Sir *Richard Greenville* General of *Virginia* arrived there with three ships, bringing relief from Sir *Walter Rawleigh* to the Colony.

Mr. *John Davies* second voyage to discover the North-west passage.

1587.

Sir *Walter Rawleigh* sent another Colony of 150 persons under the Government of Mr. *John White*.

Mr. *John Davies* third voyage to discover the North-west passage.

Sir *Francis Drake*, with four ships took from the *Spaniards* one million, 189200 Ducats in one voyage.[73]

71. John Davis (c. 1543–1605) conducted extensive explorations of the Arctic and wrote *The Seaman's Secrets* (1594). Walsingham (c. 1530–1590) was Queen Elizabeth's secretary of state.

72. Freighted with Spanish treasure, Thomas Cavendish (1560–92) returned to Plymouth shortly after England's defeat of the Spanish Armada, thus inspiring Josselyn's patriotic boast.

73. Estimates of the worth of Drake's booty ranged from £332,000 to £1,500,000. Ducats: loosely used for money or gold.

1588.

Queen *Elizabeth* opposed her Authority against the Brethrens books and writings.[74]

Sir *Francis Drake* Vice-Admiral of the *English* Fleet, the Lord-Admiral bestowed the order of Knight-hood upon Mr. *John* [p. 240] *Hawkins, Martin Forbisher* and others, *July* the Five and twentieth.

The *Spanish Armado* defeated, consisting of 130 ships, wherein were 19290 Souldiers[,] 2080 chained Rowers[,] 2630 great Ordnance, Commanded by *Perezius Guzman* Duke of *Medina Sedonia*, and under him *Johannes Martinus Recaldus* a great Sea-man;[75] The Fleet coming in like a half moon, the horns of the front extending one from the other about 7 miles asunder, it was preparing 15 years, and was blackt to make it seem the more terrible.

1589.

The *Portingal* voyage under the conduct of Sir *Francis Drake*.

Mr. *Thomas Candish* now finished his voyage about the world, as some will have it.

1590.

Now Tobacco first used in *England*, as some will have it.

1591.

The first *Englishman* that ever was in the *Bermuduze* or *Summer-Islands*, was one *Henry May*.

The voyage of Capt. *Newport* to the *West-Indies*, where upon the coast of *Hispaniola*, he took and burnt three Towns, and Nineteen sail of ships and Frigats.[76]

Mr. *Thomas Candish* last voyage, in which he dyed.

74. Probably a backlash against the Puritan polemics known as the Martin Marprelate tracts, which began appearing in this year; but see the earlier passage where Josselyn designates Quakers the "*Shunamitish* Brethren" (156).

75. Alonso Peréz de Guzman, seventh Duke of Medina Sidonia, was admiral of the Spanish Armada defeated this year by the English; Juan Martinez de Recalde was a squadron commander.

76. Christopher Newport (d. 1617), captain of the *Little John*, was part of a

1593.

[p. 241] Sir *Martin Frobisher* Commander of the *English* Fleet slain in the quarrel of *H*. King of *Navarr*.[77]

The last voyage of Sir *Francis Drake*, and Sir *John Hawkins* to the *West-Indies* with six ships of the Queens, and twelve other ships and Barks containing 2400 men and boyes, in which voyage they both dyed, and Sir *Francis Drake's* Coffen was thrown over board near *Porto bello*.[78]

1594.

Sir *Robert Duddeleys* voyage to *Trinidad*, and the coast of *Paria*.[79]

Mr. *James Lancasters* voyage to *Fernambuck* the port Town of *Olinda* in *Brazil*, in which voyage he took 29 ships and Frigats[,] surprized the said port Town, and there found the Cargazon or fraught of a rich *Indian Carack*, which together with great abundance of Sugars and Cottons he brought from thence; lading therewith fifteen sail of tall ships and barks.[80]

1595.

The voyage of Sir *Amias Preston*, & Capt. *George Sommers* to the *West-Indies*, where they took, sackt, spoiled and abandoned the Island of *Puerto Santo*, the Island of *Cock* near [p. 242] *Margarita*, the Fort and Town of *Coro*, the stately City of St.

1590 relief expedition sent to Roanoke Island. Headed by the privateer commander John Watts, the fleet first waged war and plundered Spanish ports, then reached Roanoke to find the colony vanished.

77. Frobisher received the wound from which he died in the 1594 siege and relief of Brest; Henry of Navarre (Henry III), at this time king of France (1589–1610), was first of the Bourbon line.

78. On this ill-fated voyage Drake died of yellow fever in 1596 and Hawkins of natural causes in 1595, having been unsuccessful in attempts to rescue John's son Richard Hawkins from Spanish captivity.

79. Dudley's (1574–1649) expedition included landings in Venezuela and Guiana; he was knighted in 1596.

80. The successful attack on the state of Pernambuco, along with later ravages among the Portuguese, earned Lancaster (c. 1550–1618) knighthood in 1603.

Jago de leon, and the Town of *Cumana* ransomed, and *Jamaica* entered.[81]

Sir *Walter Rawleigh's* voyage now to *Guiana*, discovered by him. In which voyage he took St. *Joseph* a Town upon *Trinidado*.[82]

The *Sabbatarian* doctrine published by the Brethren.[83]

1596.

The voyage to *Cadez*, Sir *Walter Rawleigh* Rere-Admiral.

The voyage of Sir *Anthony Sherley* intended for the Island of St. *Tome*, but performed to St. *Jago, Dominga, Margarita*, along the coast of *Terra Firma* to the Island of *Jamaica*, situated between 17 and 18 degrees of the North-poles elevation (which he conquered, but held it not long) from thence to the bay of *Hondurus*, 30 leagues up *Rio Dolce*, and homeward by *New-foundland*.[84]

1597.

The voyage to the *Azores*, Sir *Walter Rawleigh* Capt. of the Queens Guard Rere-Admiral.

Porto Rico, taken by the Earl of *Cumberland*.[85]

1599.

The grand *Canary* taken by the *Dutch* Commander *Vanderdoes*.

1600.

[p. 243] The Colonies in *Virginia* supplyed by publick purse.

---

81. The islands attacked by Amyas Preston (d. 1617?) and Somers (1554–1610) are part of the Madeira group off Morocco. In Venezuela, Santiago de Leon is now Caracas.

82. On this voyage Raleigh also explored the Orinoco River in search of the legendary El Dorado and its Gilded Man.

83. Josselyn's reference here is untraced.

84. Descended from recently impoverished gentry, Sherley (c. 1565–1635) turned to privateering as means of securing a livelihood.

85. George de Clifford (1558–1605), third Earl of Cumberland, organized many privateering expeditions against the Spanish and helped to defeat the Armada.

1602.

Queen *Elizabeth* dyed *March* the Four and twentieth.[86]
King *James* began to Raign.
The North parts of *Virginia*, i.e. *New-England* further discovered by Capt. *Bartholomew Gosnold*, some will have him to be the first discoverer.
Capt. *George Weymouth*'s voyage to discover the North-west passage.[87]
Divers of our *English* in the North of *England* entered into a Convenant of worshipping of God.

1603.

King *James* came into *England*, the fifth of *April*.
Monsieur *Champlains* voyage to *Canada*.[88]
November the seventeenth Sir *Walter Rawleigh* Arraigned and Condemned.

1604.

Monsieur *du Point* and *du Monts* voyage to *Canada*.[89]

1605.

Monsieur *du Point* and *du Monts* remove the *French* habitation to *Port-Royal*.
James Halle's voyage to *Greenland*, and to find out the North-west passage.[90]

86. 24 March 1603, following the Georgian calendar (New Style).
87. Weymouth, whose dates are unknown, sailed in 1602 under the auspices of the East India Company. He voyaged to New England in 1605, captured five Indians, and turned them over to Sir Ferdinando Gorges back in England. James Rosier, a crew member, published his *Relation* of the latter voyage that same year.
88. Samuel de Champlain (c. 1567–1635) this year explored and traded in the Gulf of Saint Lawrence, then returned and published his account entitled *Des sauvages*.
89. Pierre du Gua, sieur de Monts (c. 1588–1628) in 1603 received a grant from Henry IV of France to control virtually all trade in Canada, which was then styled Acadia. His senior officer on the 1604 expedition to Port-Royal was François Gravé du Pont (c. 1554–c. 1630).
90. In 1605, in the employ of Denmark's King Christian IV, Hall (d. 1612)

1606.

[p. 244] The province of *Main* possessed by the *English* by publick Authority King *James*, Sir *John Popham*, &c.

A Colony first sent to *New-England* by Sir *John Popham* chief Justice of the Common pleas.

James-town founded in *Virginia*.

James Halls second voyage, to find out the North-west passage.

Mr. *John Knight* his North-west voyage, lost his ship sunk by the Ice.

A Colony sent to *Virginia*, called by the *Indians Wingandacoa*, the first that took firm possession there.

1607.

Plimouth Plantation in *New-England* attempted.

St. *Georges* Fort built at the mouth of the River *Sagadahoc*, under the Presidency of Capt. *George Popham* and Capt. *Ralph Gilbert*,[91] who built the Fort.

James Halls third voyage to find out the North-west passage.

Hudsons first voyage to find out the North-west passage.

1608.

Virginia planted.

A Colony sent to *New-found-land*.[92]

[p. 245] Capt. *John Smith* fished now for *Whales* at *Monhiggen*.

Hudsons second voyage to the North-west met a *Mermaid* in the Sea. That there be such Creatures see *Plinie, Albertus Magnus, Aristotle, Elian, Theodorus Gaza, Alexander of Alexandria,*

---

and John Knight (d. 1606) sought evidence of the earlier Scandinavian settlements upon which the Danish based their claims to Greenland. The 1606 venture that Hall piloted, again to Greenland, involved a futile search for mineral riches on the west coast. His 1607 voyage proved fruitless too; yet he tried again in 1612, accompanied by William Baffin, and was slain by an Eskimo. Baffin's account of the voyage appeared in Purchas in 1625. In 1606, Knight sailed in the employ of the East India Company to Labrador, where, searching for a spot to repair his damaged ship, he was also reputedly slain by natives.

91. Raleigh Gilbert, nephew of Sir Walter and sixth son of Sir Humphrey.

92. Permanent English settlement began at Newfoundland in 1611 (Quinn 1973, 394).

Gorgius Trapozensus, Jul. Scaliger, Stows Annals in Anno Dom.
1204. at *Oreford* in *Suffolk* a *Mareman* taken.[93]

1609.

Sir *Thomas Gales* and Sir *George Summers* going to *Virginia*,
suffered shipwrack upon the *Bermudos-Islands* where they continued till 1610.

Hudsons third voyage to *New-found-land* discovered *Mohegan-*
River in *New-England*.

The *Dutch* set down by *Mohegan*-River.

1610.

Capt. *Whitburns* voyage to discover the North-west passage,
saw a *Mermaid* in the harbour of St. *Johns* at *New-found-land* by
the River side.[94]

Hudsons last and fatal voyage to discover the North-west passage, where he was frozen to death.

Dales-gift founded in *Virginia*.[95]

Sundry of the *English* nation removed out of the North of *En-*

93. The most comprehensive of Josselyn's numerous appeals to authority.
For Pliny's discussion of "Tritons, Nereids and aquatic monsters," see 3:169.
German philosopher Albertus Magnus (c. 1200–1280), sometimes known as
"Aristotle's ape," has provided the name for an institute in Cologne currently
preparing a forty-volume edition of his works, the first of which appeared in
1951. Elian is Claudius Aelianus (c. A.D. 170–235), Roman rhetorician and
author of *De natura animalium*. Teodorus Gaza (c. 1400–75), Greek scholar
and professor, wrote little himself but translated into Latin many of Aristotle's
works, including *De partibus animalium*, a project jointly undertaken with
Georgias Trapezuntius (c. 1395–1484). The most widespread Latin version of
the romance of Alexander the Great, and the one to which Josselyn perhaps alludes, was the *Historia de proeliis* (1486). The Italian physician and scholar
Julius Caesar Scaliger (1484–1558) wrote a commentary on Aristotle's history
. of animals. John Stow's (c. 1525–1605) *Annales*, which treats the whole of England's history, appeared first in 1580; it contains no such entry for 1204,
however.

94. Richard Whitbourne (fl. 1579–1626) voyaged to Newfoundland to
hunt and fish commercially in 1579; his *Discourse of the discovery of New-found-
land* appeared in 1620.

95. In 1611, Sir Thomas Dale (d. 1619) founded Dales-Gift on Smith Island near Cape Charles; he served as governor of Virginia from 1611 to 1617.

gland into the *Netherlands*, and gathered a Church at *Leyden*, where they continued until the year 1620.[96]

1611.

[p. 246] Sir *Thomas Dale* Governour of *Virginia*.
The famous Arch-Pirate *Peter Easton*.[97]

1612.

Bermudus first planted, and Mr. *R. Moore* sent over Governour, the first that planted a Colony in the *Bermudus*.

James Halls fourth voyage to discover the North west passage, was slain by the Savages.

Capt. *Buttons* voyage to discover the North-west passage.[98]

1613.

Port-Royal destroyed by Sir *Samuel Argol* Governour of *Virginia*.

Mr. *John Rolf* a Gentleman of good behaviour fell in love with *Pocahontas*, the only Daughter of *Powhaton* a King in *Virginia* and married her,[99] she was Christened and called the Lady *Rebecca*, and dyed at *Gravesend Anno Dom.* 1617. Sir *Lewis Stukely* brought up her Son *Thomas Rolf*.

1614.

Bermudus planted further.

Powhatons Daughter in *Virginia* Christened *Rebecca*.

Capt. *Gibbins* voyage to find out the North-west passage.[100]

96. The church at Leyden was that brought over by the Separatist Pilgrims to Amsterdam in 1608, to Leyden in 1609, and finally to Plymouth, Massachusetts, in 1620.

97. The predations of Easton had especial impact upon the early English settlements at Conception Bay, Newfoundland (Quinn 1977, 427–28).

98. Sir Thomas Button (d. 1634) also sailed ostensibly at this time to search for Henry Hudson, who, the previous year, had been abandoned by mutineers in the bay named for him.

99. John Rolfe (1585–1622) married Pocahontas in 1614.

100. This report presumably is based upon the spurious account of a voyage of one Bartholomew de Fonte who claimed to have sailed in 1640 through the Northwest Passage to Hudson Bay, where he encountered a ship from Boston owned by a Mr. Gibbons. Since de Fonte's account did not appear until 1708,

New-Netherlands began to be planted up- [p. 247] on *Mohegan*-River, Sir *Samuel Argol* routed them.

1615.

Sir *Richard Hawkins* voyage into those parts of *New-England*.[101]

1616.

Capt. *Gibbins* second voyage to find out the North-west passage. A new supply sent by Capt. *Daniel Tucker* to the *Bermudus*.[102] *Pocahontas* and Mr. *Rolf* her Husband went for *England* with Sir *Thomas Dale*, and arrived at *Plimouth* the 12 of *June*.

1617.

Sir *Walter Rawleighs* last and unfortunate voyage to *Guiana*, where he took St. *Thome* the only Town of *Guiana* possessed by the *Spaniards*.

1618.

The Comet or blazing-star whose motion was by some observed to be from East to West.

1619.

Sir *Walter Rawleigh* beheaded in the Parliament yard. *Bermudus-Islands* divided into Tribes and Cantreds, to each tribe a Burrough.

1620.

The *English* in *Virginia* divided into several Burroughs. [p. 248] Letters Patents obtained from King *James* for the Northern part of *Virginia* i.e. *New-England*. In *July* sundry of the *English* set sail from *Holland* for *Southampton*.

---

however, how Josselyn arrived at his information is unclear. Both Cotton Mather and Benjamin Franklin later enforced the details of this apparent hoax.

101. The son of Sir John Hawkins, Richard (c. 1562–1622) is not known to have made such a voyage.

102. Tucker (d. 1625) served as governor of Bermuda from 1616 to 1619 and was succeeded by Nathaniel Butler.

August the fift, they set sail from *Southampton* for *America*, and arrived the Eleventh of *November* at *Cape-Cod*, where they entered into a body politick, and chose one Mr. *John Carver* their Governour, calling the place where they settled *New-Plimouth*: in *January* and *February* following was a mortality among the *English*, which swept away half the Company.

Mrs. *Susanna White* delivered of a Son at *new-Plimouth*, Christened *Peregrine*; he was the first of the *English* that was born in *new-England*, and was afterwards the Lieutenant of the Military Company of *Marsh-field* in *Plimouth* Colony.[103]

New-Plimouth built, the first Town in *new-England*.

Squanto an *Indian* in *new-England*, carried into *England* by Mr. *Hunt* a Master of a Ship, but brought home again by Mr. *Dormer* a Gentleman imployed by Sir *Ferdinando Gorges* for discovery.[104]

1621.

[p. 249] *April*, Mr. *John Carver* Governour of *new-Plimouth* dyed, and Mr. *William Brandford* was chosen Governour.

The Natives in *Virginia* murdered about 340 *english*.[105]

1622.

The Fort at *new-Plimouth* built: a great drought this Summer, from *May* the Third, till the middle of *July* there was no Rain. Mr. *Thomas Weston* Merchant sent over 67 lusty men who

---

103. Peregrine White was born aboard ship during the crossing.

104. In his full account of this episode of Massachusetts history, Adams comments that "the time and place of the kidnapping of Squanto have given the authorities a great deal of trouble" (1:23n). Perhaps Josselyn was following Nathaniel Morton, who in turn followed William Bradford's then unpublished history "Of Plimmoth Plantation," which mistakenly dates Squanto's capture as 1621. Thomas Hunt, captain of a ship in John Smith's fleet of 1614, that year kidnapped twenty natives and sold them as slaves to the Spanish, a fate that Squanto somehow avoided, although he was among them. Thomas Dermer was associated first with Smith in 1615, then, after 1618, with Gorges.

105. Captain John Smith's *Generall Historie of Virginia* probably served Josselyn in these details. Smith cites a date of 22 March 1622 and a massacre tally of 347 (2:292, 302).

settled themselves in a part of the *Massachusets-bay*, now called *Weymouth*.[106]

The order of the Knights of *Novascotia* ordained by King *James* Hereditarie, they wear an *Orange* tawny Ribbin.[107]

Sir *Ferdinando Gorges* Patent for the Province of *Main* in *New-England*. The *Dutch* tortured the *English* at *Amboina*, 1623.

Westons plantation wholly ruined by their disorders.

Mr. *Robert Gorge*, Sir *Ferdinando Gorges* Brother arrived in *Plimouth*, and began a Plantation of the *Massachusets bay*, having Commission from the Council of *New-England* to be general Governour of the Countrey, carrying over one Mr. *Morrel* a Mini- [p. 250] ster but being discouraged, he returned for *England*.[108]

A fire at *Plimouth*, which did considerable dammage, several of the Inhabitants through discontent and casualities removed into *Virginia*.

Three thousand *English* now upon the *Bermudus* ten Forts, and in those ten Forts 50 pieces of Ordnance.

1624.

The number of Magistrates increased to five now at *New-Plimouth*. The first neat Cattle carried over into *New-England* to *New-Plimouth* was three Heifers and a Bull.[109]

1625.

St. *Christophers-Island* planted now by the *English* 25 leagues in compass, a great many little Rivers, in 17 degrees and 25 minutes.

106. Weston (c. 1575–c. 1644) was the chief adventurer for this abortive settlement (then named Wessagusset), whose failure is reported in Bradford, Winslow, and Morton.

107. To stimulate colonization of Nova Scotia, James created a series of baronetcies to be awarded Scotsmen who would furnish funds and laborers to settle the coastline (Andrews 1:315–17).

108. Robert Gorges was actually Sir Ferdinando's son. Little is known of the Reverend William Morrell beyond his 1623 voyage and his authorship of *Nova Anglia* or *New England* (1625), perhaps the earliest poem to treat exclusively of the New World.

109. Brought over by Edward Winslow (1595–1655).

King *James* dyed in 1625, and King *Charles* the first began his Raign *March* the seven and twentieth.

1627.

The first distribution of Lands amongst the Inhabitants of *New-Plimouth*.

A Colony of *English* planted upon the Island of *Barbados*, which in a short time increased to 20000, besides *Negroes*.

1628.

Mr. *John Endicot* arrived in *New-Eng-* [p. 251] *land* with some number of people, and set down first by *Cape-Ann*, at a place called afterwards *Gloster*, but their abiding place was at *Salem*, where they built the first Town in the *Massachusets* Patent.

The *Indians* at the *Massachusets*, were at that time by sickness decreased from 30000 to 300.[110]

Nevis or *Mevis* planted now by the *English* 3 or 4000 upon it.

Mr. *Morton* of *Merrimount* taken prisoner by the *Massachusets*, and sent into *England*.

1629.

Three ships arrived at *Salem* bringing a great number of passengers from *England*; infectious diseases amongst them.

Mr. *Endicot* chosen Governour.

Mr. *Higginson*, Mr. *Skelton* and Mr. *Bright* Ministers arrived, upon the fift of *August* was the first Church in the *Massachusets* Colony gathered at *Salem*,[111] from which year to this present year is 45 years, in the compass of these years in this Colony, there hath been gathered forty Churches, and 120 Towns built in all the Colonies of *New-England*.[112]

---

110. The greatest mortality among the Massachusetts tribes occurred from 1616 to 1617, and was followed by numerous lesser epidemics.

111. This Salem church set the pattern of Congregational polity that would be followed by the many others in Massachusetts Bay. Francis Higginson (1587–1630) otherwise is most well known today for his *New Englands Plantation* (1630). Along with Samuel Skelton (d. 1634) and Francis Bright, he had erected the church in Salem by 20 July.

112. An underestimate and another echo of Johnson (48–49).

The Church of *new-Plimouth*, was planted in *New-England* eight years before others.

The book of Common-prayer pleaded [p. 252] for, and practised in *Massachusets* Colony by two of the Patentees, but was at last prohibited by the Authority there.[113]

1630.

The Tenth of *July*, *John Winthorp* Esq; and the Assistants arrived in *New-England* with the Patent for the *Massachusets*, they landed on the North-side of *Charles* River, with him went over Mr. *Thomas Dudly*, *Isaac Johnson*, Esquires; Mr. *John Wilson*, Mr. *George Philips*, Mr. *Maverich* (the Father of Mr. *Samuel Maverick*, one of his Majesties Commissioners)[,] Mr. *Wareham* Ministers.[114]

The passage of the people in the Eagle, and nine other Vessels to *New-England* came to 9500 pounds. The Swine, Goats, Sheep, Neat and Horses cost to transport 12000 pounds, besides the price they cost.[115] The *Eagle* was called the *Arabella* in honour of the Lady *Arabella*, wife to *Isaac Johnson* Esq; they set down first upon *Noddles-Island*, the Lady *Arabella* abode at *Salem*.

Mr. *Isaac Johnson* a Magistrate of the *Massachusets*, and his Lady dyed soon after their arrival.

John Winthorp Esq; chosen Governour, for the remainder of the year, Mr. *Thomas Dudley* deputy Governour, Mr. *Simon Broadstreet* Secretary.[116]

[p. 253] *Charles-town*, the first town built.

Mr. *Higginson* Teacher of *Salem* Church dyed.

113. The patentees were Joseph and Samuel Browne. See "Second Voyage," n. 264.

114. Despite the contrary evidence of several New England historians and genealogists, Josselyn's claim that John (1578–1636) and Samuel Maverick were father and son has been vindicated by Greenlaw (236). The father was a Puritan, and the son a staunch Episcopalian. Samuel attacked the Massachusetts government in a tract unpublished until 1885, *A Briefe Discription of New England*. John Warham (d. 1670) was one of the founders of Windsor, Connecticut.

115. On these figures, see "Second Voyage," n. 263.

116. An error. Josselyn gleans Massachusetts election information freely from Edward Johnson, who often reported erroneously himself. As J. Franklin

1630.

A very sharp winter in *New-England.*

1631.

Capt. *John Smith* Governour of *Virginia*, and Admiral of *New-England* now dyed in *London.*

John Winthorp Esq; chosen Governour of the *Massachusets.* Mr. *Thomas Dudley* Deputy Governour.

Sir *Richard Saltingstall* went for *New-England*, set down at *Water-town.*[117]

Five Churches gathered this year, the first at *Boston* Mr. *John Wilson* Pastor, the second at *Water-town* by Mr. *Philips*, the third at *Dorchester* by Mr. *Maverick* and Mr. *Wareham*, the fourth at *Roxbury* by Mr. *Eliot*, the fifth at *Linn* by Mr. *Stephen Batcheler* their first Teacher.[118]

Dr. *Wilson* gave 1000 pounds to *New-England*, with which they stored themselves with great Guns.[119]

Jameson has written in his edition of Johnson's *Wonder-Working Providence*, "no election took place till spring, the time fixed by charter; and this August meeting was but a court of assistants, not a general court, competent to elect. Winthrop was governor 1629–1634, 1637–1640, 1642–1644, 1646–1649." "Dudley, a narrower and sterner Puritan, was deputy-governor during most of the years named, and four times governor [1634, 1640, 1645, 1650]. Bradstreet, a younger man but one of great ability, was governor during the last seven years under the first charter, 1679 to 1686, and from 1689 to 1692, after having been an 'assistant' (member of the council) throughout the whole period from 1630 to 1679" (65n).

117. Saltonstall (1586–1658) arrived in company with John Winthrop in 1630, then returned to England the following year; his son Richard served New England as a magistrate and military commissioner throughout his lengthy life.

118. Again, Josselyn follows Johnson's errors. Wilson (1588–1667) served as teacher, then as pastor of Boston's First Church, founded in 1630. George Phillips (1593–1644) was pastor at Watertown continuously from 1630. The Dorchester church, second of the Massachusetts churches, dates from 1630 also; the Roxbury church, headed by John Eliot (1604–90), opened its doors in 1632. Led by Batchellor, the Lynn church likewise originated in 1632.

119. See the almost identical margin note to be found in Johnson (133n). As Jameson there explains, "we find the gift acknowledged by the General Court in September, 1634, when the fortification of Castle Island in Boston harbor was begun on account of alarming news from England."

1632.

John Winthorp chosen Governour, Mr. *Thomas Dudley* Deputy Governour.

Sir *Christopher Gardiner* descended of the house of *Gardiner* Bishop of *Winchester*, Knighted at *Jerusalem* of the Sepulcher, [p. 254] arrived in *New-England* with a comely young woman his Concubine, settled himself in the Bay of *Massachusets*, was rigidly used by the Magistrates, and by the Magistrates of *New-Plimouth* to which place he retired.[120]

A terrible cold winter in *New-England*.

1633.

Mr. *Edward Winslow* chosen Governour of *New-Plimouth*.

The number of Magistrates at *New-Plimouth* increase to seven.

An infectious feaver amongst the Inhabitants of *New-Plimouth*, whereof many dyed.

Mr. *John Winthorp* chosen Governour of the *Massachusets* Colony, Mr. *Thomas Dudley* Deputy Governour.

Mr. *Thomas Hooker*, Mr. *Hains* and Mr. *Cotton* Ministers arrived in *New-England* all in one ship, and Mr. *Stone* and Mr. *William Collier* a liberal Benefactor to the Colony of *New-Plimouth*.[121]

Mr. *John Cotton* chosen Teacher of the first Church at *Boston*.

A Church at *Cambridge* gathered by Mr. *Thomas Hooker* their first Pastor.

120. This incident of New England history has gained legendary proportions. The mysterious Gardiner may have intimidated the Massachusetts Puritans with his title and lineage, but certainly he angered them with his violations of their moral law. Winthrop ordered his arrest in 1631 after receiving letters that charged Gardiner with having abandoned wives in Paris and London. Winslow claimed he was a Jesuit; others, that he was a Royalist spy. Driven from his mistress, Mary Grove, he eventually returned to England bearing accusations of ill will.

121. Hooker (1586–1647) and Samuel Stone (1602–63) led a migration to the Connecticut Valley in 1636, followed the next year by John Haynes (1594–1654), who was the colony's first governor. John Cotton (1584–1652) was teacher at Boston's First Church from the time of his arrival till his death. William Collier (d. 1670) had been a London merchant before becoming an assistant and settling in the Plymouth colony.

Great swarms of strange flyes up and down the Countrey, which was a presage of the following mortality.

1634.

[p. 255] Mr. *Thomas Prince* chosen Governour of *New-Plimouth*.[122]

Mr. *Thomas Dudley* chosen Governour of the *Massachusets* Colony, and Mr. *Roger Ludlow* Deputy-Governour.[123]

The Countrey now was really placed in a posture of War, to be in readiness at all times.

In the Spring a great sickness among the *Indians*, by the small pox.

The *Pequets* War with the *Narragansets*.

Mr. *Skelton* Pastor to the Church at *Salem* dyed.

Mr. *John Norton*, and Mr. *Thomas Shepherd* arrive in *New-England*.[124]

A Church gathered at *Ipswich*, the first Pastor Mr. *Nathaniel Ward*.[125]

A Church gathered at *Newberry*.

Capt. *Stone* turn'd Pirate, at the *Dutch* plantation.

The cruel Massacre of Capt. *Stone* and Capt. *Norton* at *Connecticut-River*, by the Pequet *Indians*.[126]

1635.

Mr. *John Haines* chosen Governour of the *Massachusets* Colony, Mr. *Richard Bellingham* Deputy Governour.

Mr. *Zachary Sims* arrived in *New-England*, and Mr. *Richard Bellingham*.[127]

[p. 256] This year Eleven Ministers arrived in *New-England*.

122. Thomas Prence (1600–1673) gave way the following year to William Bradford as governor of Plymouth.

123. Roger Ludlow (1590–c. 1649) originally immigrated to Connecticut.

124. Norton (1606–63) and Shepard (1605–49) in fact arrived in 1635.

125. During the period when Ward (c. 1578–1652) served as minister, Ipswich was known also as Aggawam or Agawam.

126. The murder of John Stone and John Norton was a contributing cause of the Pequot War. See Bradford (310–12).

127. Symmes (1599–1671) and Bellingham (c. 1592–1672) arrived in 1634, the former aboard the *Griffin* with Anne Hutchinson.

Mr. *Norton* Teacher at *Ipswich*, Mr. *Richard Mather* Teacher at *Dorchester*.[128]

Sir *Henry Vain* Junior, arrived in *New-England*, Mr. *Richard Saltingstal*, Sir *Richard Saltingstal's* Son, Mr. *Roger Harlackenden*, and *Hugh Peters*.[129]

Hugh Peters chosen Pastor of *Salem*.

A Church at *Hartford* in the Colony of *Connecticut* now gathered.

Mr. *William Bradford* chosen Governour of *New-Plimouth*.

Capt. *William Gorges*, Sir *Ferdinando Gorges* Nephew sent over Governour of the province of *Main*, then called new *Sommersetshire*.

Saturday the 15 of *August*, an Hurrican or mighty storm of wind and rain, which did much hurt in *New-England*.[130]

1636.

Sir *Henry Vane* Junior, Governour of the *Massachusets* Colony, *John Winthorp* Esq; Deputy Governour, Mr. *Roger Harlackenden* leader of their military Forces.

Connecticut Colony planted.

Mr. *John Oldham* murthered in his Barque by the *Indians* of *Block-Island*.

[p. 257] A Church gathered at *Hingham*, Mr. *Peter Hubbord* arrived now in *New-England* Teacher at *Hingham*.[131]

Mr. *Flint*, Mr. *Carter*, Mr. *Walton*, Ministers arrived now in *New-England*.

Mr. *Fenwick*, Mr. *Patrick*, Mr. *Nathaniel Rogers*, and Mr. *Samuel White*, arrived now in *New-England*.

A General Court held at *Boston* against Mrs. *Hutchinson* the *American* Jezabel,[132] *August* the 30. where the opinions and errors

128. In 1636, Richard Mather (1596–1669) received the appointment at Dorchester, where he remained throughout his life.

129. After his 1637 support of Anne Hutchinson, Vane (1613–62) returned to England; both Harlackenden (c. 1608–38) and Peter (1598–1660) prosecuted her in court. Hugh Peter became pastor at Salem late in 1636.

130. Winthrop too reports this storm (1:155–57) and alleges that the high winds turned the tides.

131. Hobart arrived, and the Hingham church was founded, in 1635.

132. The Massachusetts clergy bestowed upon Anne Hutchinson this epi-

of Mrs. *Hutchinson* and her Associats 80 errors were condemned.

A Counsel held at *New-town* about the same business *October* the second, and at *Boston* again.

1637.

Mr. *William Bradford* chosen Governour of *New-Plimouth* Colony.

Mr. *John Wenthorp* chosen Governour of *Massachusets* Colony, Mr. *Thomas Dudley* chosen Deputy Governour.

New-haven Colony began now, Mr. *Eaton* chosen Governour, *John Davenport* Pastor.[133]

Mr. *Hopkins* arrived now in *New-England.*

A second Church gathered at *Dedham*, Mr. *John Allen* Pastor.

The Pequets wars, in which war the *English* slew and took prisoners about 700 *Indi-* [p. 258] *ans* amongst which 13 of their *Sachems* to the great terror of the Natives, they sent the male children of the *Pequets* to the *Bermudus.*[134]

This year the *Antinomian* and *Familistical* errors were broached in the Countrey, especially at *Boston.*

A Synod called, which condemned these errors.

A General Court held at *New-town* against Mrs. *Hutchinson* and the rest.[135]

Mrs. *Hutchinson* and others banished by the Magistrates of the *Massachusets* Colony.

A hideous monster born at *Boston* of one Mrs. *Mary Dyer.*[136]

---

thet, which also appears in Winthrop's *Short Story . . . of the Antinomians, Familists & Libertines . . . of New England* (London, 1644). Hutchinson's arraignment and excommunication took place in 1637/38. Familists were members of the Family of Love, a sect founded in seventeenth-century Holland by Hendrick Niclaes.

133. Theophilus Eaton and John Davenport (1597–1670) arrived in 1637 with Edward Hopkins (1600–1657) but founded the New Haven colony in 1638.

134. The number of Pequot Indians killed was between 400 and 700; among the 100–200 prisoners taken—men, women, and children—most were sold as slaves and shipped to the West Indies.

135. The court was held at Newton, now Cambridge, because Hutchinson had so many supporters in Boston; it condemned eighty-two Antinomian errors.

136. See "First Voyage," n. 57.

Sir *Henry Vane* and the Lord *Lee* returned for *England*.[137]

The Ministers that went for *New-England* chiefly in the ten first years, ninety four, of which returned for *England* twenty seven, dyed in the Countrey thirty six, yet alive in the Countrey thirty one.

The number of ships that transported passengers to *New-England*, in these times was 298 supposed: men, women and children as near as can be ghessed 21200.[138]

The *Spaniards* took the Island of *Providence*, one of the Summer-Islands from the English.[139]

1638.

[p. 259] Mr. *Thomas Prince* chosen Governour of *new-Plimouth* Colony.

Mr. *John Winthorp* chosen Governour of the *Massachusets* Colony, Mr. *Thomas Dudley* Deputy Governour.

A Church now gathered at *Waymouth*, Mr. *Gennor* Pastor, Mr. *Newman* succeeded Mr. *Thomas Thatcher*.[140]

Three *English* men put to death at *Plimouth* for robbing and murthering an *Indian* near *Providence*.[141]

June the second a great and terrible earthquake throughout the Countrey.[142]

Samuel Gorton of *Warwick-shire*, a pestilent seducer, and blasphemous Atheist, the Author of the Sects of *Gortinians*, banish'd

137. James, Lord Ley, eldest son of the Earl of Marlborough, came over merely to see New England; Vane had recently lost to Winthrop his bid for reelection as governor of the Massachusetts Bay Colony.

138. Yet again Josselyn borrows from Edward Johnson's book (58), which probably mistakes the number of ships, but which appears accurate on the passenger population throughout the period of the Great Migration.

139. An error. See "First Voyage," n. 20.

140. Thomas Jenner, Samuel Newman, and Thomas Thacher, the last eventually licenser of the press set up in this year, and first minister of Boston's South Church.

141. According to Bradford (344) the three were Arthur Peach, Thomas Jackson, and Richard Stinnings; Roger Williams defended the Indian suit in court.

142. See Bradford (348).

Plimouth plantation, whipt and banished from Road-Island, banisht the *Massachusets* Colony.[143]

Now they set up a Printing-press at *Boston* in the *Massachusets*.

This year came over Mr. *William Thompson*, Mr. *Edward Brown*, Mr. *David Frisk*.[144]

Mr. *John Harvard*, the founder of *Harvard* College at *Cambridge* in the *Massachusets* Colony, deceased, gave 700 pound to the erecting of it.[145]

1639.

[p. 260] Mr. *William Bradford* chosen Governour of *new-Plimouth* Colony.

Mr. *John Winthorp* chosen Governour of the *Massachusets* Colony, Mr. *Thomas Dudley* Deputy Governour.

Mr. *Higginson* Teacher at *Salem* Church, *Skelton* pastor, and an exhorting Elder.[146] This was the first Church gathered in the *Massachusets* Colony, and it increased to 43 Churches in joynt Communion with one another, and in these Churches were about 7750 souls.

Mr. *Herbert Pelham* now arrived in *New-England*.

A Church gathered at *Hampton*, Mr. *Daulton* pastor, and Mr. *Batchelor* Teacher.[147]

Another Church gathered at *Salisbury*.

October the Eleventh and Twelfth, the *Spanish* Navy was set upon by the *Hollander* in the *Downs*, they were in all 60 sail, the *Spaniards* were beaten.

A very sharp winter in *New-England*.

143. A leader in the complex religious backlash against New England orthodoxy, Gorton (c. 1592–1677) resided most of his life in Shawomet, now Warwick, Rhode Island.

144. William Tompson, Edmund Browne, and John Fiske are intended.

145. Of his estate, valued at about £800, Harvard (1607–38) bequeathed one half together with his library of some 260 volumes, to the college.

146. An error. Francis Higginson died in 1630 and Samuel Skelton in 1634. Higginson's son, John, served as minister at Salem from 1660.

147. In 1644 Timothy Dalton and Stephen Batchellor opposed each other's authority and created a rift in the Hampton church.

1640.

Mr. *William Bradford* chosen Governour of *new-Plimouth* Colony.

Mr. *Thomas Dudley* chosen Governour of the *Massachusets* Colony, and Mr. *Richard Bellingham* Deputy Governour.

[p. 261] Civil Wars began in *England.*

Mr. *Huet* Minister arrived in *New-England*, Mr. *Peck* and Mr. *Saxton.*[148]

A Church gathered at *Braintree*, Mr. *Wheelright* pastor.[149]

Mr. *Henry Dunster* arrived in *New-England.*[150]

1641.

Mr. *William Bradford* chosen Governour of *new-Plimouth* Colony.

Mr. *Richard Bellingham* chosen Governour of the *Massachusets* Colony, Mr. *John Endicot* Deputy.

A Church gathered at *Glocester* in the *Massachusets* Colony.

A sharp winter in *New-England*, the harbours and salt bayes frozen over so as passable for Men, Horses, Oxen and Carts five weeks.[151]

1642.

Mr. *William Bradford* chosen Governour of *new-Plimouth* Colony.

Mr. *John Winthorp* chosen Governour of the *Massachusets* Colony, *John Endicot* Esq; Deputy Governour.

This Spring Cowes and Cattle fell from 22 pound a Cow, to six, seven and eight pound a Cow of a sudden.[152]

148. Ephraim Hewett, Robert Peck, and Peter Saxton.

149. John Wheelwright (c. 1592–1679), brother-in-law of Anne Hutchinson, had preached in old Braintree, now Quincy, before he was banished in 1637.

150. Henry Dunster (1609–59) served as president of Harvard from this year of his arrival till 1654, when he resigned under attack for his opposition to infant baptism.

151. Compare Johnson (207), who makes a similar observation.

152. Again see Johnson (209).

A Church now gathered at *Woeburn* in the *Massachusets* Colony.

[p. 262] Thirteen able Ministers now at this time in *new-Plimouth* Jurisdiction.

Harvard Colledge founded with a publick Library.[153]

Ministers bred in *New-England*, and (excepting about 10) in *Harvard*-Colledge one hundred thirty two; of which dyed in the Countrey Ten, now living eighty one, removed to *England* forty one.[154] *June Warwick* Parliament Admiral.[155]

1643.

Mr. *William Bradford* chosen Governour of the *new-Plimouth* Colony.

Mr. *John Winthorp* chosen Governour of the *Massachusets* Colony, Mr. *John Endicot* Deputy Governour.

May 19. the first Combination of the four united Colonies, *viz. Plimouth, Massachusets, Connecticut,* and *new-haven.*

1644.

Mr. *Edward Winslow* chosen Governour of *new-Plimouth* Colony.

John Endicot Esq; chosen Governour of the *Massachusets* Colony, *John Winthorp* Esq; Deputy Governour.

A Church gathered at *Haveril*. Mr. *Roger Harlackendin* dyed about this time.[156]

A Church gathered at *Reading* in *New-England.*[157]

A Church gathered at *Wenham*, both in the *Massachusets* Colony.

[p. 263] The Town of *Eastham* erected now by some in *Plimouth.*[158]

---

153. Founded in 1636, Harvard library circulated books to residents only.

154. Harvard's first class, 1642, graduated nine students; by the time Josselyn was writing, it had awarded some 200 degrees.

155. This perhaps alludes to the Warwick Commission to Control Plantation Affairs, founded in 1643.

156. According to Winthrop (1:281), Harlackenden died in 1638 from smallpox.

157. Actually in 1645. Again Johnson's errors (225) are perpetuated.

158. Hutchinson (1:177) has Eastham settled before 1643.

1645.

Mr. *William Bradford* chosen Governour of *new-Plimouth* Colony.

Mr. *Thomas Dudley* chosen Governour of the *Massachusets* Colony, and Mr. *John Winthorp* Deputy Governour, Mr. *John Endicot* major General.

A Church gathered at *Springfield*.

1646.

Mr. *William Bradford* chosen Governour of *new-Plimouth* Colony.

Mr. *John Winthorp* chosen Governour of the *Massachusets*, Mr. *Thomas Dudley* Deputy, and Mr. *John Endicot* major General.

Two Suns appeared towards the latter end of the year.[159]

This year they drew up a body of Laws for the well ordering of their Commonwealth (as they termed it) printed in 1648.[160]

Three men of War arrived in *new-Plimouth* harbour under the Command of Capt. *Thomas Cromwell*, richly laden, a mutiny amongst the Sea-men, whereby one man was killed.

The second Synod at *Cambridge* touching the duty and power of magistrates in matters of Religion.

[p. 264] Secondly, the nature and power of Synods.

Mr. *John Eliot* first preached to the *Indians* in their Native language, the principal Instruments of converting the *Indians*, Mr. *John Eliot* Senior, Mr. *John Eliot* Junior, Mr. *Thomas Mayhew*, Mr. *Pierson*, Mr. *Brown*, Mr. *James*, and Mr. *Cotton*.[161]

159. Johnson (242–43) reports this phenomenon in great detail.

160. Titled *The Book of the General Lawes and Libertyes Concerning the Inhabitants of the Massachusetts*.

161. The work of the Eliots among the Indians in and around Roxbury, Massachusetts is well known. Beginning in 1643, Thomas Mayhew, Jr. (1621–57) set about converting most of the 3,000 natives of Martha's Vineyard. He also published a series of letters in London to elicit support for his missionary activities. Abraham Pierson (c. 1608–78) preached to the Indians as well, probably both at Long Island and Connecticut; his prose catechism in the Quiripi dialect, *Some Helps for the Indians*, appeared in London in 1658/9.

1647.

Mr. *William Bradford* chosen Governour of *New-Plimouth* Colony.

Mr. *John Winthorp* chosen Governour of the *Massachusets* Colony, Mr. *Thomas Dudley* Deputy Governour, and Mr. *John Endicot* Major General.

Now Mr. *Thomas Hooker* pastor of the Church at *Hertford* dyed.

The *Tartars* over-run *China*.

1648.

Mr. *William Bradford* chosen Governour of *new-Plimouth* Colony.

John Winthorp chosen Governour of the *Massachusets* colony, Mr. *Thomas Dudley* Deputy Governour, Mr. *John Endicot* major General.

A Church gathered at *Andover*.

A Church gathered at *Malden* Mr. *Sarjant* pastor.[162]

A second Church gathered at *Boston*.[163]

A third Synod at *Cambridge* publishing the platform of Discipline.[164]

[p. 265] *Jan.* 30. King *Charles* the first murdered.[165]

Charles the Second began his Raign.

Their Laws in the *Massachusets* colony printed.

1649.

John Winthorp Esq; Governour of the *Massachusets* colony *March* the 26 deceased.

Mr. *William Bradford* chosen Governour of *new-Plimouth*.

Mr. *John Endicot* chosen Governour of the *Massachusets* colony.

---

162. William Sargent.

163. The Second Church of Boston, stronghold of the Mathers, was organized in 1650.

164. The Cambridge Synod convened in 1646, 1647, and 1648 to define New England doctrines; it published the Cambridge Platform in 1649.

165. By today's reckoning, the date of Charles's execution was 1649.

Mr. *Thomas Dudley* Deputy Governour, Mr. *Gibbons* major General.

An innumerable Company of *Caterpillars* in some parts of *New-England* destroyed the fruits of the Earth.

August the 25 Mr. *Thomas Shepherd* Pastor of *Cambridge* Church dyed.

Mr. *Philips* also dyed this year.

1650.

Mr. *William Bradford* chosen Governour of *new-Plimouth* colony.

Mr. *Thomas Dudley* chosen Governour of the *Massachusets* colony, Mr. *John Endicot* Deputy Governour, Mr. *Gibbons* major General.[166]

A great mortality amongst children this year in *New-England.*[167]

1651.

[p. 266] Mr. *William Bradford* chosen Governour of *new-Plimouth* colony.

Mr. *John Endicot* chosen Governour of the *Massachusets* colony, Mr. *Thomas Dudley* Deputy Governour, Mr. *Gibbons* major General.

The City *Bilbo* totally cover'd with waters for 15 days, 16 foot above the tops of the highest houses, the loss was very much to the whole Kingdom, there being their stock of dryed fish and dryed Goat the general dyet of *Spain.*

Barbados surrendred to the Parliament, its longitude 322, latitude 13 degrees, 17 or 18 miles in compass.

Hugh Peters and Mr. *Wells*, and *John Baker* returned into *England.*[168]

---

166. Dudley (1576–1653) was the father of Anne Bradstreet and sometime contender against John Winthrop for leadership in Massachusetts Bay.

167. On the epidemic among children, see Johnson 254–55.

168. An error. Hugh Peter, Thomas Welde (1595–1661), and Boston merchant William Hibbins sailed as emissaries for Massachusetts to England in 1641 to seek financial aid. Welde never returned to New England; Peter, from 1645 until his execution in 1660, remained in England embroiled in the Civil War.

1652.

Mr. *William Bradford* chosen Governour of *new-Plimouth* colony.

Mr. *John Endicot* chosen Governour of the *Massachusets* colony, Mr. *Thomas Dudley* Deputy Governour, Mr. *Gibbons* major General.

John Cotton Teacher of *Boston* Church dyed, a Comet was seen at the time of his sickness hanging over *New-England*, which went out soon after his death.

[p. 267] The Spirits that took Children in *England*, said to be set awork first by the Parliament, and *Hugh Peters* as chief Agent, Actor or Procurer.

1653.

Oliver Cromwell Usurped the Title of Protector *December* the Sixteenth.

Mr. *William Bradford* chosen Governour of *new-Plimouth* colony.

Mr. *Thomas Dudley* chosen Governour of the *Massachusets* colony, Mr. *John Endicot* Deputy Governour, Mr. *Gibbons* major General.

Mr. *Thomas Dudley* Governour of the *Massachusets* colony dyed, aged about 77 years at his house at *Roxebury, July* 31.

A great fire at *Boston* in *New-England*.

1654.

Mr. *William Bradford* chosen Governour of *new-Plimouth* colony.

Mr. *Bellingham* Governour, *Endicot* Deputy.

Major General *Gibbons* dyed this year.

1655.

Mr. *William Bradford* chosen Governour of *new-Plimouth* colony. Mr. *John Endicot* Governour of the *Massachusets, Bellingham* Deputy.

Jamaica taken by the *English*.

1656.

[p. 268] General *Mountague* taketh *Spanish* prizes.[169]

Mr. *William Bradford* chosen Governour of *new-Plimouth* colony, Mr. *John Endicot* Governour of the *Massachusets*, Mr. *Francis Willowby* Deputy.

1657.

Mr. *Thomas Prince* chosen Governour of *new-Plimouth* colony.
Mr. *William Bradford* now dyed.[170] Mr. *John Endicot* Governour, *Bellingham* Deputy.
Mr. *Theophilus Eaton* Governour of *New-haven* colony dyed. Fifth monarchy-men rebell.[171]
The Quakers arrive at *new-Plimouth*.[172]

1658.

Oliver Cromwell dyed *September* the third.
Richard Cromwell set up.
Mr. *Thomas Prince* chosen Governour of *new-Plimouth* colony.
Mr. *John Endicot* chosen Governour of the *Massachusets*, *Bellingham* Deputy.
A great Earthquake in *New-England*.
Mr. *Ralph Partrick* minister at *Ruxbury*[173] now deceased.
John Philips of *Marshfield* slain by thunder and lightning.

1659.

Mr. *Thomas Prince* chosen Governour of *new Plimouth* colony.
[p. 269] Mr. *John Endicot* chosen Governour of the *Massachusets* colony.

---

169. Edward Montagu (1625–72), first Earl of Sandwich.

170. In 1658, following the New Style.

171. This group of radical millennialists began by supporting Cromwell but in 1647 rose up against him and were imprisoned. Shortly after the Restoration they attempted to take over London, at which time most of the movement leaders were executed.

172. The first Quakers to arrive in New England were Ann Austin and Mary Fisher, who came to Massachusetts from Barbados in 1656.

173. Ralph Partridge of Duxbury.

The Quakers opinions vented up and down the Countrey.

Mr. *Henry Dunster* first President of *Harvard* Colledge deceased.

Richard Cromwell ended *May* the seventh.

The Rump Parliament *December* the six and twentieth put down.

William Robinson, *Marmaduke Stevenson*, and *Mary Dyer* Quakers of *Rhod Island* sentenced to suffer death by Mr. *John Endicot* Governour of the *Massachusets* colony, which accordingly was executed within a day or two, the prisoners being guarded by Capt. *James Oliver* with 200 Souldiers to the place of Execution, where the two men were hanged and the woman reprieved at the Gallows and banished.[174]

1660.

Mr. *Thomas Prince* chosen Governour of *new-Plimouth* colony.

John Endicot chosen Governour of the *Massachusets* colony, Mr. *Bellingham* Deputy.

James Pierce slain by lightning at *new-Plimouth*.

May the 29 King *Charles* the Second returned into *England*.

June the 20 a damnable cheat like to have been put upon *England* by a brief for *New-* [p. 270] *England*, which as it appeared was produced before the King came in, but not printed (by Mr. *Leach* in *Shoe-Lane*) till *June*, pretending that 18 *Turks-men* of War the 24 of *January* 16$\frac{59}{60}$ landed at a Town, called *Kingsword* (alluding to *Charles-town*) three miles from *Boston*, kill'd 40, took Mr. *Sims* minister prisoner, wounded him, kill'd his wife and three of his little children, carried him away with 57 more, burnt the Town, carried them to *Argier*, their loss amounting to 12000 pound, the *Turk* demanding 8000 pound ransom to be paid within 7 moneths. Signed by *Thomas Margets*, *Edward Calamy*, *William Jenkin*, *William Vincent*, *George Wild*, *Joseph Caryl*, *John Menord*, *William Cooper*, *Thomas Manton* Ministers.[175]

174. See "First Voyage," n. 57; Adams (1:407–10).

175. Neither Samuel Pepys nor John Evelyn reports this event in his diary. Indeed, the incident appears entirely to have escaped English as well as New England historical records. Turks were believed to come from *Argeire* (see Bridenbaugh 235n). Edmund Calamy was a Presbyterian minister chosen by George Monck in 1660 to serve London. Joseph Caryl was called in 1650 to

Hugh Peters put to death the 16 of *October*.

Thomas Venner a Wine-Cooper hang'd[,] drawn and quartered
Jan. 19.[176]

1661.

The fifth Monarch-men rise at *London*.

Mr. *Thomas Prince* chosen Governour of *new-Plimouth* colony.

Mr. *John Endicot* chosen Governour of the *Massachusets* colony,
Mr. *Bellingham* Deputy.

Major *Atherton* now dyed in *New-England*.[177]

1662.

[p. 271] Sir *Henry Vane* beheaded, *June* the 14.

Mr. *Thomas Prince* chosen Governour of *new-Plimouth* colony.

Mr. *John Endicot* chosen Governour of the *Massachusets* colony.

January 26 and the 28 Earthquakes in *New-England*, 6 or 7
times in the space of Three days.

1663.

John Baker unduely called Capt. *Baker*, hang'd at Tiburn, the
11 of *February*.

1663.

Mr. *Thomas Prince* chosen Governour of *new-Plimouth* colony.

Mr. *John Endicot* chosen Governour and Mr. *Thomas Leveret*
major General.

Mr. *Willowby* Deputy Governor and Mr. *Thomas Leveret*
major General.

---

leave the Council of State and to serve as a minister under Cromwell; in 1654 he
was one of thirty-eight "Triers" or Commissioners for Approbation of Publique
Preachers, a council organized by Cromwell to reform the church along Independent lines.

176. January 1661, New Style. Venner was leader of the Fifth Monarchy
rebels, all fifty or so of whom were killed or captured during their uprising.

177. Humphrey Atherton of Dorchester, founder of a trading and speculat-
ing group known as the Atherton Company, and major general of Massachusetts Bay after 1656. "Upon returning from a military review in Boston common in September 1661, he encountered a cow, was thrown from his horse, and
died within a few hours" (Hutchinson 1:119n).

April the fifth Mr. *John Norton* Teacher at the first Church in *Boston* dyed suddenly.

Mr. *Samuel Newman* Teacher at *Rehoboth* in *New-England* now dyed.

Mr. *Samuel Stone* Teacher of *Hartford* Church in *New-England*, now dyed also.

Several Earth-quakes this year in *New-England*.

[p. 272] *Charles Chancie* batchelor of Divinity, and President of *Harvard*-Colledge in *New-England*.[178]

1664.

Mr. *Thomas Prince* chosen Governour of *new-Plimouth* colony.

Mr. *John Endicot* chosen Governour of the *Massachusets* colony, Mr. *Francis Willowby* Deputy Governour, Mr. *Thomas Leveret* Major General.

May the 20 the Kings Commissioners arrived in *New-England*, *viz.* Sir *Robert Carr*, Colonel *Nicols*, Colonel *Cartwright* and Mr. *Samuel Maverich*, with whom came one Mr. *Archdale* as Agent for Mr. *Ferdinando Gorges*, who brought to the colony in the province of *Main*, Mr. *F. Gorges* order from his Majesty *Charles* the Second, under his manual, and his Majesties Letters to the *Massachusets* concerning the same, to be restored unto the quiet possession and enjoyment of the said province in *New-England*, and the Government thereof, the which during the civil Wars in *England* the *Massachusets* colony had usurpt, and (by help of a *Jacobs* staff) most shamefully encroached upon Mr. *Gorges* rights and priviledges.

The 29 of *August*, the *Manades*, called *Novede Belgique*, or New *Netherlands*, their chief Town New-*Amsterdam*, now called [p. 273] New-*Yorke*, Surrendered up unto Sir *Robert Carr* and Colonel *Nichols* his Majesties Commissioners; thirteen days after in *September* the Fort and Town of *Arania* now called *Albany*; twelve days after that, the Fort and Town of *Awsapha*; then *de la Ware* Castle man'd with *Dutch* and *Sweeds*, the three first Forts and Towns being built upon the River *Mohegan*, otherwise called *Hudsons* River.[179]

178. Chauncey (c. 1592–1672) became president of Harvard in 1654.
179. The primary purpose of this show of Royal strength—four frigates

The whole Bible Translated into the *Indian*-Tongue, by Mr. *John Eliot* Senior, was now printed at *Cambridge* in *New-England*.

December a great and dreadful Comet, or blazing-star appeared in the South-east in *New-England* for a space of three moneths, which was accompanied with many sad effects, great mildews blasting in the Countrey the next Summer.

1665.

Mr. *Thomas Prince* chosen Governour of *new-Plimouth* colony.

Mr. *John Endicot* chosen Governour of the *Massachusets* colony, Mr. *Francis Willowby* Deputy Governour, Mr. *Leveret* Major General.

Two Comets or blazing-stars appeared in 4 moneths time in *England, December* 1664. and in *March* following.

Mr. *John Endicot* Governour of the *Mas-* [p. 274] *sachusets* colony deceased, *March* the three and twentieth.

Capt. *Davenport* kill'd with lightning as he lay on his bed at the Castle by *Boston* in *New-England*, and several wounded.[180]

Wheat exceedingly blasted and mildewed in *New-England*.

A thousand foot sent this year by the *French* King to *Canada*.

Colonel *Cartwright* in his voyage for *England* was taken by the *Dutch*.

The Isle of *Providence* taken by the *English* Buccaneers, *Puerto Rico* taken and plundered by the *English* Buccaneers and abandoned.

1666.

Mr. *Thomas Prince* chosen Governour of the *New-Plimouth* colony.

---

fully armed—was to oust the Dutch from New Netherland. The expedition was less successful in its dealings with Massachusetts. On this incident see especially Andrews, who writes that "Maverick must have relished with grim enjoyment the opportunity thus furnished by the King of looking into the way Massachusetts had been conducting her government" (3:59). Note also p. 153–54. "*Awsapha*" is untraced.

180. Captain Richard Davenport was commander of the fortified castle, on Castle Island, at the mouth of Boston harbor. Hutchinson (1:217n) affirms the date and details.

Mr. *Richard Bellingham* chosen Governour of the *Massachusets* colony, Mr. *Francis Willowby* Deputy Governour, Mr. *Leveret* major General.

St. *Christophers* taken by the *French*.

July the Lord *Willowby* of *Parham* cast away in a *Hurricane* about the *Caribby-Islands*.

The small pox at *Boston* in the *Massachusets* colony.

Three kill'd in a moment by a blow of Thunder at *Marshfield* in *New-Plimouth* [p. 275] colony, and four at *Pascataway* colony, and divers burnt with lightning, a great whirl-wind at the same time.

This year also *New-England* had cast away and taken Thirty one Vessels, and some in 1667.

The mildews and blasting of Corn still continued.

1667.

Mr. *Thomas Prince* chosen Governour of *New-Plimouth* colony.

Mr. *Richard Bellingham* chosen Governour of the *Massachusets* colony, Mr. *Fr. Willowby* Deputy Governour, and Mr. *Leveret* major General.

Sir *Robert Carr* dyed next day after his arrival at *Bristow* in *England June* the first.

Several vollies of shot heard discharged in the Air at *Nantascot* two miles from *Boston* in the *Massachusets* colony.

Mr. *John Davenport* chosen pastor of the Independent Church at *Boston*.[181]

In *March* there appeared a sign in the Heavens in the form of a Spear, pointing directly to the *West*.

Sir *John Harman* defeated the *French* Fleet at the *Caribbes*.

Mr. *John Wilson* Pastor of *Boston* Church in the *Massachusets* colony 37 years now [p. 276] dyed, aged 79, he was Pastor of that Church three years before Mr. *Cotton*, twenty years with him, ten years with Mr. *Norton*, and four years after him.

1668.

Mr. *Thomas Prince* chosen Governour of *New-Plimouth* colony.

Mr. *Richard Bellingham* chosen Governour of the *Massachusets*

---

181. Davenport succeeded John Wilson as minister of Boston's First Church.

colony, Mr. *Fr. Willowby* Deputy Governour, and Mr. *Leveret* major General.

Mr. *Samuel Shepherd* Pastor of *Rowley* Church dyed.[182]

April the 27 Mr. *Henry Flint* Teacher at *Braintry* dyed.

July the Ninth Mr. *Jonathan Mitchel* Pastor of the Church at *Cambridge* dyed,[183] he was born at *Halifax* in *Yorkeshire* in *England*, and was brought up in *Harvard-Colledge* at *Cambridge* in *New-England*.

July the fifteenth, nine of the clock at night an Eclipse of the moon, till after Eleven darkned nine digits and thirty five minutes.

July the Seventeenth a great *Sperma Cæti* Whale Fifty five foot long, thrown up at *Winter-harbour* by *Casco* in the Province of *Main*.

April the Third, Fryday an Earthquake in *New-England*.

1669.

[p. 277] Mr. *Thomas Prince* chosen Governour of *Plimouth* colony.

Mr. *Richard Bellingham* chosen Governour of the *Massachusets* colony, Mr. *Fr. Willowby* Deputy Governour, Mr. *Leveret* major General.

Mr. *Oxenbridge* chosen Pastor of the Independent Church at *Boston*.[184]

The wonderful burning of the mountain *Aetna*, or *Gibella* in *Cicilia March*.

1670.

Mr. *Thomas Prince* chosen Governour of *New-Plimouth* colony.

Mr. *Richard Bellingham* chosen Governour of the *Massachusets* colony, Mr. *Fr. Willowby* Deputy Governour, Mr. *Leveret* major General.

Mr. *Fr. Willowby* Deputy Governour now dyed.

At a place called *Kenebunch*, which is in the Province of *Main*,

---

182. Shepard was only twenty-six when he died (Sibley and Shipton 1:542–44).

183. Mitchel was about forty-four (Sibley and Shipton 1:141–57).

184. John Oxenbridge (1609–74) became pastor of the First Church of Boston in 1670.

not far from the River-side, a piece of clay ground was thrown up by a mineral vapour (as was supposed) over the tops of high oaks that grew between it and the River, into the River, stopping the course thereof, and leaving a hole Forty yards square, wherein [p. 278] were Thousands of clay bullets as big as musquet bullets, and pieces of clay in shape like the barrel of a musquet.[185] The like accident fell out at *Casco*, One and twenty miles from it to the Eastward, much about the same time; And fish in some ponds in the Countrey thrown up dead upon the banks, supposed likewise to be kill'd with mineral vapours.

A wonderful number of Herrins cast up on shore at high water in *Black-point-Harbour* in the province of *Main*, so that they might have gone half way up the leg in them for a mile together.

Mr. *Thatcher* chosen Pastor of the Presbyterian Church at *Boston*.[186]

1671.

Mr. *Thomas Prince* Governour of new *Plimouth* colony.

Mr. *Richard Bellingham* chosen Governour of the *Massachusets* colony, Mr. *Leveret* Deputy, and major General.

Elder *Pen* now dyed at *Boston*,[187] the *English* troubled much with griping of the guts, and bloudy Flux, of which several dyed.

October the Two and twentieth a Ship called the flying *Falcon* of *Amsterdam*, arrived at *Dover*, having been out since the first of *January* 1669. and been in the South- [p. 279] Seas in the latitude of 50 degrees, having sailed 12900 *Dutch* leagues, the master told us he made main land, and discovered two Islands never before discovered, where were men all hairy, Eleven foot in height.

---

185. John Winthrop, Jr., made report of this explosion and sent samples of its "bullets" to the Royal Society this same year. Stearns conjectures they were "concretions in the late Pleistocene marine clay" (137n).

186. Thomas Thacher (1620–78) was the first minister of Boston's South Church, which is intended here (Hutchinson 1:223n).

187. Sir William Penn (1621–70) died in England.

1672.

Mr. *Richard Bellingham* chosen Governour of the *Massachusets* colony, Mr. *Leveret* Deputy, and major General.

1673.

Mr. *Richard Bellingham* Governour of the *Massachusets* colony now deceased.

1674.

Thomas Leveret chosen Governour.
Mr. *Simons* Deputy Governour.

Finis.

Emendations

Page	Paragraph	Original	Changed to
6	2	Jvy	Ivy
49	1	planctas	planetas
52	2	Intituled	intituled
67	2	phrases is	phrases it
77	2	simulac	simul ac
84	1	cubits,)	cubits)
90	1	Drufus	Drusus
97	1	verily	Verily
103	2	dayes	Dayes
		our	your
		Spincers	Pincers
		spoaks	spokes
104	3	Job 41.1	Job 40.20
108	2	most an end	most end
111	2	yest	yeast
119	2	ipsæ bestiæ	Ipsæ bestiæ
120	1	Prov. 26.22	Prov. 27.22
149	2	you do but	You do but
151	1	transmentitation	transmentation
158	1	the rest,)	the rest),
161	1	seconds.)	seconds).
172	1	1639	1629
173	2	Gosse	Goffe
189	1	spotted and	spotted) and
191	1	1624. hese	1624. These
199	4	Fiftenth	Fifteenth
204	1	wild-*Swins*	wild-*Swans*
214	4	steemed	stemmed

Page	Paragraph	Original	Changed to
237	6	Raign,	Raign.
242	4	8596	1596
270	1	$16\frac{58}{60}$	$16\frac{59}{60}$
270	3	hang'd	hang'd,
		Ian. 19	Jan. 19
271	5, heading	$16\frac{62}{63}$	1663
274	7	Massachusetts	New-Plimouth
276	8	g at	great

Works Consulted

Adams, Charles Francis. *Three Episodes of Massachusetts History*. 1892. Rev. ed., 2 vols. New York: Russell and Russell, 1965.

American Writers before 1800: A Biographical and Critical Dictionary. Ed. James A. Levernier and Douglas R. Wilmes. 3 vols. Westport, Conn.: Greenwood, 1983.

Andrews, Charles M. *The Colonial Period of American History*. 4 vols. New Haven, Conn.: Yale University Press, 1934–39.

Arner, Robert D. "John Josselyn." *Dictionary of Literary Biography*. Detroit: Gale, 1972–85. Vol. 24.

Axtell, James. *The European and the Indian: Essays in the Ethnohistory of Colonial North America*. New York: Oxford University Press, 1981.

———, and William C. Sturtevant. "The Unkindest Cut, or Who Invented Scalping?" *William and Mary Quarterly*, 3rd ser., 37 (1980):451–72.

Banks, Charles Edward. "Martin's or Martha's?" *New England Historic and Genealogical Register* 48 (1894):201–4.

Beck, Horace P. *The Folklore of Maine*. New York: Lippincott, 1957.

Bradford, William. *History of Plymouth Plantation*. Ed. William T. Davis. New York: Scribner's, 1908.

Bridenbaugh, Carl. *Vexed and Troubled Englishmen, 1590–1642*. New York: Oxford University Press, 1968.

Burrage, Henry S. *The Beginnings of Colonial Maine, 1602–1658*. Portland: State of Maine, 1914.

Canny, Nicholas P. "The Ideology of Colonization: From Ireland to America." *William and Mary Quarterly*, 3rd ser., 30 (1973):575–98.

Carey, George. "John Josselyn: Maine's First Folklorist." *Down East* 19 (April 1973):20, 23–25, 27–28.

Carroll, Charles F. *The Timber Economy of Puritan New England*. Providence, R.I.: Brown University Press, 1973.

Chadbourne, Ava Harriet. *Maine Place Names and the Peopling of Its Towns*. Portland, Maine: Bond Wheelwright, 1955.

Clark, Charles E. *The Eastern Frontier: The Settlement of Northern New England, 1610–1763*. New York: Knopf, 1970.

———. *Maine During the Colonial Period: A Bibliographic Guide*. Portland: Maine Historical Society, 1974.

————. *Maine: A History.* New York: Norton, 1977.

————. "The Wonderful World of John Josselyn." *Bates College Bulletin* 73 (April 1976):28–30.

Comas, Beatrice H. "John Josselyn, 'Gent,' Maine's First Folklorist." *Early American Life* 15 (February 1984):70, 83–88.

Cronon, William. *Changes in the Land: Indians, Colonists, and the Ecology of New England.* New York: Hill and Wang, 1983.

Crosby, Alfred W., Jr. *The Columbian Exchange: Biological and Cultural Consequences of 1492.* Westport, Conn.: Greenwood, 1972.

Dictionary of American Biography. Ed. Allen Johnson and Dumas Malone. 20 vols. New York: Charles Scribner's Sons, 1928–37; 7 supplements, 1944–65.

Dictionary of National Biography. Ed. Leslie Stephen and Sidney Lee. 21 vols. London: Oxford University Press, 1882–1900; 6 supplements, 1901–50.

Dorson, Richard M. *America Begins.* New York: Pantheon, 1950.

————. *American Folklore and the Historian.* Chicago: University of Chicago Press, 1971.

————. *Jonathan Draws the Long Bow.* 1946. Reprint. New York: Russell and Russell, 1970.

Felter, Harvey Wickes. "The Genesis of the American Materia Medica." *Bulletin of the Lloyd Library of Botany, Pharmacy & Materia Medica,* ser. 8, no. 26 (1927):1–64.

Frantz, R. W. *The English Traveler and the Movement of Ideas, 1660–1732.* 1934. Reprint. New York: Octagon, 1968.

Frazier, Sir James George. *The Golden Bough: A Study in Magic and Religion.* 12 vols. New York: MacMillan, 1935.

French, Elizabeth. "Genealogical Research in England: Josselyn." *New England Historic and Genealogical Register* 71 (1917):19–33; 227–57.

Godin, Alfred J. *Wild Animals of New England.* Baltimore: Johns Hopkins University Press, 1977.

Goss, Elbridge H. "Early Bells of Massachusetts." *New England Historic and Genealogical Register* 37 (1883):46–52.

Greenlaw, William Prescott. "John Maverick and Some of His Descendants." *New England Historic and Genealogical Register* 96 (1942): 232–41.

Grizmek, Bernhard, ed. *Grizmek's Animal Life Encyclopedia.* 13 vols. New York: Van Nostrand Reinhold, 1972–75.

Gura, Philip F. "Thoreau and John Josselyn." *New England Quarterly* 48 (1975):505–18.

Höltgen, Karl Josef. "Francis Quarles, John Josselyn, and the *Bay Psalm Book.*" *Seventeenth-Century News* 34 (1976):42–46.

Hutchinson, Thomas. *The History of the Colony and Province of Massachusetts-Bay.* 1767. Ed. Lawrence Shaw Mayo. 3 vols. Cambridge, Mass.: Harvard University Press, 1936.

Jantz, Harold S., ed. *The First Century of New England Verse.* 1944. Reprint. New York: Russell and Russell, 1962.

Jennings, Francis. *The Invasion of America: Indians, Colonialism, and the Cant of Conquest*. Chapel Hill: University of North Carolina Press, 1975.

Johnson, Edward. *Wonder-Working Providence of Sions Saviour in New England*. Ed. J. Franklin Jameson. New York: Scribner's, 1910.

Johnson, Thomas, and Perry Miller, eds. *The Puritans*. 1938. Rev. ed. 2 vols. New York: Harper Torchbooks, 1963.

Jones, Howard Mumford. "The Colonial Impulse: An Analysis of the 'Promotion' Literature of Colonization." *American Philosophical Society Proceedings* 90 (1946):131–61.

———. *O Strange New World: American Culture, the Formative Years*. New York: Viking, 1964.

Josselyn, John. *New-Englands Rarities Discovered*. 1672. Reprint. Boston: Massachusetts Historical Society Picture Books, 1972.

———. *An Account of Two Voyages to New-England*. 1674. Reprint. *Massachusetts Historical Society Collections*, ser. 3, no. 3 (1833):211–396.

Lemay, J. A. Leo. "The Frontiersman from Lout to Hero: Notes on the Significance of the Comparative Method and the Stage Theory in Early American Literature and Culture." *American Antiquarian Society Proceedings* 88 (October 1979):187–223.

Libby, Charles Thornton et al., eds. *Province and Court Records of Maine*. 5 vols. Portland: Maine Historical Society, 1928–64.

Little, George Thomas, ed. *Genealogical and Family History of the State of Maine*. 2 vols. New York: Lewis Historical Publishing, 1909.

Lowes, John Livingston. *The Road to Xanadu: A Study in the Ways of the Imagination*. Boston: Houghton Mifflin, 1927.

Lucanus, Marcus Annæus. *Lucan's Pharsalia: or The Civill Warres of Rome between Pompey the Great, and Julius Caesar*. Trans. Thomas May. London, 1627.

Meserole, Harrison T., ed. *Seventeenth-Century American Poetry*. Garden City, N.Y.: Anchor-Doubleday, 1968.

Miller, John C. *The First Frontier: Life in Colonial America*. New York: Laurel-Dell, 1966.

Mood, Fulmer. "Notes on John Josselyn, Gent." *Colonial Society of Massachusetts Publications* 28 (December 1930):24–36.

Morison, Samuel Eliot. *The European Discovery of America: The Northern Voyages, A.D. 500–1600*. New York: Oxford University Press, 1971.

———. *The European Discovery of America: The Southern Voyages, A.D. 1492–1616*. New York: Oxford University Press, 1974.

Morton, Thomas. *New English Canaan*. Ed. Charles Francis Adams, Jr. *Prince Society Publications*, no. 14 (1883). Reprint. New York: Burt Franklin, 1967.

Newton, Arthur Percival. *The Colonising Activities of the English Puritans*. New Haven, Conn.: Yale University Press, 1914.

Piercy, Josephine K. *Studies in Literary Types in Seventeenth-Century America, 1607–1710*. Yale Studies in English no. 91. New Haven, Conn.: Yale University Press, 1939.

Pliny. *Natural History*. Ed. and trans. H. Rackham, W. H. S. Jones, and D. E. Eichholz. 10 vols. Loeb Classical Library of Latin Authors. 1938. Rev. ed. Cambridge, Mass.: Harvard University Press, 1949–62.

Preston, Richard Arthur. *Gorges of Plymouth Fort*. Toronto: University of Toronto Press, 1953.

Prosser, Albert L. "John Josselyn." *Bulletin of the Josselyn Botanical Society of Maine* 10 (1975):1–4.

Quinn, David Beers. *England and the Discovery of America, 1481–1620*. New York: Knopf, 1973.

———. *North America from Earliest Discovery to First Settlements: The Norse Voyages to 1612*. New York: Harper and Row, 1977.

Reid, John G. *Acadia, Maine, and New Scotland: Marginal Colonies in the Seventeenth Century*. Toronto: University of Toronto Press, 1981.

Sabin, Joseph, Wilberforce Eames, and R. W. G. Vail, eds. *Biblioteca Americana. A Dictionary of Books Relating to America*. 29 vols. New York: J. Sabin, 1868–1936.

Salisbury, Neal. *Manitou and Providence: Indians, Europeans, and the Making of New England, 1500–1643*. New York: Oxford University Press, 1982.

Sandys, George. *Travels*. 1615. 7th ed. London, 1673.

Sargent, William M. "Henry Josselyn, the First and Only Royal Chief Magistrate of Maine." *New England Historic and Genealogical Register* 40 (1886):290–94.

Schutte, Anne Jacobson. "'Such Monstrous Births': A Neglected Aspect of the Antinomian Controversy." *Renaissance Quarterly* 38 (1985):85–106.

Sibley, John L., and Clifford K. Shipton. *Biographical Sketches of Those Who Attended Harvard College*. Vols. 1–3: 1642–89, Boston, 1873; vols. 4–17: 1690–1771, Boston, 1933–75.

Simmons, William S. "Cultural Bias in the New England Puritans' Perception of Indians." *William and Mary Quarterly*, 3rd ser., 38 (1981):56–72.

Smith, Isadore Leighton. *Early American Gardens: "For Meate or Medicine."* Boston: Houghton Mifflin, 1970.

Smith, John. *The Complete Works of Captain John Smith*. Ed. Philip L. Barbour. 3 vols. Chapel Hill: University of North Carolina Press, 1986.

Speck, Gordon. *Myths and New World Explorations*. Fairfield, Wash.: Ye Galleon Press, 1979.

Spiller, Robert E., et al., eds. *Literary History of the United States*. 1948. Rev. ed., 2 vols. New York: MacMillan, 1974.

Stackpole, Everett S. "Josselyn's Point." *Old Eliot* 5 (1902):30–34.

Stearns, Raymond Phineas. *Science in the British Colonies of America*. Urbana: University of Illinois Press, 1970.

Thompson, Stith. *Motif-Index of Folk-Literature*. 6 vols. Bloomington: Indiana University Press, 1955–58.

Tilley, Morris Palmer. *A Dictionary of the Proverbs of England in the Sixteenth and Seventeenth Centuries*. Ann Arbor: University of Michigan Press, 1950.

The Trelawny Papers. Ed. James P. Baxter. *Collections of the Maine Historical Society*, ser. 2, no. 3 (1884):iii–520.

Tuckerman, Edward, ed. *New-Englands Rarities Discovered*. By John Josselyn. *American Antiquarian Society Transactions and Proceedings* 4 (1860):103–238.

Tyler, Moses Coit. *A History of American Literature, 1607–1765*. 2 vols. 1878, 1897. Reprint. 2 vols. Ithaca, N.Y.: Cornell University Press, 1949.

Vaughan, Alden T. *New England Frontier: Puritans and Indians, 1620–1675*. Boston: Little, Brown, 1965.

Wardenaar, Leslie A. "Humor in the Colonial Promotion Tract: Topics and Techniques." *Early American Literature* 9 (1975): 286–300.

Wessler, Edith S., comp. *The Jocelyn-Joslin-Joslyn-Josselyn Family*. Tokyo: n.p., 1961.

Whiting, Bartlett J. *Early American Proverbs and Proverbial Phrases*. Cambridge, Mass.: Belknap–Harvard University Press, 1977.

Williams, Roger. *The Complete Writings of Roger Williams*. Ed. John Russell Bartlett et al. 7 vols. New York: Russell and Russell, 1963.

Willis, William. "Old Settlers." *New England Historic and Genealogical Register* 2 (1848):202–7.

Winsor, Justin, ed. *Narrative and Critical History of America*. 8 vols. Boston: Houghton Mifflin, 1884–89.

Winthrop, John. *History of New England, 1630–1649*. Ed. James K. Hosmer. 2 vols. New York: Scribner's, 1908.

Wood, William. *New Englands Prospect*. London, 1634.

Wright, Joseph, ed. *The English Dialect Dictionary*. 6 vols. New York: Putnam's, 1898.

Index

Obsolete forms are in *italics* (glossed in roman)